Transcription Skills for Business

Sixth Edition

Linda Mallinson
Professor, Mid Florida Tech

PEARSON

Prentice
Hall

Upper Saddle River, New Jersey 07458

Library of Congress Cataloging-in-Publication Data

Mallinson, Linda
    Transcription skills for business.—6th ed. / Linda Mallinson.
        p. cm.
    Includes index.
    ISBN 0-13-025437-1
        1. Dictation (Office practice) 2. Computer-aided transcription systems. 3. Typewriting.
    1. Title

    HF5547.5.M49 2004
    651.7'4—dc21

                                                                    2003042991

Publisher: Stephen Helba
Executive Editor: Elizabeth Sugg
Editorial Assistant: Cyrenne Bolt de Freitas
Production Liaison: Brian Hyland
Production Editor: Lori Dalberg, Carlisle Publishers Services
Director of Manufacturing and Production: Bruce Johnson
Managing Editor: Mary Carnis
Marketing Manager: Leigh Ann Sims
Manufacturing Buyer: Ilene Sanford
Design Director: Cheryl Asherman
Senior Design Coordinator: Miguel Ortiz
Cover Designer: Joseph Sengotta
Interior Design: Carlisle Communications, Ltd.
Composition: Carlisle Communications, Ltd.
Printing and Binding: Banta Harrisonburg

Prentice-Hall International (UK) Limited, *London*
Prentice-Hall of Australia Pty. Limited, *Sydney*
Prentice-Hall Canada Inc., *Toronto*
Prentice-Hall Hispanoamericana, S.A., *Mexico*
Prentice-Hall of India Private Limited, *New Delhi*
Prentice-Hall of Japan, Inc., *Tokyo*
Prentice-Hall Singapore Pte. Ltd.
Editora Prentice-Hall do Brasil, Ltda., *Rio de Janeiro*

1 0 9 8 7 6 5 4 3 2
ISBN 0-13-025437-1

Contents

SECTION THREE
Written Communication Assessment **35**

SECTION FOUR
Transcription Lessons 1–16 **47**

APPENDIX A
Machine Transcription Student Progress Record **195**

APPENDIX B
Language Arts Skill Review with Language Tapes **201**

APPENDIX C
Answers to Lesson Exercises **205**

Preface

Transcription Skills for Business, Sixth Edition, incorporates the following features:

- Format for use as either a semester or nine-week course
- Additional student progress forms
- Expanded grammar, punctuation, and proofreading exercises
- Incorporation of new features in *The Office Guide*
- A supplemental tape with 25 dictated documents for additional practice or grading
- Language arts tapes from previous editions to assist students in reinforcing acquisition of language arts skills

The lesson and dictation material for the 16 lessons (60 documents) covering a wide variety of business communications has been revised and updated. In the first eight lessons, students are given considerable assistance in transcribing through the inclusion of large chunks of the dictation in the transcription preview exercises. In later lessons, office style dictation is given where the dictator makes changes. The office style dictation has been expanded in the sixth edition of the text.

This sixth edition contains an overview of the transcription process: listening, keyboarding, using the transcriber, and proofreading. Each lesson contains the following:

- Ten or more confusing words with exercises
- Presentation of several grammar and punctuation rules with exercises requiring application of these language skills
- An integration of word usage, grammar, and punctuation rules presented in the lessons with the dictation students transcribe
- Vocabulary transcription previews that include mainstream words as well as technical and business terms
- Proofreading exercises that incorporate the word usage, grammar, punctuation, and formatting rules presented in the lesson

After every four lessons, a transcription test and a written test covering word usage, grammar, punctuation, and proofreading are given.

The sections on confusing words, grammar, and punctuation, spelling of difficult international cities, abbreviations, and word usage have been expanded in the supplemental reference text, *The Office Guide*. A section on time zones has also been added, and the index has been revised and expanded to make it easier to find information in *The Office Guide*.

The main revision for this edition centers around the transition from analog to digital transcription. Information has been included on the expanding trend of transcription being done at home. Many virtual assistants and transcriptionists work from home transcribing voice files that have been downloaded over the Internet.

ACKNOWLEDGMENTS

A thank you is extended to Maria and Bill Lupinacci from the Programmers' Consortium, Inc. for permission to include photographs of the WAVpedal and other equipment in this sixth edition.

A special thank you is given to Beverly Fain and Kim Brown who allowed me to photograph them in their at-home work environment.

Another thank you is extended to the following individuals who served as reviewers for this sixth edition:

Rochelle Kunkel, Kankakee Community College

Myrna E. Bond, Daytona Beach Community College

Kay K. Johnston, Columbia Basin College

Jacalyn J. Royal, Jonathan B. Alper, Esq.

Cynthia Galbreath, Motte Technical College

Regina Watkins Miller, Motte Technical College

Mary O'Fury, Spokane Community College

SECTION ONE
Introductory Overview

Introductory Student Information
Grading Information

INTRODUCTORY STUDENT INFORMATION

Transcribing is one of the most challenging office-related duties using information processing skills because it involves the integration of the following:

- Typing
- Grammar and punctuation
- Knowledge of word processing and transcription software
- Formatting principles
- Critical thinking
- Proofreading
- Following instructions
- Careful listening

This means, of course, that machine transcription is more than typing what you hear. It involves making decisions concerning the accuracy of what is dictated or what is typed as well as using some advanced word processing features.

In machine transcription, the transcriptionist prepares written communications by listening to recorded dictation and typing it. Sometimes, the recorded dictation may only consist of variables with instructions to the operator (transcriptionist) to merge the information with documents that have already been typed and stored. This means that the ability to follow directions is also important in the transcription process.

Most likely, you are taking machine transcription as one of the last classes in your program at school. This means that you already have learned the skills essential to success as a transcriptionist. This textbook and the tapes that accompany it are designed to provide you with instruction and practice in using this new skill along with the skills you already have.

HOW CAN YOU BECOME A GOOD TRANSCRIPTIONIST?

Strengthen Weak Skills

In addition to good typing and word processing skills, a good transcriptionist uses many other skills. If you have weak grammar, proofreading, or punctuation skills, take the time to review or remediate in these areas.

Use Your Equipment Efficiently

The manufacturer's manual for your transcription machine includes instructions for inserting tapes and using controls. Most machines have volume, speed, and tone controls, and a foot pedal that starts and stops the tape. Check the manual or ask your instructor for directions about your machine's functions.

Organize Your Workstation

Have the supplies you will need on hand: paper, textbook, and reference manuals. Common reference manuals used by machine transcription operators include dictionaries, reference format/style guides, company procedure manuals, ZIP code books, thesaurus, and reference books for specialized fields such as medical and legal. Arrange your supplies in a logical pattern based upon frequency of use so that you can find each item quickly when you need it.

Practice Good Listening Techniques

Because listening is a key skill in machine transcription, practicing good listening in your personal life will help you transcribe efficiently and accurately. When applying listening skills to machine transcription, listen to a phrase or meaningful word group, type those words, and start listening again before you have completed typing the first group of words. This listening pattern and the continuous typing that results are the keys to efficient transcription.

Think about what is being dictated and listen to the dictator's tone of voice as a guide to aid you in punctuating correctly. If you do not understand a word or phrase, listen to it again. Listen to the words before and after it. By concentrating on the meaning of the communication, you will often be able to decipher the word or phrase and avoid errors that change the meaning of the dictation. "Courses" may sound like "horses" or "bottom of this page" like "bottomless page," but *a good transcriptionist will not type something that does not make sense.*

Apply the Fundamentals of Effective Communications

A good transcriptionist will strive constantly for improvement in the use of the English language: sentence structure, word usage, spelling, punctuation, capitalization, and number usage.

Learn About the Business for Which You Are Working

Many transcription errors occur because the transcriptionist does not understand the communication. A transcriptionist in any business organization should learn as much as possible about that business—its organization, structure, personnel, products, services, and vocabulary.

Present the Final Communication Accurately and in Correct Format

A good transcriptionist is familiar with standard business formats for letters, memos, reports, and other business communications and prepares documents that are free of errors.

ORGANIZATION OF TEXTBOOK

This textbook has a reference manual, *The Office Guide,* for grammar and punctuation rules, confusing word usage, and general information concerning document formatting. This reference manual will be used in the completion of activities in the textbook. It will also prove to be a valuable resource after you complete this course.

The textbook itself is divided into four sections and three appendices:

1. Introductory Student Information (this section)
2. Machine Transcription Overview: Transcription Trends, Transcription Software and Equipment, and Dictation-Transcription Procedures
3. Written Communication Assessment
4. Transcription Practice Lessons 1–16

Appendix A: Machine Transcription Student Progress Record
Appendix B: Language Arts Skill Review with Language Tapes
Appendix C: Answers to Lesson Exercises

OVERVIEW OF TEXT SECTIONS

Section 1—Introductory Overview explains the organization and use of the textbook and grading criteria, and contains forms to use in tracking your progress.

Section 2—Machine Transcription Overview: Trends, Equipment, and Procedures gives an insight into the transcription equipment currently being used in small businesses as well as in large legal, medical, and insurance environments. Transcribing procedures and production expectations are also discussed in this section. An introductory tape is included to practice listening skills.

Section 3—Written Communication Assessment provides an assessment to determine where your strengths and weaknesses are in relation to grammar, punctuation, and language skills. A pretest is included to assess these skills. Depending upon your language pretest results, you will be instructed to work through the language tapes and exercises in Appendix B or to begin Section 4.

Section 4—Transcription Practice Lessons centers around dictated tapes containing a variety of correspondence dictated by personnel in different types of business organizations. There are 16 lessons in this section and each lesson includes a language, word usage, and proofreading review, and a transcription preview. Supplemental transcription is also provided.

Appendix A includes a student progress record that can be used as an assignment sheet and record of progress.

Appendix B contains an index to the tapes that cover grammar and punctuation rules. It can also be used as an assignment record.

Appendix C provides the correct answers to the self-check exercises in each lesson.

HOW TO USE THIS TEXTBOOK

1. Review the information concerning grading in this section. Before turning work in to your instructor, check to make sure that it is mailable quality. Use the grading information and student progress record in Appendix A to keep track of your grades.

2. Review the information in Section 2.

   Listen to the introductory/practice tape. It will review some points you have already been introduced to concerning machine transcription. After you have listened to the first side of the introductory tape, remove it, turn it over, and listen to the other side, which is called "Listening Techniques and Practice." The dictation on this side will give you examples of and practice in the special listening techniques you should develop for transcription.

   In order to help you develop good listening skills and to get used to using the foot pedal on your transcriber, complete the Introductory Listening Tape Self-Check. This self-check is at the end of Section 2. The information needed to complete the self-check is contained in the introductory tape.

3. When you have completed the introductory tape, complete the language skills pretest in Section 3. Give this pretest to your instructor for grading. Your instructor will tell you if you should do all or any of the language tapes. After you have worked through the assigned tapes, take the language skills posttest and give it to your instructor for grading.

4. Consult your instructor before working in Section 4 to find out whether you should do all lessons or only selected ones. The length of some machine transcription courses may not be long enough to allow time to transcribe all tapes.

   Tests: Four transcription and communication tests are coordinated with the transcription lessons in Section 4. Each transcription test consists of four documents to be transcribed. Communication tests cover grammar, punctuation, and proofreading skills.

TEXTBOOK CONVENTIONS FOR FORMATTING, PUNCTUATION, AND CAPITALIZATION

While the majority of punctuation, spelling, grammar, and formatting rules have not changed over time, some have. These changes have led to inconsistencies, and in some cases, no authoritative standard has been established for the capitalization of some technological and Internet words. For the purpose of this textbook, the following rules will apply for consistency. Please use these conventions when transcribing.

Punctuation

Comma or semicolon after enumerated items in a sentence: Follow rule GP 9.1 in *The Office Guide,* which uses a comma after the enumerated items introduced by numbers enclosed by parentheses within a sentence. This rule adheres to *The Gregg Reference Manual, Rule 222.*

Inclusion of commas in numbers: Follow rules GP 12.1 and GP 13.1 in *The Office Guide,* which says that including or not including the comma in four-digit numbers is correct as long as consistency is maintained. Therefore, $7000 and $7,000 are correct as long as the inclusion or noninclusion of the comma is consistent.

Use of commas before the word *which*:   Follow rule GP 3.3A in *The Office Guide* with the following modification. *Which* **usually** *indicates text that is not essential to the sentence.*

Ninety-five percent of the time the word *which* is used to introduce a nonessential phrase, so a comma is required. Occasionally it is used to introduce an essential phrase. Word processing software automatically indicates an error if a comma is not placed before the word *which* and suggests that a comma be inserted or that *which* be changed to *that.* Be careful, however, because there are times when the phrase introduced by *which* is essential to the meaning of the sentence and no comma is required.

When *The Office Guide* is revised, this rule will be clarified to show examples, such as the following, of when *which* is essential to the sentence.

The GED test given on May 1 is the test which you must pass.

Periods after items in an enumerated list: Follow rule GP 1.1 in *The Office Guide* with the following notation: Although the stem ending in a preposition always indicates that the stem is incomplete, there are times when the stem is incomplete and does not end with a preposition. Example:

These options include:

- Selling your house.
- Renting for a year.

Periods are needed to complete the stem (sentence).

Formatting

Documents: Templates in word processing software deviate from the traditional formatting of some documents. For instance, placement of items in the heading material of a memorandum differs from that of traditional memorandum formatting. Ask your instructor if template formatting is acceptable.

Placement of enclosure notations: Rule DF 10 in *The Office Guide* should be applied and notations, such as *Enclosure,* should be typed a double space below the originator's typed name. When spacing is a problem, however, the enclosure notation can be typed a single space below the originator's name to avoid the letter becoming two pages.

Capitalization

E-mail: There is no consistency in how the term E-mail is typed and no one way has been identified by an authority as the standard. Some publications use e-mail and others use E-mail or Email. For consistency when working in this textbook, use E-mail.

Words including *web*:   There is no consistency in the capitalization of terms that include the word *web*. For consistency when working in this textbook, capitalize the word *web,* for example, Web site.

GRADING INFORMATION

GRADING CRITERIA

Mailable Copy is the Grading Standard

Mailable Documents:

- Have no spelling errors.
- Have no punctuation errors.
- Have no grammatical errors.
- Contain accurate and complete information.
- Follow the originator's directions.
- Have no incorrect word usage.
- Have no typographical errors.
- Have no word division errors.
- Are correctly formatted and include all essential parts of the document (example: date, inside address, enclosure notations, reference initials).

Mailable Documents (20 Points Awarded)

If a document is turned in that does not meet the above criteria because of several errors, it will be considered **unmailable.** *Unmailable copy will result in no points awarded toward your grade.* Things that will make a document unmailable are as follows:

Unmailable Documents Have:

- Errors caused by failure to follow specific directions.
- Several uncorrected errors.
- Insertion or omission of words that change the meaning of the sentence.
- Transposed words that change the meaning of the sentence.
- Poor formatting.
- Omission of essential parts of a document.

Unmailable Documents (No Points Awarded)

If a document contains only a few minor errors that can be corrected, it will be considered **mailable with reservation.** *Documents that are mailable with reservation will receive penalty points toward grading.* Things that will make a document mailable with reservation are as follows:

Mailable with Reservation Documents Have:

- Omission of nonessential part(s) of a document (examples: reference initials, enclosure notations).
- Minor vertical or horizontal placement errors.
- Minor spacing errors.
- Inserted or omitted words that do not change the meaning of the sentence.
- Transposed words that do not change the meaning of the sentence.
- Incorrect style.
- Minor punctuation errors such as a missing comma.

Mailable with Reservation (Penalty of 5 Points per Error)

If a document has only one minor error that is easily corrected, it will be considered **correctable copy.** This means that the originator found an error that requires the transcriptionist to correct. Even though a document has only one correctable error, if a transcriptionist constantly turns in work that needs correction, he or she will soon become unemployed. Therefore, *5 points will be deducted for a correctable error.* Only **one** error is allowed for a document to be considered correctable copy.

Correctable Copy (Penalty of 5 Points per Error)

Remember:

- *Mailable copy* is worth 20 points.
- *Unmailable copy* is worth no points.
- *Mailable with reservation copy* has a penalty of 5 points per error (only two allowed).
- *Correctable copy* has a penalty of 5 points per error (only one allowed).

FINAL GRADE

Your transcription assignments will be graded according to the grading criteria previously explained. Points will be awarded for each document transcribed based upon mailability. Points received for these transcription assignments will be used to determine a grade for practice transcription, which will account for 10% of your final grade.

Grades received on the language arts/proofreading tests will account for 30% of your final grade.

Transcription production test grades will account for 60% of your final grade.

The following form will help you record information that will be used to calculate your final grade. This form can be used whether you transcribe all the documents in each lesson or transcribe only those identified for a shortened course. This is because in both the complete (standard) and abbreviated (short) courses the transcription and written tests are required.

Transcription Production | Language Arts/Proofreading | Practice Transcription

Transcription Test
Grades (60% of Final Grade)

Language Arts/Proofreading
Test Grades (30% of Final Grade)

Transcription Assignments
(10% of Final Grade)

	Pts.		Pts.	
Test #1 _____	Test #1 _____	____Les. 1		____Les. 9
Test #2 _____	Test #2 _____	____Les. 2		____Les. 10
Test #3 _____	Test #3 _____	____Les. 3		____Les. 11
Test #4 _____	Test #4 _____	____Les. 4		____Les. 12
Average _____	Average _____	____Les. 5		____Les. 13
		____Les. 6		____Les. 14
		____Les. 7		____Les. 15
Speed and Accuracy Scale:		____Les. 8		____Les. 16

Grading Scale, 16 Lessons:

NWPM	GRADE
25+	A
20–24	B
10–19	C

320–295 Pts. = A
294–269 Pts. = B
268–243 Pts. = C

Total Pts._____
Grade_____

Lesson Letterhead

When you transcribe the dictation for the lessons in Section 4, use the letterheads for the 16 organizations or businesses. These letterheads can be obtained from the Internet. If the document you are transcribing is a letter or memo, open the letterhead for the company for which you are transcribing and use the letterhead in the document.

To access the letterheads from the Internet:

Go to: **www.prenhall.com/business_studies**
click on student resources
click on Mallinson

Machine Transcription Overview

Transcription Trends

The Dictation-Transcription Process

2

TRANSCRIPTION TRENDS

The hot area in machine transcription is currently in the medical transcription field. Here the demand has increased rapidly and spawned opportunities for transcriptionists to work in small offices, large hospitals, or from their homes as individual contractors or as employees of a medical transcription company.

While the demand for transcription operators has increased in the medical field, it has decreased in the large office setting. The exact reason for the decline in the use of machine transcription in the office environment can be attributed to managers' and supervisors' increased computer usage. Although voice recognition software has become popular with some doctors, office supervisors and managers have not embraced this technology due to the time-consuming initial learning stage. Even though voice recognition software is not a major contributing factor to the decline in the use of machine transcription in large firms, refinement of voice recognition software may make it more popular in businesses.

TRANSCRIPTION HAS GONE VIRTUAL

The Internet and digital audio technology have revolutionized secretarial and administrative services. Even though machine transcription has declined in use in businesses, a demand for machine transcription skills has escalated in the virtual office setting. Hundreds of online companies offer machine transcription services, and many people are finding this to be a new career path.

New careers in online office solutions and virtual assisting have opened to individuals who have typical business/office skills that include machine transcription. Virtual assistants offer administrative support to clients without the restriction of physical location and are independent contractors who provide administrative services through the Internet, facsimile machine, and telephone.

Virtual office and business support services offer a wide range of virtual administrative assistant support, such as:

- Image and document scanning.
- Meeting arrangements.
- Answering phones/faxes/E-mails and responding to messages.
- Office management (setting up office procedures, creating filing systems, developing employee policies, etc.).
- Spreadsheet creation and maintenance.
- Travel arrangements.
- Word processing.
- Transcribing dictation.
- Business mailings (traditional and E-mail).
- Slide presentations (PowerPoint).
- Photocopying and binding.
- Editing and proofreading.
- Desktop publishing (brochures, flyers, newsletters, business cards, etc.).
- Minutes and reports.
- Business development plans.
- Seminars (motivational speaking, employee training, software assistance).
- Research.
- Accounting.
- Data entry and database management (mailing lists, labels, queries, reports, etc.).
- Web site design and maintenance.

The need to operate in a global community is one reason why virtual assistants and virtual business solution companies are growing in popularity. Other reasons include:

- Pressured deadlines.
- Reduced operating costs to the client—the client does not have to provide and maintain equipment and office space, pay for benefit packages, and keep track of payroll taxes and insurance.
- Productivity enhancement—the client does not have to spend time supervising staff.
- Convenience—service is provided 24 hours a day 7 days a week and dictation can be done wherever there is access to a phone.
- Efficiency—if the same virtual assistant is used, there is no retraining of temps and things are done according to the client's procedures and requests.
- Flexibility—a virtual assistant can be part time, full time, casual, or permanent.

- Dependability—transcription and other administrative services do not stop because someone is out sick or on vacation. Many virtual assistants are employees of virtual companies that can assign jobs through a network of online employees.

Beverly Fain is one of the many individuals who perform administrative assistant duties from home.

Administrative assistants desiring more flexible working conditions can pursue a career as a virtual assistant to one or more clients or can work for an online secretarial office solutions company. With either of these options, individuals work from home and have the choice of performing broad administrative support tasks or specializing in areas such as machine transcription, Web design, desktop publishing, or accounting.

Specialization of machine transcription in the virtual assistance field has increased. The popularity of this trend is growing and clients for virtual transcription include individuals and companies in the following fields: banking, marketing, publishing, research, public relations, radio, insurance, television, film production, medical, technology, law, financial services, and education.

Virtual transcriptionists enjoy working from home and owning their own businesses or working for virtual transcription companies. The same requirements to be a successful transcriptionst in a traditional business setting such as fast and accurate typing, stellar grammar, proofreading skill, and excellent listening ability also apply to being a successful virtual transcriptionst. In addition, self-discipline, business management, and an entrepreneurship spirit are needed. Virtual transcriptionists should also be skilled as administrative assistants, because a job may require complete product delivery such as the transcription of the notes for an entire conference, preparing camera-ready copy, and arranging for the printing and binding of the transcribed document into a book.

In this textbook you will learn broad transcription skills and apply these skills in a variety of traditional business settings. These skills should carry over into the new online machine transcription services where the types of material transcribed include more than the typical business documents such as letters, memorandums, press releases, reports, and travel itineraries. In addition to the traditional business documents, virtual transcription services include transcribing speeches, sermons, interviews, documentaries, meetings, training sessions, audio portions of films and videos, lectures, publicity interviews, teleconferences, Webcasts, news transcripts, novels, manuals, television scripts, broadcast transcription, testimonials, songs, seminars, depositions, interviews, manuscripts, screenplays, focus groups, conference proceedings, and press conferences.

C.A. Mace Transcription Services in Central New Jersey is an example of one virtual transcription company that offers verbatim transcription for in-depth interviews, media transcripts, surveillance tapes, meetings/conferences, focus groups, and general dictation. Sten-Tel is another virtual transcription service that has 45 national offices providing telephonic- and Internet-based transcription and dictation services. The company provides transcription service to the medical, legal, law enforcement, travel, education, insurance, and corporate communities. Through Sten-Tel's national network of transcription service providers, transcription is returned electronically within 24 hours.

2

2

Flash Transcription is a virtual transcription company that transcribes medical, legal, advertising, technical, and other recorded material. All transcription is reviewed by at least two individuals before being returned to the client, and an English instructor on the company's staff provides proofing services for depositions, transcripts, and other written material. Delivery of the transcribed material is in hard copy or a variety of electronic formats and E-mail.

Domenichelli Business Services is a typical virtual transcription company that produces transcripts recorded on any dictation medium: audiotapes, digital file transfer, or telephone dial-in dictation. The company has "modern-day scribes" available in every time zone in the continental United States and throughout the English-speaking world. The company believes that this global presence strengthens its ability to expeditiously produce high-quality transcripts by lengthening the production day and selecting the best transcriptionists available worldwide.

Hired Hand Transcription is an online transcription service that transcribes digital audio, .WAV, .RM, MP3, VHS video, CDs, and standard and microcassettes. The majority of the company's clients are in the fields of finance, education, research, management consulting, publishing, media, and health. The company transcribes IT conferences, interviews, recorded statements, research, speeches, executive meetings, telephone and Internet-based conference calls/Webcasts, multiple-day recorded conferences, seminars, focus groups, dissertations, sermons, and online business transactions. Finished transcripts are retrievable from an ID- and password-protected site. Transcripts are downloaded directly into a client's computer.

The Transcript Company provides closed captioning and state-of-the-art online transcription services for television, movie, banking, marketing, legal, medical, commercial, and religious industries. The company has worldwide customers ranging from individuals needing one-time service to the world's largest companies. The company transcribes and translates a variety of videotape, audiotape, computer, vinyl RPM, and 8-track formats.

Digital Transcription

Companies that have used analog tapes in the past are now switching to digital technology in order to capitalize on this technology's ability to access information quickly and to control the process of information. The transition from analog to digital technology has been the most significant development in the 100-year-plus history of dictation. Digital technology opened the doors to Internet transcription. Dictators now rapidly download work over the phone line onto the PC of someone working at home or onto a LAN where it can be routed for transcription.

Digital technology has enabled *voice messaging* to become common. Voice messaging enables employees to send, receive, and listen to voice messages through a telephone messaging network. Employees can distribute a voice message to an entire group and request that the message be transcribed and sent to the sender and recipients as a follow-up hard copy. Integrated communications now allow for the following to happen from a PC:

- Recording and playback of voice messages
- Creating and faxing of documents

- Recording a voice message to accompany faxes
- Listening to E-mail messages as they are read by using text-to-speech conversion
- Forwarding of E-mail messages with a voice message

The surprise is that using nothing more than the telephone keypad does all this. Digital transcription involves the capturing of data through a telephone, into a handheld digital recorder, via a microphone or other input device and transferring of the captured data in digital format to transcriptionists.

Dictation and transcription can take place anywhere in the world, as data files are automatically allocated to available transcriptionists across a WAN or the Internet, facilitating faster document turnaround.

Most online virtual transcription services provide transcription from standard cassette tape, microcassette, reel-to-reel, and 4-track to new technology such as magneto-optical disk, CD-audio, and digital transcription. Digital transcription takes advantage of current technology that allows audio files (wave files) to be downloaded from a client's computer to the virtual transcription service provider's computer. This allows transcription to be done directly from the computer and to be sent via E-mail to the destination requested by the client.

Kim Brown is one of the many transcriptionists who use digital transcription technology. Although employed by a company that does medical transcription, Kim works from home. When she began her career eight years ago, Kim transcribed analog tapes. She now transcribes dictation downloaded from the Internet.

There are numerous ways to make a digital recording. One way is to use a handheld recorder that is similar to the traditional microcassette recorder. The main difference is the audio is recorded directly into the memory of the machine. When the recorder is connected to a computer, the audio file is uploaded for transcribing.

Another method to make a digital recording is to use a microphone with a computer that has a built-in audio function. It is recommended that the system have good compression so quality is maintained. Because even highly compressed digital audio files are too large to send as E-mail attachments, File Transfer Protocol (FTP) is used to quickly transfer files across the Internet.

VoiceDoc enables a person to dictate directly to a PC using a microphone or by downloading from a cassette/tape recorder. When the dictator is finished, the files are compressed and transferred to a transcriptionist's PC.

Now with telephone and Internet access and computers, the transcription process has become quick and easy. Here is an overview of the process:

1. The client calls an 800 number and enters a password or account number. At the beep, the client starts dictating. Numbers on the telephone are used similar to commands on traditional dictation units: For example, pressing 1 activates a pause; pressing 2 resumes dictation; pressing 3 plays back the last four seconds of the dictation; pressing 7 allows the client to replay everything dictated; pressing the # signifies the end of the dictation and checks that the job has been received.

2. As soon as the client is finished dictating, the dictation is stored as a voice file on an FTP site and is ready immediately to be transcribed.

2

3. The transcriptionist accesses the FTP site and downloads the client's voice file(s) to his or her computer and transcribes the dictation. The documents are transcribed in formats such as word processing, PDF, plain text, or HTML.

4. The client then accesses the FTP site and downloads the transcribed documents onto his or her computer.

Digital voice technology solved the problems associated with endless loop technology and has introduced a new era in recording media. It captures voice digitally on computer disks or mini CD-ROM, enabling several dictators to simultaneously record, store, and access hundreds of dictated documents and voice messages through a central source. The digital system eliminates the time-consuming exercise of scanning, searching, and handling tapes. Documents can be left "open" to allow for interruptions or approvals before approving them for transcription.

Digital voice technology is a software-based technology that offers the most advanced dictation capabilities because it allows instant access to any dictated work at any time in any order for transcription. Work can be routed automatically for transcribing in the order of importance determined by the user. The system can be programmed by station, user, work type, record number, or department.

Digital voice processing is used in many hospitals because it provides an advanced system for clinical reporting with immediate access. This technology eliminates reporting delays caused by a lag between dictation and transcription time. Digital voice technology allows physicians and diagnostic personnel to hear the latest report on a patient in the diagnostician's own voice before the transcribed copy of the report is delivered. This is done by calling the hospital's phone access numbers and entering the patient's ID number.

New systems allow for the identification of job identification data via bar code technology for faster entry and greater accuracy. This technology includes a light pen, a laser scanner, or hand microphone and built-in light pen. These input accessory tools help ensure accuracy of data input. The pen is swiped across bar codes for instant identification, eliminating the need for keypad input.

One feature of digital processing is a *call alert* capability that allows the dictating physician to have the verbal dictated report automatically transmitted and stored in the referring physician's voice mailbox as it is sent for transcribing.

Voice-generated digital technology is used in many hospitals. This technology allows a clinician to dictate a radiology report and have it appear on the computer screen. By saying "print report," the clinician can get an instant printout of the report without writing or waiting for the report to be transcribed. This system combines three of the most exciting new concepts in hospital communications technology—digital voice storage, voice recognition, and speech synthesis.

As radiologists dictate their reports, each word appears on the computer screen where it can be proofread and edited. The system provides one- or two-word *trigger phrases* that can call up a predefined sentence or paragraph. In dictating a bone exam, for example, saying "normal" displays the on-screen entry, "No bony or soft tissue abnormality noted. Impression: Normal examination." Physicians can customize the system's vocabulary. Before a report is printed, the computer electronically spell-checks the document. Radiologists and other users of the system can opt for conventional dictation and transcription by touching a button.

Does this mean that machine transcriptionists will be out of work soon? Does this mean that voice-generated documents will be the standard method used to process documents? No, this advancement in digital technology opens many possibilities for document processing; and the transcription skills you are learning now will be in demand for a long time. Digital voice technology means that you will have sophisticated tools to help you transcribe more efficiently and have the opportunity to work from home doing "virtual transcribing."

DIGITAL TRANSCRIPTION SOFTWARE AND HARDWARE

Word counting software is frequently used with machine transcription. Virtual transcriptionists are frequently paid by the amount of words transcribed, so accurate word and line counting is essential. There are several word/line counting software programs available. Sylcount is the original document counting program for transcriptionists that allows for counts of lines, pages, characters, words, headers, footers, tabs, indents, underlines, blank spaces, font changes, footnotes, bold, capitalized characters, superscript, subscript, italics, small caps, and hard returns. Various versions of the software allow for separate counting options and billing rates for each client, automatic billing calculations for each document, and invoice totals.

The word count feature in word processing programs is not as sophisticated as the one used in official word count software, but it is close to the count calculated by counting characters to obtain a word count.

In addition to word count software, the hardware in digital transcription systems uses software. Examples of the software used with various equipment components are discussed next.

Hardware for Digital Transcription

Recorders: Recorders are only one component of a digital transcription system. Following are two examples of recorders used with digital transcription systems.

The Quikscribe Recorder has software with an external hand control that includes a built-in microphone which allows it to record and edit behind Windows applications.

Sony ICD-MS1 Digital Recorder with removable Memory Stick media is an example of a digital recorder that allows for easy download of dictation to a PC for transcription or transmission as audible E-mail. The Memory Stick media is a small, convenient flash memory device that is interchangeable with other digital devices including PCs and digital cameras. The 16MB Memory Stick provides up to 63 minutes of recording time in standard mode and 2.1 hours in long play mode. Some unique features of the ICD-MS1 are the playback edit function which makes it easy to correct the dictation and a highly efficient file folder system allowing the creation of up to 340 folders.

Storage such as the Sony MSAC-US5 Memory Stick PC Adaptor Reader/Writer enables the transfer of files from a Memory Stick to a PC in a standard 3.5-inch floppy disk drive.

WAVpedal allows for flexibility in the transcription process. WAVpedal works with word processing software and controls playback of .wav-formatted files. The foot pedal controls playback to accommodate fast dictators.

2

Foot Pedals A special foot pedal and software is needed to transcribe directly from the computer. WAVpedal (as shown) is an example of an interface that allows the operator to control the playback of any .wav-formatted file on the computer. Transcription equipment is not needed because the pedal controls the volume and playback of voice files. The interface automatically loads the word processing software.

Digital Systems

PC-based digital dictation and transcription software such as Quikscribe's Digital Transcription System reduces dictation and transcription time. Features of the system include insert audio, cut and paste text, capture screen shots, add file attachments, and undo and redo unlimited audio edits in real time. The Quikscribe Player used to transcribe audio files utilizes software that applies a triple-action foot switch.

WinScribe is a digital workflow system that allows users to dictate by speaking into a telephone/cellular phone, microphone, PC, or a handheld digital recorder. Data in digital format are then automatically routed to a transcriptionist anywhere in the world through a WAN or the Internet.

Following are example components of digital transcription systems.

Components of a digital transcription system for a large transcription company and hospital: VoiceDoc, VoiceScribe, and VoiceWare server.	Components of digital transcription system for a small company (a couple of dictators and a couple of transcriptionists) or for a single at-home transcriptionist.
This would be a fully automated system:	This would be the typical hardware needed:
VoiceDoc used by the dictator in conjunction with VoiceScribe (WAVpedal with a small database and built-in communications software) used by the transcriptionist in a modem-to-modem or DSL connection or with VoiceWare Server. When used directly with VoiceScribe, either the dictator (VoiceDoc) or the transcriptionist (VoiceScribe) is designated as the Host and the other party initiates getting and sending dictations and transcribed reports.	WAVpedal and digital recorder. Files are sent and received via E-mail or downloaded directly if they are in the same location.

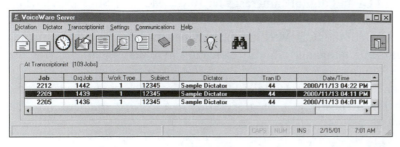

Screen capture of the VoiceWare Server

The following VoiceWare Server replaces the *supervisor's console* in traditional transcription systems.

The VoiceWare Server screen has eight types of dictation (pending, completed, to send, at transcription site, awaiting QA, at QA, pre-transcribed, and transcribed). A toolbar consisting of 12 Windows icons that display the status of documents and error dictations makes it easy to track documents. The VoiceWare Server is the central hub that interfaces to dictation machines, Dragon Naturally Speaking™ speech recognition products, a variety of slideswitch and bar code–enabled microphones, and handheld digital recorders.

TRADITIONAL DICTATION EQUIPMENT

Although dictation equipment comes in many sizes, it has common characteristics. These common characteristics allow the dictator to record dictation for a specified amount of time; review what has been dictated; make corrections; mark the end of the dictation; and through indexing and cueing features, give special instructions to the person who will transcribe.

There are three main categories of dictation equipment: portable units, desktop machines, and centralized dictation systems. The location and use of the dictation equipment determine which category should be used.

Portable Dictation Units

Portable dictation units run on batteries and can easily be transported from one location to another. They are ideal for the person who travels and are designed to fit in a briefcase or pocket. Portable dictation units generally are small enough to be held in one hand and use standard cassettes, minicassettes, and microcassettes.

The features on portable dictation units have increased in recent years. Only 2.5 by 5.25 inches or smaller and weighing 5.9 ounces or less, these portable units provide the dictator with the capability to use voice-activated recording, which means the unit starts recording when the dictator speaks and stops recording when the dictator stops talking. Most portable dictation units also have an indexing feature which allows the dictator to give instructions to the transcriptionist, an LED light indicating that the batteries are low, a charging unit to recharge batteries, and end-of-tape signal to let the dictator know how much dictation time is left, and a pause control to let the dictator reference materials.

Desktop Units

Companies that are not large enough to require centralized dictation systems use dictation units that are small enough to be placed on the dictator's desk. Small and mid-size companies use desktop units that are for dictating only, for transcribing only, or for a combination of both. These new features have made desktop units multifunctional:

- Controls that record date, time, dictator identification, and length of dictation
- Two-way recording capability that allows the dictator to record both sides of a phone conversation
- Telephone answering machine functions that allow callers to leave messages on the unit
- Cordless units that allow the dictator to leave his or her desk while dictating
- Visual displays that provide the dictator with information about his or her dictation location on the tape

- Electronic cueing devices that allow the dictator to place a tone at the end of dictation or to give special instructions
- Calculator functions for the computing of client telephone charges
- Calendar capabilities that remind the dictator of appointments
- Fast erase capabilities for simultaneously erasing and rewinding of an entire cassette
- Conference control to clearly pick up all voices at a meeting

Centralized Dictation Systems

Centralized dictation systems are used by large organizations because they provide the most cost-effective means to serve a large volume of dictators. There are four basic parts to a centralized dictation system: *dictation unit, recorder, transcription unit,* and *supervisor's console.* These components are quickly changing as technology advancements are made. For instance, new systems have now eliminated the supervisor's console.

The *dictation unit* may be a hand microphone or telephone receiver that allows the dictator to dictate work that is transmitted through wires to a recording unit. This method of dictating allows dictators to use dictation units or telephones to generate work at many different areas in a building or outside of the building.

The *recorder* is the unit that receives and stores the dictation. Dictation is recorded in either *discrete* media, which requires the supervisor to handle cassettes when removing them from the recorder, or in a medium that does not require cassette handling. *Endless loop* recording was one of the first analog systems used that eliminated the need to handle cassettes. The main disadvantage of endless loop technology is its rigidity; only one person can transcribe at a time, and dictation has to be transcribed in the order it was received. Although handling and tracking dictation recorded on many cassettes is a problem with discrete media, it allows the supervisor to address rush items first and to distribute dictation to be transcribed by several operators at the same time, which greatly reduces turnaround time.

The *transcription unit* is a machine that the operator uses to listen to recorded dictation. The transcription unit has a headset that allows the operator to hear the dictated text, a foot pedal that plays, fast forwards, or backs up the tape, and the machine itself that allows the operator to control the volume and tone of the dictation. If digital technology is used, the transcriber station displays critical record information such as the user, work type, record number, and job number. With digital voice technology, the transcription station also has a display window and the capability to keep track of the transcriptionist's name, originator's (dictator's) name, originator's number, work type, record number, date of dictation, time of dictation, and length of the job. Each transcription station credits work to the operator and accumulates accurate and comprehensive production statistics.

Another feature of digital voice technology that makes the transcription unit easier to use is instant positioning. Instant positioning eliminates fast forward and rewind because by touching a button you can locate a voice file or a location within one.

The *supervisor's console* is used to control the workflow of the dictation recorded. If digital technology is used, the console provides summary reports on department productivity. Job information such as the transcriptionist's name, dictator's name and number, work type, record number, date and time of dictation, and productivity information are displayed on the console. The supervisor can decide how, when, and where each dictated document could best be handled for maximum efficiency for document processing. Because it is software based, the supervisor can route dictation to individual secretaries within a specific department or to a centralized word processing center. Work can also be prioritized and distributed according to author, status, subject, department, time/date, special designations, or work type. The supervisor can also print a hard copy of reports produced by the system that are displayed on the console. The last 65,000 jobs are stored on hard drive, and historical information is backed up on disk.

New technology has made dictation management control easier, and the supervisor's console is not always needed. Items such as transcription status, job list, and work routing assignments are displayed at the PC station, so it is no longer necessary to go to the management console to view this type of information.

THE DICTATION-TRANSCRIPTION PROCESS

Many aspects of the dictation-transcription process were discussed in the preceding information; therefore, the remainder of this section will focus on dictation and transcription procedures.

DICTATION GUIDELINES

Most organizations have training sessions to assist their employees in how to operate the dictation equipment they will use and how to dictate effectively. When a centralized dictation system is used, dictators are usually given written instructions on how to use the system and the procedure and codes used when dictating from inhouse or from locations outside of the building.

Frequently, companies use a dictation format to help guide new dictators. Using a standard format is also beneficial to the transcriptionist because it speeds up the transcribing process. Using consistency in the dictating process frees the transcriptionist from time spent figuring out what type of document the transcribed material will be and how to treat special instructions. For instance, the dictator needs to know how to instruct the transcriptionist to type something in initial caps or all caps. Guidelines to help the originator do this may be written as follows:

Desired Action	What to Say/Example
Capitalize the first letter of the next word.	Capital (Example: The invoice number is [Capital] P1287.)
Capitalize the first letter of each major word in a group of related words.	Initial Caps (Example: The meeting will take place in the [Initial Caps] Presidential Room.)
Capitalize all letters in each word that follows until you want to stop.	All Caps (Example: The state organization [All Caps] FVA [End all Caps] will meet on Thursday.)

Some companies use forms to assist their employees in dictating. This is especially helpful to the novice dictator. Following is an example of such a form.

Dictation Format

Operator, this is _____ from _____
(Name) (Department)

This is to be a _____
(Specify letter, long memo, report, outline, etc.)

Operator, special instructions _____

_____
(Store longer, rough draft, special format, additional originals, letterhead other than company, etc.)

This is to be addressed/sent to _____
(Addressee's name and address/dept.)

Regarding _____ and/or subject _____

Greeting (if applicable)

Dictate body of document

Dictate closing (your name and title)

Copies to _____ _____ _____

End of document (dictate next document or specify end of dictation)

Pronounce a word before spelling it. Spelling is necessary only for words that are unusual or can be spelled more than one way. We have found that words with letters *b-c-d-g-f-m-n-p-s-t-v-y-z* are the most difficult to understand and would encourage you to use the phonetic alphabet below for these letters:

b as in *bravo*	*g* as in *golf*	*s* as in *Sam*
c as in *Charlie*	*m* as in *Mike*	*t* as in *Tango*
d as in *delta*	*n* as in *November*	*v* as in *Victor*
f as in *fun*	*p* as in *papa*	*y* as in *Yankee*

TRANSCRIPTION LOGGING GUIDELINES

The large number of documents transcribed and stored through the use of computer software has made it necessary for a systematic method of logging and retrieving these documents. It is not unusual for document retrieval information to be printed a double space below the closing information on a document. The coded information about the document transcribed varies from company to company, but each firm is consistent in following the procedure established. Correspondence that does not need to be stored permanently is still coded and stored for one week. Following are two examples of document coding.

EXAMPLE 1

Should you have any further questions, please feel free to contact me at (813) 275-7883, Ext. 2814.

Sincerely,

Juanita Responte
Program Assistant

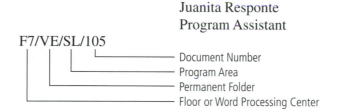

EXAMPLE 2

Sincerely,

Wayne Charlton
Marketing Director

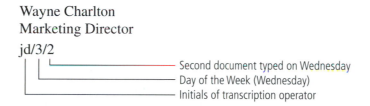

Document or transcription coding has been placed on letters for 10 years or more, but the appearance of these codes on documents has only now been considered acceptable by many businesses. Document coding in legal documents is handled much the way blind copy notations are made; that is, the coding only appears on the file copy.

TRANSCRIPTION LOGS

Transcribed documents are usually logged in the same manner as word processing documents. Most firms use specific log sheets to record and keep track of transcription documents if they do not have a computerized system that does this. Most transcriptionists have production quotas that must be met for employment. Some large organizations such as hospitals pay transcription operators a bonus for each word they transcribe over their established quota. Although an operator's pay may be affected by the amount of work transcribed, the quality of the transcribed work is equally important.

Some transcription instructions are given to the transcriptionist on a work requisition form. This is done when hard copy text is part of dictated material. When this is the case, originators complete the usual work requisition form used. Following is a modified version of a work requisition form. This transcription instruction form can also be used by a novice transcriptionist to record information about how to format documents.

Transcription Instruction Form

Name of Originator/Dictator_____

Document: _____Block Letter _____Modified Block Letter

_____AMS Letter _____Block Letter/Paragraph
_____Press Release _____Minutes
_____Form Letter _____Variable Information
_____Memo _____Report

Send Copies to: _____

Margins _____ Special Paper _____

Special Instructions _____

MACHINE TRANSCRIPTION TERMS

Adaptor A device that makes media compatible.

Aural Having to do with hearing.

Cassette Magnetic tape that is encased in a holder. A standard cassette holds up to 120 minutes of dictation. Mini- and microcassettes, although much smaller, can also hold up to 120 minutes of dictation.

Centralized System Used primarily in large companies. Allows dictators to call a central recording device to dictate from areas within the company or outside of the physical facility.

Desktop Dictation Units Small dictation machines that easily fit on the dictator's desk. May have strictly dictation capabilities or a combination of dictation and transcription capabilities. Uses cassette storage.

Digital Technology Software-based technology that allows random access to dictated text instantly and requires no media handling. Digital portable recorders store on DAT or mini CD-ROM and information can be downloaded via phone or rapid download to a LAN.

Discrete Media Removable media such as cassettes that are used to record dictation.

Endless Loop Nonremovable media used to record dictation. Similar to the tape used in reel-to-reel tape recorders that has spliced ends so that it forms a continuous loop. The oldest dictation is automatically erased as new dictation replaces it.

Enunciation The manner in which words or syllables are pronounced.

Index Slip A slip of paper used on older transcription units to indicate the length of dictation.

Indexing Feature   Used on a dictation unit to mark points where corrections or instructions are given. Usually done electronically with a cueing feature on most current dictation units.

LCD Window Display   Shows the location and length of each document and instruction as well as the dictator's or transcriptionist's location on the tape.

LED (Light-Emitting Diode)   An electronic display that lets the dictator see the dictation place on the cassette.

Letter/Instruction Counters   Indicate the number of letters and instructions recorded and also count down to indicate the number of documents left to be transcribed.

Operator   The person who is transcribing.

Originator   Dictator; the person who dictates the work.

Portable Dictation Unit   Small, usually handheld dictation machines that use discrete media (cassettes).

Principal   The person who originates or dictates the work.

Private Wire   A system of wires dedicated to connecting parts of a dictation system in a company.

Recorder   The unit that records the dictation onto magnetic tape or digital storage.

Remote   Dictation recorders and stations that are in separate locations from the transcription units.

Search Feature   Enables the operator to quickly locate and preview instructions before transcribing to avoid having to make changes after a document is typed.

Supervisor's Console   The component of a centralized dictation unit that controls the workflow of the recorded dictation.

Tank   Digital unit that stores voice on hard disk.

Telephone Lines   A system wired so that any telephone can be used for dictating purposes.

Transcription   The process of playing recorded dictation and typing a hard copy.

Transcriptionist   Operator; the person who types (transcribes) dictated communications.

Trigger Phrases   One- or two-word phrases that, when dictated, call up a predefined sentence or paragraph.

Turnaround Time   The amount of time between the recording of dictated work and the time it is transcribed and returned to the originator.

Verbal Insertion   Allows the dictator to insert changes, additions, or corrections at any point within the dictation process instead of recording over the dictation.

Voice-Activated Recording (VOR)   Dictation is recorded when the dictator speaks and automatically stops when the dictator stops speaking.

Voice-Generated Digital Technology   Technology that allows spoken words to be translated into text that appears on a computer monitor.

Well, this has been a lot to absorb. To help you review some of the information that has been presented, complete the machine transcription terminology exercise that follows.

Refer to Appendix C to check your answers.

2

Machine Transcription Terms Self-Test

Directions: Apply your knowledge of machine transcription terminology by correctly identifying the word that should be used in each of the following sentences.

1. His foreign accent makes his _____ unclear, and it is difficult to transcribe his work.

2. Prior to digital technology, the nonremovable media used to record dictation called _____ was commonly used in large organizations.

3. The dictator used the _____ feature on her transcription unit to automatically insert a change in the dictation.

4. Another name for the person dictating besides originator/dictator is _____.

5. The transcription operator used the _____ feature on her transcriber to locate and preview instructions before transcribing.

6. The _____ was improved when the dictators and transcription operators learned how to use 70 _____, which eliminated a great deal of typing.

7. The _____ for the endless loop tape system took up one corner of the room.

8. Metro-Plex will install a _____ that will allow all its employees to dictate 24 hours a day from _____ locations.

9. By monitoring the _____, the supervisor can tell how much work each transcription operator has been assigned.

10. You have to know _____ in order to correctly divide words.

11. _____ are used by many individuals in sales because they can easily be carried while working in the field.

12. An _____ is needed in order to allow the transcriber to interface with the computer.

13. The direction machine transcription technology is taking is _____, which allows software to randomly access dictated text without media handling.

14. The _____ on the transcription unit shows the location and length of each document as well as the dictator's location on the tape.

15. Many new transcription units have _____ capabilities that automatically stop the dictation when the dictator stops speaking.

✓ *Refer to Appendix C to check your answers.*

INTRODUCTION TO THE MACHINE TRANSCRIPTION PROCESS

The machine transcription process involves listening to dictated material with instructions, typing, and then proofreading the typed text. Several skills are integrated into this process.

Listening

Although listening is a large part of the communication process, it is also one of the weakest links. Hearing is different from listening in that it requires information to be received, recognized, comprehended, and retained. In essence, listening implies that we are able to make sense out of what we hear. Listening is a critical factor in the machine transcription process. Below are some tips to help you become a better listener.

- Remove distractions
- Pay attention to voice inflection
- Determine the main idea of the message
- Concentrate by listening for facts, accuracy, and meaning of information

In the machine transcription process you will learn to listen to instructions and develop what is commonly known as "listening in phrases."

Listening for Instructions

Receiving verbal instructions on the job instead of written ones takes awhile to get used to. Receiving instructions in a dictated format may take a little while to adjust to because the dictator is not present to ask for clarification if something is not understood. The dictator will usually preface instructions with the word *operator* to alert you to the fact that what follows is instructions and should *not* be typed. The dictator will usually include the following information in the instructions given at the beginning of each item.

■ His or her name (title or dept. are sometimes given)	■ Document type (letter, memo, agenda, report)
■ Special instructions (store for longer period of time, use special paper)	■ How many copies are needed and how they should be distributed
■ Additional information (such as merge information)	■ Special mailing instructions

Throughout the dictated material the dictator will also give you instructions. Sometimes these instructions are introduced by the word *operator* to alert you to the fact that what follows should not be typed. Instructions given within the dictated information include:

2

▪ Corrections	▪ End of dictation
▪ Spelling of names, technical terms, foreign words	▪ End of paragraphs and sometimes punctuation

An example follows of dictation with instructions indicated in bold and parentheses. Frequently you can distinguish instructions from the dictated material by the change in voice inflection of the dictator. Listening to voice inflection will also help you determine breaks that signify phrases, which will assist you in punctuating and determining whether a sentence is a statement or question.

(This is Roberto Martinez, merchandise manager. This will be a memo to division managers. Subject: Sales Projections) Congratulations on reaching your projected sales **(exclamation point).** The efforts of you and your staff are appreciated, and there will be a small bonus in your next month's paycheck. **(paragraph)** As you know, the Eastern Region will be restructured; and two new sales managers will be hired. In order for this restructuring to be successful, we will have to work together as a team. This restructuring will result in the following **(colon) (Operator please use an enumerated list format)** (1) new sales projections for ten instead of eight regions (2) sales projections based upon calculations of past performance shown in each city (3) a newly created position of district manager **(Operator, this ends enumerated items)** If any of you are interested in the position of district manager, please notify me within the next two weeks. Interviews for the position will be conducted in about a month. Once the restructuring of divisions is done, you will receive a copy of the proposal. Please give me your honest feedback including concerns you may have regarding the fairness of the restructuring. **(paragraph)** We have such a strong team now and want the restructuring to be a positive step in helping you develop your assigned area and reach its sales potential. The goal of the restructuring is to make it easier for you to do so by concentrating your efforts on a smaller territory. Please note that we see no elimination of jobs through this restructuring or a reduction in any region's sales staff. **(paragraph)** Once again, congratulations on reaching your sales projections. If you can think of any way that we at corporate headquarters can help you in the field please let us know. You know the strengths and weaknesses of your staff as well as the needs of your clients, so let us know the type of assistance you need including training and marketing campaigns. **(Operator, this is the end of the memo.)**

The transcribed memo follows:

MEMORANDUM

DATE: Current

TO: Division Managers

FROM: Roberto Martinez, Merchandise Manager

SUBJECT: Sales Projections

Congratulations on reaching your projected sales! The efforts of you and your staff are appreciated, and there will be a small bonus in your next month's paycheck.

As you know, the Eastern Region will be restructured; and two new sales managers will be hired. In order for this restructuring to be successful, we will have to work together as a team. This restructuring will result in the following:

1. new sales projections for ten instead of eight regions
2. sales projections based upon calculations of past performance shown in each city
3. a newly created position of district manager

If any of you are interested in the position of district manager, please notify me within the next two weeks. Interviews for the position will be conducted in about a month. Once the restructuring of divisions is done, you will receive a copy of the proposal. Please give me your honest feedback including concerns you may have regarding the fairness of the restructuring.

We have such a strong team now and want the restructuring to be a positive step in helping you develop your assigned area and reach its sales potential. The goal of the restructuring is to make it easier for you to do so by concentrating your efforts on a smaller territory. Please note that we see no elimination of jobs through this restructuring or a reduction in any region's sales staff.

Once again, congratulations on reaching your sales projections. If you can think of any way that we at corporate headquarters can help you in the field please let us know. You know the strengths and weaknesses of your staff as well as the needs of your clients, so let us know the type of assistance you need including training and marketing campaigns.

Typing/Transcribing

Typing involves the process of listening for phrases in dictation, stopping the dictation and keying (typing) these groups of words or phrases, and then starting the dictation and repeating the process. Essentially these steps are the heart of the transcription process. You will use your transcriber to start and stop the dictation and your computer to keyboard and store the dictated documents.

With experience you will be able to listen to longer phrases before typing, and with practice you will be able to eliminate the pauses between stopping and typing so that listening and typing overlap thus producing one continuous action.

Typing Transcribing	Press the center foot pedal to start the tape.	Listen to as much of the dictation as you can remember at once.	Take your foot off the foot pedal to stop the tape.	Type the words or phrases.	Repeat the process.

Preparing the Transcriber

1. Plug in the unit.
2. Connect the foot pedal to the transcriber and put the foot pedal on the floor.
3. Connect the headset to the transcriber.

4. Put the dictation tape into the transcriber.

5. Reset the tape counter to zero.

6. Adjust the volume control to your comfort.

7. Set the tone/speed control to the middle. This control determines the speed of the dictation. If it is set too slow, the dictation will be distorted. If it is set too fast, the dictator may sound like Donald Duck. You can use this control any time to adjust the speed that the dictation tape is played.

Using the Transcriber

The foot pedal on the transcriber is used to start, stop, rewind, and fast forward the dictation tape.

Start: Press the center of the foot pedal.
Stop: Take your foot off the foot pedal.
Rewind: Press the left side of the foot pedal.
Fast Forward: Press the right side of the foot pedal.

You should *only* use the rewind function to listen to a phrase you did not understand. Some transcribers have an automatic recall feature, but it is better to use the rewind function of your foot pedal to avoid accidentally rekeying words.

Proofreading

Proofreading is the final step in the transcription process. Proofreading involves making sure that:

- The transcribed document makes sense.
- There are no inconsistencies such as references made to a name, price, or date.
- Grammar, punctuation, and format are correct.
- Word usage is correct.
- There are no typographical errors such as *in* for *it.*
- Placement is correct.
- Enclosure notation and other needed notations are included.

Proofreading Procedures

Proofreading usually involves comparing your work to the original manuscript. Transcriptionists, however, cannot compare their transcribed work to the original work because they have not been given original work in a typewritten or handwritten format. Proofreading also involves identifying errors in grammar, punctuation, formatting, content accuracy, and word usage. Therefore, you normally proofread by listening to part or all of the dictation a second time to verify the words and by reading the copy to compare it with your perception of accuracy. Your "perception of accuracy" is dependent upon your knowledge of the organization, understanding of language skills, and ability to use secondary sources such as dictionaries, reference manuals, and postal guides. These qualifications are necessary whether you are proofreading on a computer screen or a printout.

Proofreading on a Computer Screen

Short, simple communications can be proofread quickly on the screen. You should:

- Read line by line.
- Listen to part or all of the dictation to verify that the copy is verbatim.
- Use software spelling, thesaurus, and grammar checkers.
- Use secondary sources to verify the accuracy of word usage and writing mechanics.

Proofreading Hard Copy

When a communication is long, complex, or formal (with footnotes, quotes, and references) you usually print a hard copy so the proofreading job is physically easier to perform. You can write on the copy, manipulate it easily, or transmit it to another place or person for discussion or verification.

Proofreading Responsibility

Both you and the originator (dictator) should proofread each communication. The originator has this responsibility because he or she signs the document and, therefore, is responsible for the content.

Proofreader's Marks

When text has to be revised, changed, or moved, these format and text changes are shown by proofreader's marks. These symbols explain to the person typing the work corrections or revisions needed that the originator wants made. Machine transcription operators should be able to understand these proofreader's marks so that they can make the changes requested. As a transcriptionist, you will also use these marks to indicate questions or suggestions for originators of the work you transcribe.

There are several proofreader's marks, and the most commonly used are shown in *The Office Guide.*

Tired of reading? Well, let's practice. Set up your transcriber and put in the introductory practice tape. Information about this tape and all future dictation lesson tapes will be noted next to a tape icon.

TAPE: INTRODUCTORY PRACTICE TAPE

Tape Counter: Start 2 Stop 120

Refer to Appendix C to compare your practice transcription to a correct hard copy.

2

Introductory Tape Self-Check

Directions: Listen to the Introductory Tape for directions and information needed to complete this self-check.

1. The three basic controls that most transctription units have are:

   1. _____

   2. _____

   3. _____

2. Which of the three basic controls sets the voice so that it is as clear as possible?
   _____

3. Stepping on what side of the foot pedal will reverse the tape? _____
   _____

4. If the dictation is slow or dragging, what control is set too slow? _____
   _____

5. What word precedes directions and is used by the dictator to alert the transcriptionist that instructions are to follow?

6. The abbreviation of Rural Route is _____.

7. The proofreader's mark for center is _____.

8. Which of the following arrangements is correct for the heading of a second page of a letter?

   a. Page 2   Ms. Susan Shankley   March 13, 20–

   b. Ms. Susan Shankley   Page 2   March 13, 20—

   c. March 13, 20—   Page 2   Ms. Susan Shankley

9. The two-letter state abbreviation for Minnesota is _____.

10. Where should the subject line be typed in a letter? _____
    _____

11. Where should the attention line be typed in a letter? _____
    _____

12. Is the body of a press release single spaced, double spaced, or triple spaced?
    _____

13. What is the proper division of the following name? Ms. Linda C. Anderson?
    _____

14. Where is the date typed on a modified block-style letter?

    a. centered

    b. starting at the center

    c. at the left margin

15. The name of the letter style that does not have a salutation or complimentary close is _____.

16. anyway   any way
17. ascent   accent
18. roll   role
19. assistants   assistance
20. capitol   capital
21. chronical   chronicle
22. confident   confidant
23. principle   principal
24. Who's   Whose
25. compliment   complement

✓ *Refer to Appendix C to check your answers.*

2

SECTION THREE
Written Communication Assessment

Language Arts Pretest

Language Arts Posttest

3

In the previous section you were introduced to the machine transcription process and vocabulary associated with machine transcription. The introductory tape provided you with an opportunity to learn about listening techniques and to review some grammar and word usage rules that will help you transcribe more accurately. The focus of this section is to provide you with an opportunity to assess your language arts skills and to practice transcribing.

Strong grammar and punctuation skills are essential if you are to be successful as a transcriptionist. Therefore, if you do not do well on the Language Arts Pretest, your instructor may require you to transcribe the language arts tapes that review grammar and punctuation rules. These rules are also introduced in the 16 transcription lessons, so even if you do well on the Language Arts Pretest, you will have an opportunity to review and practice punctuation and language skills.

Take the Language Arts Pretest that follows and give it to your instructor for grading. Your instructor will direct you as to what to do next.

LANGUAGE ARTS PRETEST

Apply your knowledge of grammar and punctuation on the following Language Arts Pretest. Circle the correctly punctuated and grammatically correct sentence from the two choices.

PUNCTUATION

1. **a.** Will you please submit your ballot in the enclosed envelope?
   b. Will you please submit your ballot in the enclosed envelope.

2. **a.** I would like to know your charges for the installation of the Brandt trash compactor?
   b. I would like to know your charges for the installation of the Brandt trash compactor.

3. **a.** The customer asked when the fall sale would begin?
   b. The customer asked when the fall sale would begin.

4. **a.** We received your check on September 1 but it was not signed.
   b. We received your check on September 1, but it was not signed.

5. **a.** The printers will demonstrate at 4 p.m. and will strike at midnight if the contract does not contain an acceptable cost-of-living clause.
   b. The printers will demonstrate at 4 p.m., and will strike at midnight if the contract does not contain an acceptable cost-of-living clause.

6. **a.** The personnel director of the Palmer Company, and the training officer of the Comber Company will be on the panel.
   b. The personnel director of the Palmer Company and the training officer of the Comber Company will be on the panel.

7. **a.** In January of next year, employees will be eligible for the new retirement benefits.
   b. In January of next year employees will be eligible for the new retirement benefits.

8. **a.** To be eligible for this scholarship the applicant must have a 3.0 average.
   b. To be eligible for this scholarship, the applicant must have a 3.0 average.

9. **a.** Having worked in the receiving department of the Browner Company, Joe understood the importance of accurate recordkeeping.
   b. Having worked in the receiving department of the Browner Company Joe understood the importance of accurate recordkeeping.

10. **a.** Evaluating this department's cost effectiveness is a full-time job.
    b. Evaluating this department's cost effectiveness, is a full-time job.

11. **a.** By subscribing before November 15, you can obtain one free issue of *Horizon* magazine.

    b. By subscribing before November 15 you can obtain one free issue of *Horizon* magazine.

12. **a.** When an applicant is hired, he or she is placed on probation for six months.

    b. When an applicant is hired he or she is placed on probation for six months.

13. **a.** All operating employees will be given a holiday on Friday, if the quota is met.

    b. All operating employees will be given a holiday on Friday if the quota is met.

14. **a.** To have repaid the loan within five years is remarkable.

    b. To have repaid the loan within five years, is remarkable.

15. **a.** Next turn the dial.

    b. Next, turn the dial.

16. **a.** In my opinion the money for the new jail should be raised by a sales tax.

    b. In my opinion, the money for the new jail should be raised by a sales tax.

17. **a.** This clause in your policy, I admit, is open to interpretation.

    b. This clause in your policy I admit is open to interpretation.

18. **a.** The word *check* has many meanings.

    b. The word *check,* has many meanings.

19. **a.** An employee, from the branch office in Santa-Fe, will be transferred to the home office.

    b. An employee from the branch office in Santa-Fe will be transferred to the home office.

20. **a.** Ms. Bibbons, who was an information specialist at the Gameon Company, has been hired as the new information manager.

    b. Ms. Bibbons who was an information specialist at the Gameon Company, has been hired as the new information manager.

21. **a.** The examination will be held on Tuesday, February 18, in Room 401.

    b. The examination will be held on Tuesday, February 18 in Room 401.

22. **a.** This applicant graduated from high school in Modesto, California, in 1996.

    b. This applicant graduated from high school in Modesto, California in 1996.

23. **a.** John Salas the production manager is a member of the Executive Committee.

    b. John Salas, the production manager, is a member of the Executive Committee.

24. **a.** This company which has been in business for forty years, is a good prospect for a merger.

    b. This company, which has been in business for forty years, is a good prospect for a merger.

25. **a.** She has strong managerial qualities, such as dependability, flexibility, and leadership experience.

    b. She has strong managerial qualities such as dependability, flexibility, and leadership experience.

3

26. **a.** Yes Mr. Billingly, your application for credit has been approved.

    b. Yes, Mr. Billingly, your application for credit has been approved.

27. **a.** Ms. Cameron is an enthusiastic, diligent employee.

    b. Ms. Cameron is an enthusiastic diligent employee.

28. **a.** Memphis, Tennessee, Little Rock, Arkansas, and Orlando, Florida are fast growing states.

    b. Memphis, Tennessee; Little Rock, Arkansas; and Orlando, Florida, are fast growing states.

29. **a.** Some legislators are in favor of increasing the Social Security rate; other legislators, however, are in favor of maintaining the current rate.

    b. Some legislators are in favor of increasing the Social Security rate, other legislators, however, are in favor of maintaining the current rate.

30. **a.** Daily College is on the quarter system, however, other institutions in the state are on the semester system.

    b. Daily College is on the quarter system; however, other institutions in the state are on the semester system.

31. **a.** Henri DeCresentis, records manager; Paul Romaine, advertising consultant; and Mimi Fornas, training director, were promoted this month.

    b. Henri DeCresentis, records manager, Paul Romaine, advertising consultant, and Mimi Fornas, training director, were promoted this month.

32. **a.** The seminar will be held on: Monday, Tuesday, Thursday, and Friday.

    b. The seminar will be held on Monday, Tuesday, Thursday, and Friday.

33. **a.** The customer wrote, "I will pay $80 this month and the remainder next month."

    b. The customer wrote, "I will pay $80 this month and the remainder next month".

34. **a.** Did Ms. Simpkins actually say, "I expect a $1500 compensatory payment?"

    b. Did Ms. Simpkins actually say, "I expect a $1500 compensatory payment"?

35. **a.** Eric Mason is a well known economist.

    b. Eric Mason is a well-known economist.

36. **a.** Each department must submit its budget before June 1.

    b. Each department must submit it's budget before June 1.

37. **a.** A months annual leave is given to each employee who has worked in this organization for twenty years.

    b. A month's annual leave is given to each employee who has worked in this organization for twenty years.

38. **a.** The three company's lawyers met to discuss the charges.

    b. The three companies' lawyers met to discuss the charges.

39. **a.** Four companies assets qualify them for inclusion in this list.

    b. Four companies' assets qualify them for inclusion in this list.

40. **a.** Since I attended the meeting, I will report to the president.

    b. Since I attended the meeting I will report to the president.

CAPITALIZATION

1. **a.** Please send your application to the personnel department of our branch in Portland.
   b. Please send your application to the Personnel Department of our branch in Portland.

2. **a.** Ms. Angeria has been elected president of the Musser Company.
   b. Ms. Angeria has been elected President of the Musser Company.

3. **a.** This company is in conformance with the equal employment opportunity act.
   b. This company is in conformance with the Equal Employment Opportunity Act.

4. **a.** The company library subscribes to *U.S. News And World Report.*
   b. The company library subscribes to *U.S. News and World Report.*

5. **a.** The Mississippi River divides the Eastern part of the United States from the Midwest.
   b. The Mississippi River divides the eastern part of the United States from the Midwest.

NUMBER USAGE

1. **a.** Barton Company has three overseas branches.
   b. Barton Company has 3 overseas branches.

2. **a.** The accrediting committee prepared 2 400-page reports.
   b. The accrediting committee prepared two 400-page reports.

3. **a.** Forecasters predict 12 inches of snow will fall before the storm is over.
   b. Forecasters predict twelve inches of snow will fall before the storm is over.

4. **a.** The minimum checking account balance is $250.00.
   b. The minimum checking account balance is $250.

5. **a.** The cost of gasoline jumped nearly $.50.
   b. The cost of gasoline jumped nearly 50 cents.

6. **a.** Expenditures for the candidate's campaign exceeded $1,000,000.
   b. Expenditures for the candidate's campaign exceeded $1 million.

7. **a.** According to a recent survey, 40 percent of the voters favor the resolution.
   b. According to a recent survey, 40% of the voters favor the resolution.

8. **a.** We have reached three-fourths of our fund-raising goal.
   b. We have reached 3/4 of our fund-raising goal.

9. **a.** You have an appointment for 2 p.m. on September 5.
   b. You have an appointment at 2:00 p.m. on September 5.

10. **a.** Paula Givens has been employed at the Baker Company for 20 years.
    b. Paula Givens has been employed at the Baker Company for twenty years.

3

ABBREVIATIONS

1. **a.** The CPA examination has six parts.
   b. The C.P.A. examination has six parts.
2. **a.** Professor Jane Irwin will speak at the seminar.
   b. Prof. Jane Irwin will speak at the seminar.
3. **a.** The tax regulations have been changed by the IRS.
   b. The tax regulations have been changed by the I.R.S.
4. **a.** The company is planning to change to the F.I.F.O. method of charging inventory.
   b. The company is planning to change to the FIFO method of charging inventory.
5. **a.** George Santana has been promoted to news director of KRA-TV.
   b. George Santana has been promoted to news director of KRATV.

AGREEMENT

1. **a.** Typing, plus proofreading and editing, are part of every transcriptionist's job.
   b. Typing, plus proofreading and editing, is part of every transcriptionist's job.
2. **a.** Neither of the transcription operators was trained in medical terminology.
   b. Neither of the transcription operators were trained in medical terminology.
3. **a.** Every transcription operator have a procedures manual to follow.
   b. Every transcription operator has a procedures manual to follow.
4. **a.** The backed-up copies of the transcription for last month is in the storeroom.
   b. The backed-up copies of the transcription for last month are in the storeroom.
5. **a.** Have the supervisor and her assistant arrived yet?
   b. Has the supervisor and her assistant arrived yet?
6. **a.** The transcription operator seen an example of the document formatting guide.
   b. The transcription operator saw an example of the document formatting guide.
7. **a.** In fact, the supervisor had written a procedures manual explaining transcription formats.
   b. In fact, the supervisor write a procedures manual explaining transcription formats.
8. **a.** The transcription department recently received the hard copy of the proposal.
   b. The transcription department recently receive the hard copy of the proposal.
9. **a.** Either Mr. Tyson's secretary or one of the transcription operators are responsible for transcribing his work.
   b. Either Mr. Tyson's secretary or one of the transcription operators is responsible for transcribing his work.
10. **a.** All of the transcription operators meet their production quotas regularly.
    b. All of the transcription operators meets their production quotas regularly.

LANGUAGE ARTS POSTTEST

Only take this posttest if directed to do so by your instructor. Apply your knowledge of grammar and punctuation on the following Language Arts Posttest. Circle the correctly punctuated and grammatically correct sentence from the two choices.

PUNCTUATION

1. **a.** Will you please send us 1500 career brochures before May 1?
    b. Will you please send us 1500 career brochures before May 1.

2. **a.** I am interested in the Model B Turntable advertised in yesterday's paper?
    b. I am interested in the Model B Turntable advertised in yesterday's paper.

3. **a.** The representative from the Employees' Council asked when we could schedule a meeting?
    b. The representative from the Employees' Council asked when we could schedule a meeting.

4. **a.** Construction on the annex was started in July and the foreman promised completion by November 10.
    b. Construction on the annex was started in July, and the foreman promised completion by November 10.

5. **a.** Mr. Anderson sold candy at football games and worked as a janitor in a manufacturing plant when he attended college.
    b. Mr. Anderson sold candy at football games, and worked as a janitor in a manufacturing plant when he attended college.

6. **a.** The treasurer of the Acme Company, and the vice president of the Lando Company are among the eight members of the President's Energy Council.
    b. The treasurer of the Acme Company and the vice president of the Lando Company are among the eight members of the President's Energy Council.

7. **a.** On both Labor Day and Thanksgiving, all state offices will be closed.
    b. On both Labor Day and Thanksgiving all state offices will be closed.

8. **a.** To be considered for promotion you must work here three years.
    b. To be considered for promotion, you must work here three years.

9. **a.** As an auditor, Ms. Booker has the experience for this job.
    b. As an auditor Ms. Booker has the experience for this job.

10. **a.** Being a door-to-door salesperson requires perseverance.
    b. Being a door-to-door salesperson, requires perseverance.

11. **a.** By working hard, you can complete the book in less than a month.
    b. By working hard you can complete the book in less than a month.

12. **a.** Internet transcription, which is now the norm, requires special equipment.

   b. Internet transcription which is now the norm requires special equipment.

13. **a.** Employees who have been with the company for one year are eligible to enroll for this insurance, if they have the proper classifications.

   b. Employees who have been with the company for one year are eligible to enroll for this insurance if they have the proper classifications.

14. **a.** Achieving a 3.5 grade point average as a freshman is a requirement for appointment to this organization.

   b. Achieving a 3.5 grade point average as a freshman, is a requirement for appointment to this organization.

15. **a.** Second place the paper in the tray to the right of the machine.

   b. Second, place the paper in the tray to the right of the machine.

16. **a.** By the way this film should be processed for forty minutes.

   b. By the way, this film should be processed for forty minutes.

17. **a.** All your children, you see, are covered under this policy until they are the legal age of 21.

   b. All your children you see are covered under this policy until they are the legal age of 21.

18. **a.** The word *fast* was misinterpreted by the customer.

   b. The word *fast,* was misinterpreted by the customer.

19. **a.** One person, from each school in this state, will be given the Eaton award.

   b. One person from each school in this state will be given the Eaton award.

20. **a.** Ms. Harrison, who is the city attorney, will become the independent candidate's campaign manager.

   b. Ms. Harrison who is the city attorney will become the independent candidate's campaign manager.

21. **a.** Staff employees will have a holiday on Monday, July 5.

   b. Staff employees will have a holiday on Monday July 5.

22. **a.** The corporate headquarters will be transferred to Tucson, Arizona, in August.

   b. The corporate headquarters will be transferred to Tucson, Arizona in August.

23. **a.** Jane Allen the personnel officer formerly worked for the Bascom Company.

   b. Jane Allen, the personnel officer, formerly worked for the Bascom Company.

24. **a.** This computer which is ten years old has been fully depreciated.

   b. This computer, which is ten years old, has been fully depreciated.

25. **a.** Personnel in this department are urged to take quantitative courses, such as mathematics, statistics, and econometrics.

   b. Personnel in this department are urged to take quantitative courses such as mathematics, statistics, and econometrics.

26. **a.** Under the circumstances, Ms. Baxter we shall expect your check by return mail.

    b. Under the circumstances, Ms. Baxter, we shall expect your check by return mail.

27. **a.** He prepared a concise, well-written report.

    b. He prepared a concise well-written report.

28. **a.** Rocky Mountain High School, Texas; Littleton High School, Florida; and Rover High School, Utah, are in the Class B tournament.

    b. Rocky Mountain High School, Texas, Littleton High School, Florida, and Rover High School, Utah are in the Class B tournament.

29. **a.** Taxpayers in this county did not vote for the bond; taxpayers in adjacent counties, however, favored it.

    b. Taxpayers in this county did not vote for the bond, taxpayers in adjacent counties, however, favored it.

30. **a.** Corley Company employees work on a traditional schedule, however, they have petitioned management to establish flexible scheduling.

    b. Corley Company employees work on a traditional schedule; however, they have petitioned management to establish flexible scheduling.

31. **a.** ICR Company, Madison; NCM Corporation, Philadelphia; and Egram's, Ltd., St. Paul, are subsidiaries of the Apex Drilling Company.

    b. ICR Company, Madison, NCM Corporation, Philadelphia, and Egram's, Ltd., St. Paul, are subsidiaries of the Apex Drilling Company.

32. **a.** The Farmers' Elevator is now storing: corn, soybeans, and wheat.

    b. The Farmers' Elevator is now storing corn, soybeans, and wheat.

33. **a.** The supervisor wrote on the memo, "I approve your leave."

    b. The supervisor wrote on the memo, "I approve your leave".

34. **a.** Did the police officer write in his report, "Security at the experiment station is deplorable?"

    b. Did the police officer write in his report, "Security at the experiment station is deplorable"?

35. **a.** The procedure manual for this operation contains easy to follow directions.

    b. The procedure manual for this operation contains easy-to-follow directions.

36. **a.** Each unit in this division must show that its hiring policies conform to the company-wide policies.

    b. Each unit in this division must show that it's hiring policies conform to the company-wide policies.

37. **a.** One years work experience is required by an applicant for this position.

    b. One year's work experience is required by an applicant for this position.

38. **a.** Two subsidiary's annual reports have not been received.

    b. Two subsidiaries' annual reports have not been received.

39. **a.** Three companies presidents have been indicted for fraud.

    b. Three companies' presidents have been indicted for fraud.

40. **a.** The semester deadlines (December 10 and June 19) are months apart.

b. The semester deadlines (December 10 and June 19) are month's apart.

CAPITALIZATION

1. **a.** Our marketing department will send five direct mail pieces during the next two months.

b. Our Marketing Department will send five direct mail pieces during the next two months.

2. **a.** Helen Weaver, treasurer of Lang Company, will be the keynote speaker.

b. Helen Weaver, Treasurer of Lang Company, will be the keynote speaker.

3. **a.** Congress is expected to amend the social security act this year.

b. Congress is expected to amend the Social Security Act this year.

4. **a.** Personnel in this department should read periodicals such as *Business And Economic Trends.*

b. Personnel in this department should read periodicals such as *Business and Economic Trends.*

5. **a.** The Western half of the state has had little precipitation during the summer.

b. The western half of the state has had little precipitation during the summer.

NUMBER USAGE

1. **a.** This department has scheduled two employees for the course.

b. This department has scheduled 2 employees for the course.

2. **a.** The line extension will require two hundred 10-foot poles.

b. The line extension will require 200 ten-foot poles.

3. **a.** The temperature is expected to drop below 10 degrees Fahrenheit by morning.

b. The temperature is expected to drop below ten degrees Fahrenheit by morning.

4. **a.** A down payment of $25.00 will hold your purchase until Christmas.

b. A down payment of $25 will hold your purchase until Christmas.

5. **a.** You can obtain a copy of the pamphlet for $.75.

b. You can obtain a copy of the pamphlet for 75 cents.

6. **a.** The company's third-quarter profit was nearly $2,000,000.

b. The company's third-quarter profit was nearly $2 million.

7. **a.** The new program drew 30 percent more viewers than expected.

b. The new program drew 30% more viewers than expected.

8. **a.** The company pays one-half of the employees' health-insurance premiums.

b. The company pays 1/2 of the employees' health-insurance premiums.

9. **a.** The meeting time has been changed to 10 a.m. on June 8.

b. The meeting time has been changed to 10:00 a.m. on June 8.

3

10. **a.** The Business Math Fundamentals course is 12 weeks.

 b. The Business Math Fundamentals course is twelve weeks.

ABBREVIATIONS

1. **a.** Ms. Jamison received the LPS (Legal Professional Secretary) certification.

 b. Ms. Jamison received the L.P.S. (Legal Professional Secretary) certification.

2. **a.** Governor Harris will speak at the ceremony.

 b. Gov. Harris will speak at the ceremony.

3. **a.** The regional office of the EPA is in the Customs Building.

 b. The regional office of the E.P.A. is in the Customs Building.

4. **a.** Don is taking a class in C.O.B.O.L. (Common Business Oriented Language).

 b. Don is taking a class in COBOL (Common Business Oriented Language).

5. **a.** Radio Station WAS-FM discontinues broadcasting at 6 p.m.

 b. Radio Station WASFM discontinues broadcasting at 6 p.m.

AGREEMENT

1. **a.** The number of transcription operators has increased.

 b. The number of transcription operators have increased.

2. **a.** Supervisors must design their training programs so that each operator can become productive and proofread their own work.

 b. Supervisors must design their training programs so that each operator can become productive and proofread his/her own work.

3. **a.** Every month each of the transcription operators contribute $5 toward the fund.

 b. Every month each of the transcription operators contributes $5 toward the fund.

4. **a.** Neither the supervisor nor his staff members write legibly.

 b. Neither the supervisor nor his staff members writes legibly.

5. **a.** Information on production logs show that operators are meeting their quotas.

 b. Information on production logs shows that operators are meeting their quotas.

6. **a.** Either of those reports is acceptable.

 b. Either of those reports are acceptable.

7. **a.** A former transcription operator has apply for a promotion.

 b. A former transcription operator has applied for a promotion.

8. **a.** Operators receive a bonus base on the number of words transcribed over a quota.

 b. Operators receive a bonus based on the number of words transcribed over a quota.

3

9. **a.** Each transcriptionist who had a low number of transcription revisions will receive a bonus in their paycheck.

   b. Each transcriptionist who had a low number of transcription revisions will receive a bonus in his or her paycheck.

10. **a.** Both transcription operators have passed their probation requirements.

   b. Both transcription operators has passed their probation requirements.

3

SECTION FOUR
Transcription Lessons 1–16

INTRODUCTION TO SECTION 4

4

The development of good listening techniques and the improvement of transcription speed and accuracy are the result of PRACTICE. In the transcription lessons that follow, you will be able to obtain this practice and to develop the detail proofreading, command of word usage, and application of good communication skills needed to be successful in transcribing. Your goal will be to create error-free transcripts and to develop both speed and accuracy.

The person who dictates the communications is called the **dictator, principal,** or **originator.** You are the **transcriptionist,** the person transcribing (typing) the information that the principal dictated. Occasionally during the dictation, the originator may insert instructions to you. These instructions are *not* to be transcribed; the dictators in these lessons will use the word *operator* to alert you to these instructions.

The 16 lessons in this section provide you with the opportunity to obtain practice while "working" for 16 companies or agencies. The organizations are representative of the divisions that make up our free enterprise economy. Lesson 16 introduces international correspondence. In addition to learning about correspondence associated with a variety of businesses, you will also transcribe a variety of documents including letters, memorandums, press releases, reports, and itineraries. Complex transcription requiring merging is also dictated. In Section 4, you will also strengthen communication and proofreading skills and become familiar with business terminology.

Appendix A contains forms to use to help you pace yourself and record your progress through the 16 lessons in this section. Pages 6–8 discuss how your work will be graded. You should review this information before you submit work to your instructor to make sure that you are turning in work that is accurate and mailable.

The path through each lesson in this Transcription Practice section is similar. To give you an idea of how to work through each lesson, an overview of the elements in each lesson follows.

Every lesson contains an exercise that will help you master troublesome and confusing words that give beginning machine transcription operators difficulty. All words in section GR 1 of *The Office Guide* are reviewed, and the majority of these words are included in the dictation you will transcribe.

Every lesson contains an exercise that reviews grammar and punctuation rules. All the language arts rules in the Grammar and Punctuation Section of *The Office Guide* are reviewed, and the majority of these communication rules are applied in the dictation you transcribe.

Every lesson contains a formatting exercise, which requires you to apply knowledge of document formatting rules and other information presented in the General Reference Section of *The Office Guide.*

Every lesson contains a proofreading exercise, which will require you to apply knowledge of all the grammar, punctuation, formatting, word usage, and other rules presented.

Information related to the documents and the company for which you will transcribe is given at the beginning of each lesson. To give you an idea of this overview material, we examine the first lesson, Lightning Catering. The information below explains the contents of the Transcription Overview with the information for Lightning Catering.

Progress Assignment Record
Grade Record

Word Usage Review

Language Skill Review

Formatting Review

Proofreading Review

Transcription Overview

4

The Organization

The beginning of each lesson provides an orientation to the company and the goods or services it offers. Example:

Lightning Catering provides both informal and formal catering services ranging from family reunions to private sit-down dinners for as few as 10 people to as many as 500 people. The company, started by a husband and wife, has been in business for ten years and recently moved to larger quarters. Lightning Catering is a sole proprietorship that is hoping to expand into the franchise market.

Personnel for Whom You Will Be Transcribing

The names and job titles of the individuals for whom you will transcribe documents are explained in the next section. The names and titles are to be used in the transcribed documents as they are shown. Example:

Timothy Fennel is the General Manager
Alice Anthony is the Special Events Manager

Your Job

Needed information about your duties is given in the job section. You will occasionally receive hints about the correspondence, such as technical vocabulary, symbols, and confidentiality. Example:

You are working with the office manager, Nancy Baltus, and your primary responsibility is to transcribe correspondence concerning catering orders and contracts.

Vocabulary Preview

Specialized and business vocabulary, as well as general vocabulary used in business context, is listed in alphabetical order and defined. You will be able to transcribe more rapidly and accurately if you learn how to spell these words, practice typing them, and study their meanings.

The first word (or term) in the Vocabulary Preview for Lightning Catering is *banquet*.

Transcription Preview: Self-Check

Sentences from the actual dictation are the basis for these exercises. You should punctuate the sentences, complete the exercises, and check your answers against the appropriate key in Appendix C. Each answer is followed by a code in parentheses. These codes correspond to the rules in the Grammar and Punctuation section of *The Office Guide.* If you make a mistake, turn to the section to review the rule to which the code corresponds. How would you punctuate the first sentence in the Transcription Preview for Lightning Catering shown below?

> We understand the strict adherence to the no smoking policy and we will advise our staff to follow this policy and the other restrictions that Mr. Andrews gave us regarding use of the building.

Formatting Preview

The first time a certain format is encountered, it is illustrated in this section. Thereafter, when you need to use the same format, you can refer to the Document Format section of *The Office Guide.* Studying this section and practicing the formats prior to transcribing will save you a great deal of time. The Formatting Preview for Letter 1 provides information about letter placement.

4

Tape Count

TAPE: LESSON 1: LIGHTNING CATERING

Tape Counter: Start ___3___ Stop ___36___ Doc. 1
Start ___37___ Stop ___65___ Doc. 2
Start ___66___ Stop ___99___ Doc. 3

You can use this information to estimate the length of various items on the tape. A count is given for the beginning of each dictated item. If your tape counter is set to zero, you should be able to advance the tape to the count that corresponds to the beginning of each item.

Procedures

When working through the 16 lessons, use the Student Progress Record in Appendix A to keep track of the exercises and transcription that you have completed.

For each lesson, complete the confusing words, language review, formatting, and proofreading exercises. Then work through the exercises related to the transcription. Check your answers in Appendix C. Finally, transcribe the letters for the lesson and give them to your instructor for grading.

4

1   LIGHTNING CATERING

276 West Blvd.
Atlanta, GA 34890
Phone: 756-329-7022
Fax: 756-329-7743
E-Mail: LC@magic.com
Internet: www.lightning.com

Lightning Catering provides both informal and formal catering services ranging from family reunions to private sit-down dinners for as few as 10 people to as many as 500 people. The company, started by a husband and wife, has been in business for ten years and recently moved to a larger facility. The company is a sole proprietorship that is hoping to expand into the franchise market.

PERSONNEL FOR WHOM YOU WILL BE TRANSCRIBING

You will be transcribing dictation from:

Timothy Fennel, General Manager
Alice Anthony, Special Events Manager

YOUR JOB

You are working with the office manager, **Nancy Baltus,** and your primary responsibility is to transcribe correspondence concerning catering orders and contracts.

JOB PREPARATION

Before you begin transcribing the documents for this lesson, complete the following exercises. Make certain that you review the rules identified in *The Office Guide* first.

WORD USAGE REVIEW 1

CONFUSING WORDS

Review GR 1 Confusing Words in the General Reference section of *The Office Guide*. Study words *accede* through *advice*.

Directions: Circle the correct word choice in each of the following sentences. Check your answers in Appendix C. Review the material in *The Office Guide* again if you missed more than three items.

1. We will (ad, add) two more members to our staff.
2. He could not gain (access, excess) to the password.
3. Please do not (accede, exceed) the amount budgeted for software.

4. We will (adapt, adept, adopt) two children.

5. Every employee (accept, except) those newly hired will have a two-week vacation.

6. His fast (accent, ascent) into management has been criticized by many.

7. She had an (adverse, averse) reaction to the medication.

8. Please (advice, advise) employees that the deadline date is May 10.

9. The supervisor has many (adherents, adherence) in favor of the change.

10. Thomas is very (adapt, adept, adopt) at machine transcription.

11. Martha's heavy (accent, ascent) makes it difficult to transcribe her work.

12. The Sales Department's budget included $50,000 for the (ad, add).

13. The new manager will have to (adapt, adept, adopt) his former marketing strategies to meet the needs of a much different customer base.

14. It took a long time for him to (accede, exceed) to the new procedures.

15. Because Nancy miscalculated the number of chairs needed, the department now has an (access, excess) of 30 chairs.

16. The best (advice, advise) she could give her sister was to work hard.

17. (Adherence, Adherents) to the no-smoking policy is mandatory for continued employment.

18. She had a difficult time deciding whether or not to (accept, except) the position because of the salary difference.

19. Her family was (adverse, averse) to her taking the new job because it would require moving to a different state.

20. The board of directors has decided not to (accept, except) the committee's recommendation.

21. The next (addition, edition) of the guide should include information on all the new tax laws.

22. In (addition, edition) to taking five courses at the university, she is working 35 hours a week.

LANGUAGE REVIEW 1

The Office Guide

Review GP 3.1, GP 3.2A, GP 3.2D, GP 3.3A, GP 3.4, GP 3.7, GP 3.8, GP 4.2, GP 7.1, GP 8.2, GP 10.1, GP 12.1, GP 12.2, GP 13.1, and GP 15.1 in the Grammar and Punctuation section of *The Office Guide.*

Directions: Review the rules below in *The Office Guide* and then complete the following exercises.

GP 3.1   **Use a comma before the coordinate conjunction (*and, but, for, so, or, yet, nor*) that connects the two independent clauses of a compound sentence.**

Write a compound sentence that requires a comma similar to the example in *The Office Guide*.

1) _____

_____

_____

GP 3.2A and 3.2D   **Place a comma after an introductory phrase and after an introductory dependent clause.**

Write one sentence that includes an introductory prepositional phrase and write one sentence that includes an introductory dependent clause. Use the examples shown in *The Office Guide* as guides.

1) _____

_____

_____

2) _____

_____

_____

GP 3.3A   **A parenthetical phrase or clause, such as those beginning with *which*, that is not necessary to the meaning of the sentence should be set off by commas.**

Write one sentence that includes a parenthetical expression that begins with *which* that is not essential to the sentence. Refer to the example shown in *The Office Guide* if you need assistance.

1) _____

_____

_____

GP 3.4   **Separate an element in apposition (word, phrase, or clause that provides further information) when it is NOT needed. This rule applies no matter where the apposition is placed in the sentence. Phrases and clauses beginning with *this, these, those, which,* and *such as* are usually set off with commas. States, dates, days, names, and titles of people and publications should be set off with commas when they are *not* necessary to the sentence.**

Write two sentences with appositions similar to the examples shown in *The Office Guide*.

1) _____

_____

_____

2) _____

_____

_____

GP 3.7   **When three or more items are listed in a series and the last item is preceded by *and, or,* or *nor*, separate the items with a comma. Include a comma before the conjunction.**

4

Write a sentence that includes a series similar to the example shown in *The Office Guide.*

1) _____

_____

_____

GP 3.8 **If the adverb *too* (meaning "also") comes anywhere in the sentence *except* at the end of the sentence, set it off with commas. Do not use commas to set off *too* when it is used to mean "excessively."**

Write two sentences similar to those shown in *The Office Guide* as examples of when to use commas with the adverb *too* and when not to use a comma.

1) _____

_____

2) _____

_____

GP 4.2 **When one or both independent clauses in a compound sentence contain internal punctuation, use a semicolon before the coordinate conjunction.**

Write one sentence similar to those shown in *The Office Guide* as examples of when to use a semicolon before the coordinated conjunction with internal punctuation.

1) _____

_____

_____

GP 7.1 **Use a hyphen to join compound adjectives before a noun they modify.**

Write a sentence that includes a compound adjective modifying a noun. Use the example shown in *The Office Guide* as a guide.

1) _____

_____

_____

GP 8.2 **Add an apostrophe and "s" to form the possessive of most words *not* ending in "s."**

Using the examples shown in *The Office Guide,* write a sentence using an apostrophe to form a possessive of a word not ending in "s."

1) _____

_____

_____

GP 10.1 **Proper nouns (words that identify specific persons, places, and things) are capitalized.**

Write a sentence that includes proper nouns. Refer to the example shown in *The Office Guide* if you need assistance.

4

1) _____

_____

GP 12.1   **Express numbers through ten in words unless they are used in tables, dates, or statistical text. Express numbers above ten in figures. In some formal situations, numbers above ten may be written as words. The general rule, however, is to use figures unless otherwise directed to do so or for more formal emphasis such as in the instance of "a hundred and one reasons." The current trend is to not use a comma in four digit numbers (1000) but to use commas in numbers of five digits or more (23,658).**

Write a sentence using a number lower than ten.

1) _____

_____

_____

Write a sentence using a number that is in the thousands.

2) _____

_____

_____

GP 12.2   **Express numbers used in a sentence in the same style. If one or more numbers in the sentence are above ten, use figures for all numbers.**

Write a sentence that includes numbers under ten and over ten.

1) _____

_____

_____

GP 13.1   **Express amounts of $1 or more in figures preceded by a dollar sign. Express even dollar amounts without a decimal point and zeros unless there are amounts with decimals in the same sentence. Although the trend is to not put a comma in four-digit numbers, many people still think it looks awkward to not include the comma in monetary amounts. Whatever method you choose to use, be consistent and either put the comma in or leave it out in all four-digit dollar amounts.**

Write a sentence that includes two amounts: one amount more than $1 that is not an even amount and one that is more than $1 that is an even amount. Refer to the examples shown in *The Office Guide* if you need assistance.

1) _____

_____

_____

GP 15.1   **Express time in figures when the abbreviation a.m. or p.m. or the word *o'clock* follows the time. Use words to express time when it is not followed by a.m., p.m., or o'clock. Do not use zeros for time that is "on the hour."**

4

Write a sentence that includes meeting someone at a specific time.

1) _____

_____

_____

Directions: Punctuate and correct the following sentences if needed. Check your answers in Appendix C. Review the rule in *The Office Guide* again for each incorrect answer.

1. Region Five placed first in sales and every employee in that region will receive a bonus.

2. Mr. Runnels former chairman of the committee resigned last month.

3. Mr. Smith and Ms. Anderson both are candidates for the position and they will be interviewed next week.

4. You too are qualified and should apply for the position.

5. The new director believes that ergonomic concerns such as eyestrain and wrist pain can be alleviated with better equipment and peripheral selection.

6. The deadline was last week and at that time there were 57 applicants.

7. Should we open another branch in Ohio too?

8. The no-smoking policy which is not popular with employees takes effect on Monday.

9. We will reimburse you for the cost of the incorrect part and will ship the correct part at no cost.

10. Ms. Smith the vice president will remodel his old office which was once the conference room.

11. The associations dues will increase this year in order to cover the cost of hiring an administrative assistant.

12. The leatherwood manufacturing company will hold its convention in August.

13. We only have 6 chairs and 9 people are coming.

14. The new concert hall can hold one thousand people which should be adequate seating for each of the thirty scheduled shows.

15. Sally made a last minute attempt to finish before 5 p.m.

16. The new transcriptionist had to learn the software transcription equipment and office rules.

17. As soon as the new president took over employee morale improved.

18. We could not locate the reference manual ZIP code book style guide or thesaurus.

19. When Juan and Nancy volunteered to do Mary's work while she was on vacation they didn't know that they were expected to take over her responsibilities for the mail too.

20. Unless someone tells Ms. Henson to slow down when she dictates we will continue to have difficulty transcribing her dictation.

21. The cost of the item was two dollars and he made $2,000 selling it.

4

22. The transcription operator transcribed five memos, six reports, and 15 letters.

23. She will not be home until 8:00 p.m.

24. Mr. Adams who was the last manager transferred will be available to assist the new employees at three o'clock.

25. The business started with eighty employees.

FORMAT REVIEW 1

Review the information about proofreading on page 30 in this textbook. Review sections DF 1 and DF 10 in the Document Format section of *The Office Guide*.

Directions: Write a T in front of the statement if it is true or an F if it is false. Check your answers in Appendix C. Review the rule in *The Office Guide* again for each incorrect answer.

_____ **1.** All letters except simplified should include a return address, date, inside address, salutation, closing, and writer's identification.

_____ **2.** All letters regardless of their style are double spaced.

_____ **3.** The letter style that uses indented paragraphs is simplified.

_____ **4.** Block-style letters have the date and closing starting at the left margin.

_____ **5.** "Dear Ms. Anderson" is the writer's identification.

_____ **6.** The inside address is the same address used on the envelope.

_____ **7.** If the letter style uses indented paragraphs, you don't need to double space between paragraphs.

_____ **8.** The two-letter state abbreviation for Alaska is AL.

_____ **9.** Reference initials are the writer's initials.

_____ **10.** Reference initials are typed in lower case.

_____ **11.** Reference initials are typed a double space below the typed signature (name of the writer).

PROOFREADING EXERCISE 1

This proofreading exercise covers the rules identified and reviewed in The *Office Guide* for this lesson.

Directions: Review the information about proofreading on page 30 of this textbook. Use proofreader's marks shown in GR 4 of the General Reference section of *The Office Guide* to indicate needed corrections. There are **15** errors. Check your answers in Appendix C.

4

Current Date

Mr. Thomas Whitney
2976 West Street
Orlando, FA 3870

Dear Mr. Thomas:

We are sorry that we couldn't respond to your earlier request faster. Our add acceded our expectations in reaching new customers, and we didn't have enough parts on hand to fill orders quickly. We have since resolved the problem, and can now except and fill orders in a timely manner. We are pleased to announce that, due to an access of parts in stock, we can repair the six printers and two monitors, too.

We do not have the part needed to repair the switch on the surge protector, but we can adopt a lever from an older model to repair the switch. Let us know if your would like us to do so at no cost. We will except your Purchase Order 450 in replacement or the original purchase order sent in May.

Sincerely,

Nancy Jones

LM

VOCABULARY PREVIEW

banquet	Feast, an elaborate meal for numerous people
biennial	Occurring every two years
buffet	A meal set on a table to be eaten without formal service
cater	Supply a banquet
complimentary	Given at no cost as a courtesy
cuisine	Specially prepared food
defray	Pay; payment of expenses
dignitaries	Individuals with positions of power; celebrity or political status
fare	Food
suffice	Be enough; adequate
utensil	Instrument used particularly in the kitchen; tool
verbal	Oral, spoken

TRANSCRIPTION PREVIEW: SELF-CHECK

Directions: Insert punctuation marks in the following sentences. Check your answers in Appendix C.

1. We understand the strict adherence to the no smoking policy and we will advise our staff to follow this policy and the other restrictions that Mr. Andrews gave us regarding use of the building.

2. We look forward to serving Orange City Association's catering needs and we hope that our quality professional service and outstanding cuisine will result in repeat business.

3. The festival backyard tent which until this week was only available in blue and white is now available in a variety of colors.

4. Your office manager Ms. Martha Anderson faxed her entry in to our "Delivering the Best" contest last week and her entry was chosen as one of ten lucky winners.

Directions: If an item below is correct, write "C" in the blank at the right; if the item is not correct, write the correct form in the blank.

1. 6 menu selections _____

2. Orange City Association's catering needs _____

3. for every 100 dinners _____

4. the ten tables _____

5. except Sunday _____

6. mouth watering cuisine _____

7. Biennial Celebration _____

FORMATTING PREVIEW

Documents 1, 2, and 3: Block-Style Letters

As discussed in *The Office Guide,* letters are typed in different styles. Block-style letters have all parts typed at the left margin. Most letters use the default 1-inch margins unless they are adjusted to keep a letter from becoming two pages.

STANDARD COURSE AND SHORT COURSE:

Transcribe all three letters.

Transcribe the first three documents for Lightning Catering on Tape 1. The three letters you are to transcribe for this lesson are all block-style letters. Use your standard default margins and add your reference initials at the end of each letter.

You may want to use a block-style letter template that is included with your word processing software instead of formatting the letter yourself.

Use the tape count below to quickly locate the beginning and ending of the documents on the tape.

4

TAPE: LESSON 1: LIGHTNING CATERING

Tape Counter: Start __3__ Stop __36__ Doc. 1
Start __37__ Stop __65__ Doc. 2
Start __66__ Stop __99__ Doc. 3

4

2   THE CAMBERLEY ANDERSON RESORT

The Camberley Anderson Resort is a five-star hotel with meeting and lodging accommodations large enough to attract major conventions. This luxurious resort was once the private retreat of a wealthy family. Following an 18-month renovation, the resort now has 750 rooms and offers all the comforts and amenities of world-class hotels.

6986 Niumalu Loop
Honolulu, HI 96825
Phone: (808) 298-1754
E-mail:
CamberleyA@mgnet.com
Internet:
www.CamberleyA.com

PERSONNEL FOR WHOM YOU WILL BE TRANSCRIBING

You will be transcribing dictation from:

Tony Perez, Convention Director

YOUR JOB

You will be working in the sales office. Most of your time will be spent transcribing letters from Tony Perez, Convention Director. The main emphasis of the work in this department is to generate convention business. Hawaii has several top-notch hotels and resorts, so the hotel/resort industry in the area is very competitive.

JOB PREPARATION

Before you begin transcribing the documents for this lesson, complete the following exercises. Make certain that you review the rules identified in *The Office Guide* first.

WORD USAGE REVIEW 2

CONFUSING WORDS

Review GR 1 Confusing Words in the General Reference section of *The Office Guide*. Study words *affect* through *allowed*.

4

Directions: Circle the correct word choice in each of the following sentences. Check your answers in Appendix C. Review the rule in *The Office Guide* for each incorrect answer.

1. Employees in the building were allowed to leave early because there was a problem with the (heir, air) system.

2. The fire inspector noted several safety violations including equipment blocking the (I'll, isle, aisle).

3. The department had to hire someone from a temporary staffing agency to (aide, aid) Mary so she could catch up.

4. There was (a lot, allot) of controversy over the new schedule.

5. The new policy will not (effect, affect) the transcription procedures currently used.

6. She was (all ready, already) knowledgeable of transcription procedures.

7. Did he (allot, a lot) enough money in the budget for software purchases?

8. The new (aid, aide) did not know where the reference manuals were kept.

9. (Aisle, I'll, Isle) be late getting home from the meeting.

10. The new employee was not (aloud, allowed) access to the files.

11. Timothy was (all ready, already) to give his presentation when the power went out.

12. As an (aid, aide) in the proofreading department, Mary read the typed text (aloud, allowed) while Vernita followed along on the original draft.

13. The merger will have a major (affect, effect) on the employment status of the staff.

14. She was originally listed as his (air, heir) in the will.

15. The supervisor was the new employee's mentor and (alley, ally).

16. She didn't realize that her transcriber was set to speaker so the dictation was heard (aloud, allowed).

17. There were (a lot, allot) of complaints about her transcription.

18. The reference material did not mention the location of the (I'll, Isle, Aisle) of Capri.

19. The error was found when the brochure was (all ready, already) at the printers.

20. The new employee did not know enough to (aide, aid) John in preparing the report.

21. (Air, Heir, Err) on the conservative side if you must do so.

22. The Kardon Brothers band (almost, all most) signed a contract with a different recording studio.

LANGUAGE REVIEW 2

Review GP 3.2B, GP 3.3A, GP 3.3C, GP 3.9, GP 10.12, GP 12.6, GP 14.1, and GP 15.2 in the Grammar and Punctuation section in *The Office Guide*.

Directions: Review the rules below in *The Office Guide* and then complete the following exercises.

GP 3.2B **Participial phrases (phrases that begin with a verb form used as an adjective) should always be set off with commas.**

Write a sentence using commas to set off a participial phrase similar to the example shown in *The Office Guide.*

1) _____

_____

_____

GP 3.3A **Use commas to set off a parenthetical phrase or clause that is not essential to the meaning of the sentence.**

Write a sentence containing a nonessential parenthetical phrase other than *which* or *that.* Review the examples shown in *The Office Guide* for assistance.

1) _____

_____

_____

GP 3.3C **Use commas to set off transitional expressions used to carry the thought of a sentence.**

Write two sentences that contain a transitional expression similar to those shown in *The Office Guide* as examples.

1) _____

_____

_____

2) _____

_____

_____

GP 3.9 **When the year follows the month and day, set it off with a comma after the day and a comma after the year.**

Write a sentence using commas with dates similar to the example shown in *The Office Guide.*

1) _____

_____

_____

GP 10.12 **Capitalize the formal name of ethnic groups and names of languages and heritages.**

Write a sentence that includes the name of a language or race. Use examples shown in *The Office Guide* as a guide.

1) _____

_____

_____

4

GP 12.6 **Express weights in figures.**

Write a sentence that includes figures (numbers) with weights. Use examples shown in *The Office Guide* as a guide.

1) _____

_____

_____

GP 14.1 **Express the percent in figures and spell out the word *percent*.**

Write a sentence similar to the one shown in *The Office Guide* as an example of using percents.

1) _____

_____

_____

GP 15.2 **Express periods of time in words except: (1) when the number cannot be expressed in one or two words, (2) when the time period is part of credit terms, discount periods, interest rates, or significant contractual terms.**

Write a sentence that includes figures in credit terms similar to the one shown as an example in *The Office Guide.*

1) _____

_____

_____

Directions: Punctuate and correct the following sentences if needed. Check your answers in Appendix C. Review the rule in *The Office Guide* for each incorrect answer.

1. The black, white, Haitian, and Spanish students attended the seminar.
2. Only ten percent of the photographs came out.
3. The merger took place on Thursday May 18 2001.
4. He was not aware of the policy, however, because he was a new employee.
5. Consequently he was able to apply the profit he made on the sale of the house toward paying his college loan.
6. Of the three new employees Mary is the best qualified to assume Beth's duties.
7. Because he missed the meeting it is important that you get the minutes to him.
8. Sally's mother of course will be there to see her get the award.
9. According to my records she was absent 7 times this month.
10. It is vital therefore that she signs the contract before tomorrow.
11. If you are a college student you can get a fifteen percent discount on the first months rent.
12. Finally she was able to take her vacation.
13. Striving to become a better transcriptionist she spent hours reviewing grammar and punctuation rules.

4

14. The lower sales in our department in my opinion were caused by inexperienced staff.

15. Working steadily toward perfection is the only way to achieve the desired results.

16. The new supervisor is too much of a stickler on rules.

17. She is an expert in corporate management portfolio development and stock analysis.

18. The new president will take office on Monday May 10.

19. She is a very well known consultant and speaker.

20. The quartz clock which was given to him as a retirement gift was stolen.

FORMAT REVIEW 2

Review section DF 10 (closing, items 1–4) in the Document Format section of *The Office Guide*. Review GR 6 in the General Reference section of *The Office Guide*.

Directions: Write a T in front of the statement if it is true or an F if it is false. Check your answers in Appendix C. Review the rule in *The Office Guide* for each incorrect answer.

1. This is the correct abbreviation for U.S.A.

2. Space once after the first period in a.m.

3. One space is used after the period in a person's title, such as Mr.

4. This is the correct form of the abbreviation for post office: PO.

5. If initials are used in a name, one space should be left after the period in the initials.

6. Space once after a semicolon.

7. Two spaces should be left after the colon in the figure form of "six, twenty" p.m.

8. Two spaces are now commonly used after a period at the end of a sentence.

9. One space should be left after an asterisk and the text that follows.

10. One space should be left before and after a dash.

11. There should be no space left before and after a hyphen.

12. When parentheses are used, there should be no space left after the first parenthesis and before the last parenthesis.

13. Letters are single spaced except when they are short.

14. Double space between the last line of the inside address of a letter and the salutation.

15. The complimentary close is typed a double space below the last line of the body of the letter.

4

16. Press return (enter) once after the writer's typed name in a letter and type the reference initials.

17. The enclosure notation is typed after the reference initials.

18. The enclosure notation is always typed at the left margin.

PROOFREADING EXERCISE 2

This proofreading exercise covers the rules identified and reviewed in *The Office Guide* for this lesson.

Directions: Review the information about proofreading on page 30 of this textbook. Use proofreader's marks shown in GR 4 of the General Reference section of *The Office Guide* to indicate needed corrections. There are **13** mistakes. Check your answers in Appendix C.

Current Date

Mr. Thomas Henson
598 East Elm Street
Atlanata, GA 85093

Dear Mr. Thomas Henson:

This is to confirm your registration for the week of October 24. We have reserved a suite on the fourth floor close to the isle leading to an outdoor balcony which overlooks the Atlanta skyline. We have reserved an adjoining suite for your aid. According to the schedule we received, your assistant will allready be in Atlanta prior to your visit, so we will be able to handle any last minute details or changes regarding meeting rooms and accommodations.

We are certain that you will enjoy the warm, friendly atmosphere of the community and the spectacular nightlife and activity Atlanta has to offer. We look forward to your visit.

Sincerly,

Martha Barlow
slm

4

VOCABULARY PREVIEW

awesome	Impressive, grand
bid	A proposal or offer to do specific tasks for a specified price
breakout rooms	Smaller rooms that are used for meetings and presentations
candidate	Applicant, competitor
coincide	Correspond, match
facilities	Lodging, rooms, buildings
high season	The busiest time of the year
irresistible	Tempting, charming
multifunctional rooms	Large rooms that can be rearranged to make smaller rooms that can be used for a variety of purposes
perks	Advantages, privileges
roll out the red carpet	A term used for providing special, royal treatment
spectrum	Range
submitting	Placing an offer
technicolor	Vivid colors
veranda	Large porch

TRANSCRIPTION PREVIEW: SELF-CHECK

Directions: Insert punctuation marks in the following sentences and make any other corrections. Check your answers in Appendix C.

1. At the request of Mr. Randy Simms we are submitting a bid to host the Regional Association of Information Systems Supervisors 2010 conference.

2. Since we are a five star resort you can be assured that we pamper our guests and do everything possible to make their stay enjoyable and memorable.

3. First we're offering an incentive travel award that could put you your boss or a superstar attendee on an 8 day/7 night vacation anywhere in the United States.

4. As a result we are offering your group a $5,000 Bonus Dollars Certificate which may be applied towards your master account for guest and meeting room charges banquet food beverage expenses and audiovisual rentals.

4

Directions: If an item below is correct, write "C" in the blank at the right; if the item is not correct, write the correct form in the blank.

1. multifunctional breakout rooms _____

2. Bonus dollars certificate _____

3. fivestar resort _____

4. perks _____

5. "roll out the red carpet" _____

6. 8,500 sq. foot ballroom _____

FORMATTING PREVIEW

Document 4: Block-Style Letter with Enclosures

There are two enclosures for this letter. Use the following style to show this:

Enclosures (2)

Document 5: Block-Style Letter with Enclosure

Document 6: Block-Style Letter with Enclosure

STANDARD AND SHORT COURSES:

Transcribe all three letters.

Transcribe the three letters for The Camberley Anderson Resort on Tape 1. Use block style and the standard default margins for all of the letters. Be sure to include your reference initials on the letters and enclosure notations if needed.

You may want to use a block-style letter template that is part of your word processing software rather than formatting the letter yourself. Use the tape count below to quickly locate the beginning and ending of the documents on the tape.

TAPE: LESSON 2: THE CAMBERLEY ANDERSON RESORT

Tape Counter: Start __100__ Stop __138__ Doc. 4
              Start __139__ Stop __173__ Doc. 5
              Start __174__ Stop __210__ Doc. 6

4

3   SWEET HOLLOW LANDSCAPING

Sweet Hollow Landscaping provides full-service lawn care and landscaping for individual homes and private businesses. The owner, Mary Page, and her assistant, Martha Dunn, oversee a landscaping and lawn maintenance crew of 50 employees. The company has established a good reputation in the community during its 15 years of operation.

313 North End Drive
Maryville, TN 37801
Phone: 378-275-7988
Fax: 378-236-7921
E-mail: shl@Magic.com
Internet: www.shl.com

PERSONNEL FOR WHOM YOU WILL BE TRANSCRIBING

You will be transcribing dictation from:

Mary Page, Owner

YOUR JOB

Most of the correspondence you will transcribe is related to bids for potential landscaping and lawn maintenance jobs.

JOB PREPARATION

Before you begin transcribing the documents for this lesson, complete the following exercises. Make certain that you review the rules identified in *The Office Guide* first.

WORD USAGE REVIEW 3

CONFUSING WORDS

Review GR 1 Confusing Words in the General Reference section of *The Office Guide*. Study words *altar* through *awhile*.

4

Directions: Circle the correct word choice in each of the following sentences. Check your answers in Appendix C. Review the rule in *The Office Guide* for each incorrect answer.

1. There was not enough time to (altar, alter) the proposal before the meeting.

2. We didn't know which program (annalist, analyst) would be able to come on such short notice to debug the software programming error.

3. We needed some (assistance, assistants) with the final report.

4. It was essential that the supervisor be (appraised, apprised) of policy changes.

5. The (annul, annual) stockholders' report should be available soon.

6. There will be ten (assistance, assistants) working on the project.

7. (Any one, Anyone) of the employees can transfer to the new branch.

8. Mr. Turner will be the (alternate, alternative) member on the committee.

9. If everyone pays his or her dues, we will have $150 (altogether, all together).

10. If she isn't careful, the insurance company will (annual, annul) her policy.

11. An opening becomes available once in (awhile, a while).

12. Before the company is sold, the building will be (appraised, apprised).

13. She tripped during her wedding on her way to the (alter, altar).

14. Did you see (any one, anyone) take the file folder?

15. Did you (appraise, apprise) him that you would be late?

16. Since she is not eligible for retirement (any way, anyway), she will not attend the meeting.

17. The only (alternate, alternative) to transferring is to stay and take a salary cut.

18. The (alternate, alternative) date for the meeting will be Tuesday.

19. It will be (a while, awhile) before we can get the information for you.

20. The contract given to the consulting firm is an (annual, annul) one.

21. The (analyst, annalist) made a scrapbook detailing the history of the organization's fifty years of service.

22. The desert heat sometimes gives travelers an (allusion, illusion, elision) of shimmering water holes.

23. The students were (already, all ready) to give their presentation when the power went out.

24. The new staff member was (always, all ways) punctual.

25. Mary tried to (arrange, arraign) the files in alphabetic order.

26. The (attendance, attendants) who worked in the clerk's office received less pay than employees in other departments.

27. Juan's remarks implied that his supervisor was unethical, and this (allusion, illusion, elusion) of improper conduct started an investigation.

28. The company had (already, all ready) won an award for outstanding customer service and was surprised to receive the prestigious Baldridge Leadership award.

4

29. The (attendance, attendants) at the school dropped by 50 percent on Senior Skip day.

30. Students in every generation have been said to be (ante-, anti-) establishment, but I don't think this is true.

LANGUAGE REVIEW 3

Review GP 3.2C, GP 3.5, GP 3.6, GP 3.11, GP 6.3, and GP 10.10 in the Grammar and Punctuation section of *The Office Guide*.

Directions: Review the rules below in *The Office Guide* and then complete the following exercises.

GP 3.2C **Infinitive phrases (phrases that begin with "to" plus a verb) should always be set off with commas** *if they are not the subject of the sentence.*

Write a sentence using commas to set off an infinitive phrase similar to the example in *The Office Guide.*

1) _____

_____

_____

GP 3.5 **Set off a noun in direct address with commas.**

Write a sentence that includes a direct address similar to the example shown in *The Office Guide.*

1) _____

_____

_____

GP 3.6 **Use a comma to separate two consecutive adjectives that modify the same noun.**

Write a sentence with two consecutive adjectives similar to the example shown in *The Office Guide.*

1) _____

_____

_____

GP 3.11 **Use a comma when the word *that* has been omitted causing a break in the sentence.**

Write a sentence with the word *that* omitted similar to the example shown in *The Office Guide.*

1) _____

_____

_____

4

GP 6.3 **Underline or italicize titles of complete published works (books, newspapers, plays, operas, poems, magazines, pamphlets). Use italics when a computer is used. Place quotation marks around parts of published work (chapters, articles, sections, essays, poems, newspaper columns).**

Write a sentence that includes the title of this textbook. Refer to *The Office Guide* for examples.

1) _____

_____

_____

GP 10.10 **Capitalize the word preceding an identifying letter. Capitalize the word preceding an identifying number with the following exceptions:** *line, page, paragraph,* **and** *size.* **Abbreviate the word** *Number* **if it is used.**

Write a sentence similar to one shown in *The Office Guide* as an example of correctly capitalized letters and numbers.

1) _____

_____

_____

Directions: Punctuate and correct the following sentences if needed. Check your answers in Appendix C. Review the rule in *The Office Guide* for each incorrect answer.

1. We apologize Mrs. Anderson for the delay in filling your order.
2. She was transferring the information from Brochure no. 576 to the new multimedia format.
3. The new supervisor suggested that every employee become familiar with the book Merriam Webster's Guide to International Business Communications.
4. The problem we found is many of the new employees don't know the policy.
5. She worked in a cold dreary office.
6. To become a good transcriptionist you should practice listening and using good grammar.
7. We could not locate purchase order no. 578.
8. The top ranking salesperson is a hardworking conscientious employee.
9. You should be delighted to know Susan that you have met your transcription quota.
10. To become a professional transcriptionist is a goal that all transcriptionists should have.
11. Mary and Joan are revising the "Dictation Policy" section of our handbook.
12. It is apparent that Appendix C needs to be reviewed.

4

FORMAT REVIEW 3

Review DF 1 (simplified letter) in the Document Formats section of *The Office Guide*. Review GR 6 and GR 7 (Numbers Used as Street Names) in the General Reference section of *The Office Guide.*

Directions: Write a T in front of the statement if it is true or an F if it is false. Check your answers in Appendix C. Review the rule in *The Office Guide* for each incorrect answer.

1. Do not space before or after a dash.
2. Space twice after a colon except when it is used within a time context (Example: 6:30).
3. Space once before and once after a hyphen.
4. In the Simplified letter, all lines begin at the left margin.
5. The complimentary closing and the date are typed centered in modified-block style letters.
6. The first and second pages of a letter usually have a 1″ top margin.
7. Numbers above ten used as street names are spelled out.
8. This is the correct format to use in a street name: 6200-23rd Avenue North.
9. This is the correct format: The package was mailed to 387 3rd Avenue North.

PROOFREADING EXERCISE 3

This proofreading exercise covers the rules identified and reviewed in *The Office Guide* for this lesson and previous lessons.

Directions: Use proofreader's marks shown in GR 4 of *The Office Guide* to indicate needed corrections. There are **14** errors. Check your answers in Appendix C.

4

Ms. Paula Atkinson   Page 2   April, 10, 20—

We will send out your merchandise for Order no. 3760 by United Parcel immediately so it should arrive about the time you receive this letter. We are sorry Ms. Atkinson for any inconvenience this delay has caused you.

You are a very loyal dependable customer; and we strive to make our service as efficient as possible. Once in awhile however we slip up as we did in this case. Please accept our apology and let us know if we can be of assistant in anyway.

Sincerely,

Peggy Jones

lm

VOCABULARY PREVIEW

alkaline soil	"Heavy" wet soil, which holds a lot of water
amenities	Features, comforts
annuals	Plants that live only one year or season
bedding plants	Plants planted in flower boxes or flower beds
bid	Proposal to do a job or project for a specific amount
distinguish	To recognize from others by some characteristic
expertise	Aptitude, ability
in leafing	Bearing leaves
interspersed	Scatter between
luxuriant	Lush, flourishing
majestic	Grand, stately
miscalculated	Judge incorrectly, erroneous conclusion
perennials	Flowers that die and then renew themselves the next season
preliminary	Introductory
reputation	Recognition of character or ability, good name
scaled back	Reduction, made smaller
Snow Mold	Disease of close-cut bent grasses
soot	Black powder, ash
sunscald	Patches of a lawn that have been killed by waterlogged soil
tile drainage	Spiking and turning the soil for better drainage
wholesalers	Business that sells items in quantities for resale by a retail merchant

4

TRANSCRIPTION PREVIEW: SELF-CHECK

Directions: Punctuate and correct the following sentences if needed. Check your answers in Appendix C.

1. The bedding plants arrived in excellent condition and we were able to plant them at a clients house within hours of your delivery.

2. These are majestic trees that are hardy to the cold and are able to survive drought flooding smoke and soot.

3. I have chosen 8 perennials interspersed with annuals to add color to the courtyard and garden area.

4. Since the restaurant business is as competitive as the landscaping business I know you understand that although there are many competitors not just any one can provide you with quality.

5. From touring other developments built by your company I notice that large picture windows glass walls glassed in sun porches and terraces all combine to make the outdoors part of the house.

6. Beautiful gardens luxuriant turf and healthy blossoming trees add as much to the exterior appeal of a home as the wallpaper and other amenities add to the interior appeal.

Directions: If an item below is correct, write "C" in the blank at the right; if the item is not correct, write the correct form in the blank.

1. Purchase Order 5430 _____
2. The new edition of *Landscaping* _____
3. fifteen years _____
4. 1890 7th Avenue _____
5. first class eating establishment _____
6. ten percent _____
7. three hundred and fifty acres _____

FORMATTING PREVIEW

Make sure that you have done the Transcription Preview Self-Check and Vocabulary Preview. This will help you transcribe the letters for this lesson. All three of the letters for this lesson are modified block style so you should review section DF 1 and DF 10 in *The Office Guide*. You may want to use the modified block-style letter template included in your word processing software rather than formatting the letters yourself.

Document 7: Modified Block-Style Letter

Below are some terms or words used in this letter that you should review.

Polovtsian, Snow Mold disease, sunscald

Document 8: Modified Block-Style Letter with Enclosure Notation

Make sure that you have done the Transcription Preview Self-Check and reviewed the Vocabulary Preview.

Document 9: Modified Block-Style Letter with Enclosure Notation

Adjust margins, if needed, so that this letter fits on one page. In addition to the vocabulary words and transcription preview information, names of the following trees and flowers will help you transcribe this letter:

Moraine Locust trees

chrysanthemum

zinnias

scabiosa

nasturtium

cosmos

candytuft

lily of the valley

dwarf daffodil

sweet pea

hollyhock

STANDARD AND SHORT COURSES:

Transcribe the three documents for Sweet Hollow Landscaping.

TAPE: LESSON 3: SWEET HOLLOW LANDSCAPING

Tape Counter: Start ___3___ Stop ___30___ Doc. 7

Start ___31___ Stop ___62___ Doc. 8

Start ___63___ Stop ___100___ Doc. 9

4

4　EVERGREEN PRODUCTS, INC.

12708 Pike Street
Seattle, WA 98104
Phone: 801-655-2712
Fax: 801-655-7854
E-mail: Evergreen@
netstream.com
Internet:
www.EvergreenPI.com

Evergreen Products, Inc. specializes in making clothing from fabric made from recycled plastic soda bottles and discards from fabric mills. The company also makes recycled paper products and a variety of other "green" products, such as notebook, bond, and computer paper; furniture; and newsprint. The company is relatively new, having been in business for only six years. The clothing portion of the company is the smallest division with only ten employees operating from a small warehouse. Furniture and paper are manufactured at other sites to achieve maximum efficiency in production with minimum cost. All paper products are sold to wholesalers who, in turn, sell them to retailers for resale to customers. Evergreen Products, Inc. sells its clothing, furniture, and paper products primarily on the West Coast and throughout the Pacific Northwest; however, it also markets to wholesalers in Hawaii, Florida, and Alaska.

PERSONNEL FOR WHOM YOU WILL BE TRANSCRIBING

You will be transcribing dictation from:

Jarrett Floyd, President/Owner
- Primary responsibilities focus on overall operation of the business and managing the clothing production line.

Ronald Gates, Credit Manager
- Investigates the credit of potential customers; establishes line of credit; handles collection procedures.

George Markham, Marketing Manager
- Responsible for planning, organizing, directing, and controlling all activities in the Marketing Department.

YOUR JOB

As a transcriptionist in the Marketing Department, you transcribe dictation from the marketing manager and his subordinates. You also transcribe special correspondence from the president of the company.

The Marketing Department is responsible for the following functions.

4

Function	Description	Tasks
Planning	Determining 1. nature of product and demand for it. 2. distribution channel to get the product from the seller to the buyer. 3. methods to obtain customer reaction to product.	Researching the product (size, content, features, etc.) and the market. • Investigating sources to finance manufacturing; deciding on credit relationships with buyers. • Investigating the method of transporting the product to purchasers and selecting carriers to handle it enroute. • Deciding how to motivate the potential purchaser to buy the product.
Organizing	Setting into motion the plan to sell the product.	Selecting the procedures and the people who will carry them out by distributing and selling the product.
Directing	Motivating the employees at all levels to contribute to the efficient and effective promotion of the product.	Setting up training programs on sales techniques; presenting demonstrations; holding meetings; creating incentives; offering recognition.
Controlling	Evaluating the marketing function from beginning to end to ensure that sales volume is maintained or increased and that the product satisfies the users.	Checking sales volume against competitors, cooperating with production department to correct defects in product; monitoring advertising to comply with federal regulations.

JOB PREPARATION

Before you begin transcribing the documents for this lesson, complete the following exercises. Make certain that you review the rules identified in *The Office Guide* first.

WORD USAGE REVIEW 4

CONFUSING WORDS

Review GR 1 Confusing Words in the General Reference section of *The Office Guide*. Study words *bare* through *broach*.

Directions: Circle the correct word choice in each of the following sentences. Check your answers in Appendix C. Review the rule in *The Office Guide* for each incorrect answer.

1. The employees are given two 15-minute (brakes, breaks) during the day.

2. Tyler used the DeskTop Publishing features of the software to make the brochure advertising the (bizarre, bazaar).

3. The office was (bear, bare) prior to his occupancy.

4. She put a (boarder, border) around the chart to make it easier to read.

5. He was seated (beside, besides) the office manager at the meeting.

6. The (breath, breathe, breadth) of the desk prohibited moving it into the office.

7. The (biannual, biennial) stockholders' meetings are held in the fall and spring.

8. The office manager was very (board, bored) at the meeting.

9. No one (beside, besides) the manager knew the combination to the safe.

10. The (bread, bred) served in the cafeteria was stale.

11. She did not know how to (broach, brooch) the subject of a salary raise.

12. She was (beat, beet) from working all day and taking night classes.

13. The (boarder, border) did not pay his rent last month.

14. The (bases, basis) for the companies to merge was financial.

15. The (bare, bear) was the school's mascot.

16. The fact that was so (bizarre, bazaar) was that he had no need to embezzle the funds since his father would have loaned him the money.

17. We need to get the (brakes, breaks) fixed on the company van.

18. The (brooch, broach) was worth $5,275.

19. He could not (breath, breathe, breadth) because of a strong odor from the carpet glue.

20. Contract negotiations are (biannual, biennial) so we can't bargain for better salaries next year.

21. The audience waited with (baited, bated) breath as the trapeze artist walked on the tight rope.

22. Should we (billed, build) a new house or should we remodel this one?

23. John was (born, borne) in July.

24. She (baited, bated) him with her cooking ability.

25. Nancy should not have (born, borne) the burden of doing Jane's work and her own, but she had no choice.

26. The clerk (billed, build) Ron twice for the same purchase.

LANGUAGE REVIEW 4

Review GP 1.2, GP 2.1, GP 3.10, GP 4.1, GP 4.2, GP 4.3, and GP 12.4 in the Grammar and Punctuation section of *The Office Guide.*

4

Directions: Review the rules below in *The Office Guide* and then complete the following exercises.

GP 1.2 **Use a period after each item in a list if it is used to complete the sentence introducing the list. For instance, if the introductory stem ends in a prepositional phrase, periods should be placed after the items in the list. Do not use a period after items in a list if the sentence is complete.**

Write two sentences similar to the examples shown in *The Office Guide* for both types of list formats.

1) _____

_____

_____

2) _____

_____

_____

GP 2.1 **Use question marks in place of commas when a series of questions is used. Space once after these internal question marks.**

Write a sentence using commas to set off questions used in a series. Use the examples in *The Office Guide* as a guide.

1) _____

_____

_____

GP 3.10 **Do not use commas to set off Jr. or Sr. unless this is requested.**

Write a sentence that includes Jr. or Sr. Use examples in *The Office Guide* to assist you.

1) _____

_____

_____

GP 4.1 **Use a semicolon between independent clauses that are NOT joined by connecting words, such as coordinating conjunctions (*and, but, or, for, yet, so,* or *nor*).**

Write one sentence similar to the example shown in *The Office Guide* when it is necessary to use a semicolon because there is no conjunction used.

1) _____

_____

_____

GP 4.2 **Use a semicolon before the coordinate conjunction when one or both independent clauses in a compound sentence contain internal punctuation.**

Write a sentence similar to the examples shown in *The Office Guide* using a semicolon because a comma has been used in the sentence.

1) _____

_____

_____

GP 4.3   **Use a semicolon preceding transitional expressions that connect two independent clauses.**

Write a sentence that uses a transitional expression to connect two independent clauses. Use the transitional words and examples shown in *The Office Guide* to assist you.

1) _____

_____

_____

GP 12.4   **Express dates in figures. Use one of these endings (*st, nd, rd, th*) when the day precedes the month or is used alone.**

Write two sentences: one where the date precedes the month, and one where the month is followed by the day.

1) _____

_____

_____

2) _____

_____

_____

Directions: Punctuate and correct the following sentences if needed. Check your answers in Appendix C. Review the rule in *The Office Guide* for each incorrect answer.

1. Mr. Smith and his nephew John Jones, Jr. did not attend the conference.
2. Because there were so many customers interested in the sale it was extended.
3. The outgoing president will not leave office until May the incoming president will begin her term then.
4. Since she had so much experience she was promoted to manager and John became her assistant.
5. JoAnne took the CPS exam in August and she passed on her first try.
6. If you continue to practice you will become a good transcriptionist.
7. Sally attended night classes to get her associate degree as a result she got a salary increase.
8. If he doesn't improve his proofreading he will be fired and then we will have to do his work.
9. Should Paul Thomas Sr. be introduced at the banquet?

4

10. How much money did it cost to operate the booth at the conference the meeting afterward the transportation shuttles for the board members

11. Unless the product has better sales we will discontinue manufacturing it and then some consumers will be angry.

12. Although it took us nine months to prepare the report we were able to meet the deadline but we still were unprepared for some of the questions.

13. We will be going to the office at noon therefore we should be finished before dinner.

14. In addition to the pay increase some of the operators received a bonus for exceeding their quota and this enabled them to have extra money at Christmas.

15. I don't remember the books name but I think it was written by Paul Jones Jr. and sells for one dollar and 98 cents.

16. She donated $6.00 to the school fund.

17. The deadline for applying was August 10th.

18. Each employee was asked to bring one of the following items to the party:

    dessert.

    casserole.

    soft drinks.

    chips.

FORMAT REVIEW 4

Review sections DF 4, DF 9, and DF 11 in the Document Formats section of *The Office Guide*. Review GP 1.2 in the Grammar and Punctuation section. Review GR 6 (Enumerated items in the "Spacing with Punctuation Marks" chart) and GR 7 (Abbreviations in Addresses).

Directions: Write a T in front of the statement if it is true or an F if it is false. Check your answers in Appendix C. Review the rule in *The Office Guide* for each incorrect answer.

1. It is correct to abbreviate the name of the city in the inside address.

2. The word "Saint" should not be abbreviated in American cities.

3. Due to space restrictions on an envelope, it is acceptable to abbreviate some items that should not be abbreviated in the inside address.

4. Ft. Lauderdale is the correct style to use in the inside address.

5. Ft. Lauderdale is the correct style to use on the envelope.

6. If the individual to whom the letter is addressed is no longer working for a company and an attention line is used, someone in the company may open the letter.

7. It is better to address a letter directly to an individual rather than use an attention line.

8. An attention line is frequently used when the writer does not know the name of the individual but knows the title of the person such as marketing director.

9. The attention line may be typed as the first line of the address.

10. Enumerated items consisting of more than one line are single spaced.

11. One blank line is left before and after each enumerated item.

12. Enumerated items usually are not indented from the left and right margin.

PROOFREADING EXERCISE 4

This proofreading exercise covers the rules identified and reviewed in *The Office Guide* for this lesson and previous lessons.

Directions: Use proofreader's marks shown in GR 4 of the General Reference Section of *The Office Guide* to indicate needed corrections. There are **19** errors. Check your answers in Appendix C.

July 10, 20—

Attention: Sales manager
Applehouse Magic
3899 10th Street
Mt. Dora, FK 3392

Gentlemen:

We recently send you a demo copy of our our CD-Rom, *The Rolling Que* which provides instructions for making music. To date we have not heard from you regarding the introductory offer outlined in the brochure that accompanied the demo CD-Rom. Because this introductory offer is only for a limited amount of time we need a response from you within the next few weeks if you would like to purchase the software at the fifteen percent discount. If you do not wish to take advantage of quantity discounts for a site license you may purchase single user versions of the software however this is more costly.

Sincerely,

George Markham, Marketing Manager

lm

4

VOCABULARY PREVIEW

accrue	To accumulate over a period of time
anticipate	Predict, expect
barrier	Obstacle, hindrance
cordial	Friendly, congenial
dilemma	Problem, predicament
downside	Negative effects
exacts a toll	Negative effects of doing something
hold cargo	Freight stored in a large open area at the bottom of the ship
hurdles	Barriers, obstacles
polyester	Type of fabric used in clothing production
portray	Represent, picture
prototype	Model, example
Ptarmigan	A bird that is common to Alaska
reimbursement	Money paid back, compensation
salvage	Money paid for damaged or unclaimed goods (cargo)
strife	Conflict, struggle
submit	Put in, give
Tanana	River in Alaska (named for an Alaskan Indian tribe)

TRANSCRIPTION PREVIEW: SELF-CHECK

Directions: Punctuate and correct the following sentences if needed. Check your answers in Appendix C.

1. You have the largest wholesaling operation in the state and Evergreen appreciates your business.

2. Upon the basis of your payment record we are increasing your line of credit by $10,000.

3. The newsprint school and office paper products and computer printout paper should be at your Matanuska warehouse in five days but this schedule may be altered if this bizarre weather continues.

4. For instance each mass produced T-shirt exacts a toll on the environment either through the pesticides used by farmers to produce the cotton or the chemical bleaching and dyeing of the fabric during manufacturing.

5. Our dilemma however is how to take advantage of this interest after the Eco-Expo convention.

6. We know that in addition to your catalog you also produce the *Enviro Business Letter* and an article in this newsletter might educate the general consumer about the environmental hazards of standard clothing manufacturing.

7. We would like to advertise our clothing line Enviro Duds in your *Green Business* catalog.

8. The carrier Ptarmigan Fast Freight called our Anchorage representative Tom Broers who contacted three private insurance appraisers to determine the extent of the damage.

9. When Tom called me about this shipment I immediately made these decisions: (1) to offer the furniture on the next salvage sale and (2) to send a duplicate shipment by air freight.

10. Bob we have had a long and cordial business relationship and I am truly sorry about having to submit this claim.

Directions: If an item below is correct, write "C" in the blank at the right; if the item is not correct, write the correct form in the blank.

1. 315 Fourth Avenue _____
2. thirty percent _____
3. your June 15th order _____
4. pier 14 _____
5. 2:30 p.m. _____
6. T. McGee _____
7. three appraisers fees _____

FORMATTING PREVIEW

Document 10: Modified Block-Style Letter

Adjust top and bottom margins, if necessary, to fit this letter on one page.

Document 11: Modified Block-Style Letter with Attention Line

Adjust margins, if needed, so that this letter fits on one page. Refer to section DF 4 in *The Office Guide* for information on attention lines.

Document 12: Modified Block-Style Letter with Enclosure and Enumerated Items

Adjust margins, if needed, so that this letter fits on one page. Indent enumerated items five spaces from the left and right margins. Review DF 9 in *The Office Guide* to see examples of enumeration styles. *Use the indention feature on your word processing software or the numbering feature to align the items.* Example:

These are some of the items we have discussed so far in our Monday evening class:

1. Income tax evasion and the penalties for this type of crime.
2. Illegal copying of text, graphics, and photos and procedures to take to stop copyright violations.

4

SHORT COURSE:	STANDARD COURSE:
Transcribe Documents 11 and 12	Transcribe the three documents for Evergreen Products, Inc.

TAPE: LESSON 4: EVERGREEN PRODUCTS, INC.

Tape Counter: Start __102__ Stop __131__ Doc. 10
Start __132__ Stop __187__ Doc. 11
Start __189__ Stop __247__ Doc. 12

TEST TIME

After your instructor has graded your transcribed letters for Lesson 4, review the confusing words and language rules presented in the first four lessons. Ask your instructor for the first written test covering confusing words, punctuation, grammar, and proofreading. Then ask your instructor for the tape for Transcription Test 1.

INTRODUCTION TO TEST 1

The following are words used in the test dictation that you may need assistance in spelling or understanding.

asphalt	Pavement or road surface
entrée	Main course in a meal
fungicide	A spray used to kill fungus
fungus	A moldy-type growth
reciprocate	To return a favor, exchange
shredded	Torn into small strips or pieces
sophisticated	Worldly, refined
susceptible	Open to or vulnerable

It may be helpful to review the first four lessons in Section Four to know how to spell dictators' names.

LETTER STYLES

Use block style for letters 1 and 2.

Use modified block style for letters 3 and 4.

5   PC ANSWERS/MULTIMEDIA, DESKTOP PUBLISHING, AND PC SUPPORT

PC Answers
Suite 129, Maitland Center
Hightman's Drive
Clearwater, FL 33602
Phone: (813) 343-7312
Internet:
www.PCAnswers.com
E-mail:
RichardsonS@nova.com

PC Answers was formed by three computer experts to perform consulting services for business and individuals. These consulting services include direction in purchasing personal computer hardware and software, designing offices, answering technical questions, and installing personal computer network systems. The company employs four technicians who perform troubleshooting and installation services. The owners do most of the consulting work and rely on an office staff consisting of one full-time and one part-time employee to handle all support activities.

PERSONNEL FOR WHOM YOU WILL BE TRANSCRIBING

You will be transcribing dictation from the three owners and partners in the firm:

Jane Samson, Barry Switzer, and **Jerry Yost**

YOUR JOB

You will be filling in for the part-time office employee and will transcribe work dictated by the firm's three partners. The company uses modified block with paragraph indention letter style.

JOB PREPARATION

Before you begin this lesson, review procedures for using template forms that come with your word processing software programs. Most word processing programs contain several memorandum formats that can quickly be accessed through templates.

Before you begin transcribing the documents for this lesson, you should also complete the following exercises. Make certain that you first review the rules identified in *The Office Guide.* Your instructor may want to see these completed exercises before you transcribe the documents for this lesson.

4

> **WORD USAGE REVIEW 5**
>
> CONFUSING WORDS
>
> Review GR 1 Confusing Words in the General Reference section of *The Office Guide*. Study words *burrow* through *choose*.

Directions: Circle the correct word choice in each of the following sentences. Check your answers in Appendix C. Review the rule in *The Office Guide* for each incorrect answer.

1. His (census, senses) were dulled by the drug.
2. Eating (carats, carets, carrots) is supposed to help your vision.
3. Sally (cannot, can not) miss the deadline; her job is at stake if she does.
4. People complained about how expensive it was to build the new (capital, capitol).
5. In order to meet the United Way goal, managers were asked to (canvas, canvass) their department's staff for donations.
6. Did she (choose, chose) to work the late shift?
7. A (carat, caret, carrot) is also used as a proofreader's mark.
8. We (cannot, can not) meet our transcription quota unless we work Monday.
9. The report discussed the glass (ceiling, sealing) on promotions for women.
10. Marty was asked to (cease, seize) contract negotiations.
11. The (canvas, canvass) had mildew on it.
12. He made a large (capital, capitol) investment in the company.
13. Her property was (ceased, seized) during the investigation.
14. The police were looking for a (cereal, serial) killer.
15. Why did she (choose, chose) to work the night shift?
16. He was (ceiling, sealing) the package, but the tape wouldn't stick.
17. The students (cannot, can not) work on the network because of maintenance repairs.
18. He (choose, chose) to transcribe from his house rather than work in the office.
19. He was a (canvas, canvass) worker during the last (census, senses) and went door-to-door requesting people to fill out forms.
20. The county is looking at building a new park in the (burrow, borough) where there is a large population of children.
21. The (calendar, calender, colander) was missing the month of October because Tom had torn out the picture of the alligators to use in his report.
22. His (cash, cache) of old books was acquired from purchases made on eBay.
23. Tomaka was glad to receive a (calendar, calender, colander) as a wedding gift since she cooked (a lot, allot) of pasta.
24. Jon did not have enough (cash, cache) to purchase the bed.

4

LANGUAGE REVIEW 5

Review GP 4.4, GP 4.5, GP 5.1, GP 6.2, GP 8.1, GP 8.8, GP 10.2, and GP 11.2 in the Grammar and Punctuation section of *The Office Guide.*

Directions: Review the rules below in *The Office Guide* and then complete the following exercises.

GP 4.4   **Use a semicolon to separate items in a series that already contains commas.**

Write a sentence that requires the use of a semicolon because commas are already used to set off items in a series. Use the example in *The Office Guide* as a help.

1) _____

_____

_____

GP 4.5   **Use semicolons between a series of dependent clauses.**

Write a sentence that includes several dependent clauses used in a series that are punctuated with semicolons to separate each clause. Use the example shown in *The Office Guide* as a help.

1) _____

_____

_____

GP 5.1   **Use a colon before words that complete the thought or add to the clarity of the sentence.**

Write a sentence that includes a colon to make the sentence clearer. Use the examples shown in *The Office Guide* as a help.

1) _____

_____

_____

GP 6.2   **Enclose with quotation marks technical terms, business jargon, and other words that the reader may not know. Also enclose slang expressions and words given special emphasis with quotation marks.**

Write a sentence to demonstrate this rule. Use the examples given in *The Office Guide* as a help.

1) _____

_____

_____

GP 8.1   **Use an apostrophe to indicate where letters have been omitted in contractions, words, or figures.**

Write a sentence using at least one contraction. Use the examples in *The Office Guide* for help.

1) _____

_____

_____

GP 8.8   **Add only an *s* to form plurals of all capital abbreviations.**

Write a sentence that contains a plural all-capital word. Use the examples shown in GP 8.8 Abbreviations for assistance.

1) _____

_____

_____

GP 10.2   **Capitalize titles of departments, divisions, sections, committees, boards, and other subdivisions of the company where the individual is employed. Do *not* capitalize these titles when used to refer to another company or when they do not refer to a specific organization.**

Write two sentences as examples of this rule. Write one sentence where the Accounting Department is referred to within the organization and one where the Human Resource Division is referred to outside of the organization. Use the examples in *The Office Guide* as a help.

1) _____

_____

_____

2) _____

_____

_____

GP 11.2   **Dashes can be used in place of commas, semicolons, colons, and parentheses. Generally dashes are used in place of other punctuation or words when more emphasis is desired.**

Write a sentence using a dash in place of a word or punctuation. Use the examples in *The Office Guide* for help.

1) _____

_____

_____

Directions: Punctuate and correct the following sentences if needed. Check your answers in Appendix C. Review the rule in *The Office Guide* for each incorrect answer.

1. The transcription handbook did not include the procedures for reporting absences making personal telephone calls or working overtime.

2. All of the department heads failed to request reimbursement for travel meals and supplies.

3. Your the main candidate for the promotion.

4. Since we arrived after 1 p.m. since we had no idea of what our responsibilities were since we did not know where to display the computer equipment the conference day was of little value.

5. If its approved we will get a salary increase in June.

6. The supplies were shipped to Kansas City Missouri Orlando Florida Maryville Tennessee and Dayton Ohio.

7. The new advertising logo stressed one theme relaxation.

8. The name of the CD was Rock Rap N Roll.

9. Do not tell you're supervisor that you will be gone that week.

10. The members of the quality circle were: Agatha Eastrurn Nancy Evans and Samantha Robinson.

11. Our Advertising Department is way over budget.

12. When she was offered the opportunity to transfer from the finance department to the personnel department, Sally decided to stay with the company instead of taking a position with a competing firm.

13. When Jon transferred to the Becker Corporation he was put in charge of the Finance Division.

14. Many transcription operators were unprepared when the company went through its downsizing.

15. It was Jon not Mary who transcribed the document.

FORMAT REVIEW 5

Review sections DF 12 and DF 17 in the Document Format section of *The Office Guide.*

Directions: Write a T in front of the statement if it is true or an F if it is false. Check your answers in Appendix C. Review the rule in *The Office Guide* for each incorrect answer.

_____ 1. The memorandum templates found in some word processing software programs do not conform to traditional memorandum format.

_____ 2. Titles such as Mr., Mrs., or Ms. should be used in the "To" and "From" sections of a memorandum.

_____ 3. No matter what style is used for a memorandum To, From, Date, and Subject are always included.

_____ 4. Memorandums are sent to people outside the company.

_____ 5. If a memo is going to more than one person, a distribution list may be used at the bottom of a memo or the names can be listed after the word "To."

_____ 6. If the memo is confidential, the word *Confidential* is typed in initial caps in bold.

4

_____ **7.** The body of a memorandum is double spaced.

_____ **8.** Usually memorandums do not include signature lines.

_____ **9.** Reference initials are typed on the memo a double space below the last line of the memo.

_____**10.** The same second-page heading format used for letters is used for memos.

_____**11.** Triple or double space after the word *Subject* before typing the body of the memo.

_____**12.** The heading information (To, From, Date, Subject) is typed in all capitals.

_____**13.** The body of the memo is typed at the left margin.

_____**14.** The body of a report is single spaced.

_____**15.** The first page of a report should be numbered.

_____**16.** The first page of a report should have a 2-inch margin.

PROOFREADING EXERCISE 5

This proofreading exercise covers the rules identified and reviewed in *The Office Guide* for this lesson and previous lessons.

Directions: Use proofreader's marks shown in GR 4 of the General Reference section of *The Office Guide* to indicate needed corrections. There are **12** errors. Check your answers in Appendix C.

MEMORANDUM

TO: Dr. Mary Thompson
        John anderson
        Aretha Fain

FROM: Alison DeChant

RE: New Procedures for Submitting Payroll information

There are new guidelines that will be used beginning on the first of next month for turning in payroll information. These guidelines are explained in the attached documentation.

Its important that every one in your department be familiar with these guidelines and follows them. Failure to follow these procedures will result in possible delay in paychecks. If you have questions concerning these procedures please contact the supervisor in the accounting department Martha Jeptson at extension 876.

lm

Attachment

VOCABULARY PREVIEW

accustomed	Used to, familiar with
asynchronous	Having each operation start only after the preceding one is completed
annotate	Add notes, explanations, or comments
acoustical	Having to do with hearing and sound
alleviate	Lessen, ease
array	An arrangement
components	Parts, pieces
concluded	Formed an opinion
circumvention	Avoidance, evasion
encryption	Data converted to code
ergonomics	Study of health and safety issues related to use of equipment and facilities
fatigue	Weariness, tiredness
in depth	Careful analysis, deep review, in detail
internet protocols	Method of connecting to the Internet
intrusive	Distracting, annoying
lifeblood	The element that sustains or animates something
morale	Spirit, attitude
needs assessment	Study done to determine an organization or department's needs
network port	A connector, usually at the back of a computer, that allows a cable from a peripheral device or a network to be attached
nonlinear	Ability to move sequencing in any order
obsolete	Out-of-date
options	Choices
pivot	Swivel
sanctum	Place, retreat, chamber, office, or other area regarded as private or special
scanner	A piece of equipment that converts text or graphic images into a digital form that can be used on the computer
stock photos	Royalty-free photos that can be purchased from a company that has paid the photographer for their copyright
versatility	Flexibility

4

TRANSCRIPTION PREVIEW: SELF-CHECK

Directions: Insert punctuation marks in the following six items. Items 4 and 5 are part of an enumerated list so they are not complete sentences. Check your answers in Appendix C.

1. Technology enabled information exchange is now the lifeblood of an organization. Information and the growing knowledge base of an organization have become increasingly audiovisual in nature.
2. Via voice data and video links users can see and speak with customers and competitors.
3. Interactive brainstorming can be instantly E-mailed printed or stored.
4. Electric copyholders with foot-pedal control of copy movement text magnifying lens place-keeping line cursor and built-in task lighting.
5. Adjustable modular desks with shelves file cabinet and personal locker.
6. Works not owned by anyone through an expired copyright or those that have been identified as such are public domain.

Directions: If an item below is correct, write "C" in the blank at the right; if the item is not correct, write the correct form in the blank.

1. PDA's _____
2. indepth analysis _____
3. touch screen panel _____
4. workstations _____
5. some personal space _____
6. built in wrist support _____
7. full motion video _____
8. CD-Rom _____
9. DVD _____
10. web-streamed content _____
11. e-mailed _____
12. PC monitors _____
13. If the essence or expression of the work

4 FORMATTING PREVIEW

Document 13: Long One-Page Modified Block Paragraph Indented Style Letter.

If available, use the modified-block letter style with indented paragraphs template from your word processing software. Adjust margins so this letter fits on one page.

Document 14: One-Page Modified Block Paragraph Indented Style Letter with Enumerated Items and Enclosure Notation.

Review DF 9 in *The Office Guide* for examples of enumerated items. Adjust margins so this letter fits on one page.

Document 15: Memorandum

Use a memorandum template from your word processing software program or type the heading information using the information in section DF 12 in *The Office Guide* and the examples shown in DF 20.

The following are Internet sites that the dictator has given you in hard copy form to type at the end of the memorandum.

Authorit-e (www.authorit-e.com)

Publish One (www.publishone.com)

Aries Systems DocuRights (www.docurights.com)

iCopyright (www.icopyright.com)

Aladdin Knowledge Systems (www.aks.com)

Scandiplan Technology (www.scandiplan.dk)

Document 16: Two-Page Report with Bulleted Paragraphs

Single-space bulleted paragraphs and double space between them. Review DF 9 in *The Office Guide.*

SHORT COURSE:	STANDARD COURSE:
Transcribe documents 14, 15, 16	Transcribe the four documents for PC Answers.

TAPE: LESSON 5: PC ANSWERS

Tape Counter: Start __2__ Stop __53__ Doc. 13
Start __54__ Stop __91__ Doc. 14
Start __92__ Stop __111__ Doc. 15
Start __112__ Stop __174__ Doc. 16

4

6 ROCKY MOUNTAIN HIGH REALTY

Mile High Building
One Denver Plaza
Denver, CO 80200
E-mail:
RMHR@novajet.com
Internet: www.RockyMt.com
Phone: 832-222-8963
Fax: 832-254-8966

Rocky Mountain High Realty is a full-line realty company with customers throughout the nation. It is organized to perform a wide range of services. It sells, rents, and purchases private and commercial property (for example: houses, store buildings, plants, farms, mountain land, apartments, townhouses, and condominiums). In addition, the company contracts with owners to manage their property: secure the lease, collect the rent, and maintain the interior and exterior of this property—all for a fee.

PERSONNEL FOR WHOM YOU WILL BE TRANSCRIBING

You will be transcribing dictation from:

Joe Crossman, Sales Manager, Residential Property
- Determines the guidelines that govern the sales associates in the purchasing and selling of homes.

Don Dobbs, Marketing Manager
- Develops advertising for the various media and researches the market conditions.

Mark Emerson, President
- Has final responsibility for the overall operation of the company.

Bob Pemberton, Administrative Vice President
- Handles problems that develop from sales or rental transactions; determines branch office territories; helps branch office managers improve their administrative procedures.

YOUR JOB

4

The president and his family own the company. No stock is sold; therefore, it is called a closed corporation. The president manages the company; other management and supervisory personnel assist him. The company employs over 500 people who work either in the home office or in the metropolitan or state branch offices. At least 400 of these employees are sales associates.

- **Home Office:** This office occupies the first five floors of the company-owned Mile High Building at One Denver Plaza. The executives located here plan and direct the diverse activities of the company.
- **Branch Offices:** These offices are managed by a supervising broker who directs the sales associates assigned to his or her territory (geographic area that encompasses the location of the branch office).

You are one of ten transcriptionists in the Information Processing Center located on the second floor of the Mile High Building. You transcribe dictation from the executives, managers, supervisors, and sales associates. The format used for letters is generally full block. Use this letter style unless the dictator tells you otherwise.

JOB PREPARATION

Before you begin transcribing the documents for this lesson, complete the following exercises. Make certain that you first review the rules identified in *The Office Guide.* Your instructor may want to see these completed exercises before you transcribe the letters for this lesson.

WORD USAGE REVIEW 6

CONFUSING WORDS

Review GR 1 Confusing Words in the General Reference section of *The Office Guide.* Study words *chord* through *confidently.*

Directions: Circle the correct word choice in each of the following sentences. Check your answers in Appendix C. Review the rule in *The Office Guide* again for each incorrect answer.

1. His (confidant, confident) in planning the surprise party was his neighbor.
2. Mr. Raymond's (commence, comments) had a major impact on his behavior.
3. The extreme weather changes made her asthma more (chronic, chronicle).
4. Working on the computer for long periods of time made her (cite, sight, site) blurry.
5. All the transcription operators took the language (coarse, course).
6. The new software was delivered to the correct (cite, sight, site) but to the wrong department.
7. Mr. Thomas was (confidant, confident) that the transcription operators would meet their quotas.
8. A lot of office accidents could be avoided if (chords, cords) were not left exposed for people to trip over.
9. She spent $350 on (clothes, cloths, close) that she could wear at her new job.
10. The new procedures will (commence, comments) on January 1.
11. She did not have enough information to (cite, sight, site) a price quote.
12. There are special cleaning (clothes, cloths, close) to use to clean computer equipment.
13. When he retired, the staff gave him a (chronic, chronicle) overview of his years with the company, which included some photographs.
14. His (complement, compliment) started her day off on a positive note.
15. The (command, commend) to shorten the turn-around time for transcription by 5 percent was met with much grumbling.
16. Mary was told (confidently, confidentially) that she would be given a raise.

17. The door to her office would not (clothes, cloths, close) properly.

18. The two blue chairs (complement, compliment) the new desk and go well with the carpet.

19. You have to interview (confidently, confidentially) for the job.

20. The cleaning compound was (coarse, course) and left a film on the desk.

21. In preparation for the (comptroller's, controller's) scheduled visit to audit Orange County's expenditures, all employees had to complete new reimbursement forms.

22. The (course, coarse, corpse) was found several days after he was reported missing.

23. Most of the employees in the office were local residents who had lived in Tokyo most of their lives, so it took a long time for Juanita to become part of the office (click, clique, cliché) since she was from Copenhagen.

24. (Click, Clique, Cliché) on the Internet address for Realtor.com to find information about new homes for sale in your area.

25. The (collision, collusion) between the van and truck resulted in two seriously injured people.

26. The office manager, Sara Kolenski, (commanded, commended) Joan on her transcription.

27. The old (click, clique, cliché) "a woman's work is never done" is still true today.

28. George Fierro was in (command, commend) when the battle was fought.

29. The government was trying to decide if there was a (collision, collusion) between the two companies to form a monopoly.

30. The (comptroller, controller) reviewed the school's accounting procedures to make sure they adhered to the new policy.

LANGUAGE REVIEW 6

Review GP 1.1 and GP 3.12 in the Grammar and Punctuation section of *The Office Guide.*

Directions: Review the rules below in *The Office Guide* and then complete the following exercises.

GP 1.1 **Periods are used instead of question marks when the question asked is a polite request (requires action).**

Write a polite request sentence similar to the example in *The Office Guide.*

1) _____

_____

_____

GP 3.12 **When words are repeated, they should be separated with a comma.**

Write a sentence similar to the one shown in *The Office Guide* that includes repeated words and punctuate it correctly.

1) _____

_____

_____

Directions: Punctuate and correct the following sentences if needed. Check your answers in Appendix C. Review the rule in *The Office Guide* for each incorrect answer.

1. You are requested to bring the following items with you

    Minutes of the last meeting

    Comprehensive report

    Schedule of projects

2. We couldn't find any of the old old houses shown in the book.

3. Several new branch offices will open in

    Florida

    Maine

    California

4. Can you please pass along the information in the memo to Jim?

5. The water level in the lake was very very high due to the heavy rain.

FORMAT REVIEW 6

Review sections DF 1 (Letter Styles, Document Spacing), DF 2, DF 6, and DF 20 in the Document Formats section of *The Office Guide.*

Directions: Write a T in front of the statement if it is true or an F if it is false. Check your answers in Appendix C. Review the rule in *The Office Guide* again for each incorrect answer.

In letters *other* than simplified:

_____ **1.** The subject line is always centered.

_____ **2.** The salutation comes before the subject line.

_____ **3.** The titles "Subject," "In re," "Re" or "Refer to" are used at the beginning of the subject line.

_____ **4.** Double space before and after the subject line.

_____ **5.** In a block-style letter, the subject line begins at the left margin.

_____ **6.** A colon is used after the word *Subject* in the subject line.

_____ **7.** The subject line may be typed in initial caps or all caps.

_____ **8.** The second-page heading of a letter should start 1 1/2 inches from the top of the page.

_____ **9.** It is acceptable to put the complimentary close and signature line on the second page alone.

4

_____ **10.** Triple space between the second-page heading and the body of the letter.

_____ **11.** The page number is the first thing to put in the second-page heading.

_____ **12.** There should be at least two lines of a paragraph left at the bottom of the first page and at least two lines carried over to the top of the second page of a letter.

_____ **13.** Leave at least 1 1/2 inches at the bottom of the first page of a letter.

PROOFREADING EXERCISE 6

This proofreading exercise covers the rules identified and reviewed in _The Office Guide_ for this lesson and previous lessons.

Directions: Use proofreader's marks shown in GR 4 of _The Office Guide_ to indicate needed corrections. There are **13** errors. Check your answers in Appendix C.

Date

Ms. Mary Hamilton
1 Anderson Street
Sharpsburg, GA 3027

Dear Mary

Subject Performance Evaluation

Tuesday morning at 9:30 a.m. has been set aside for us to go over your yearly performance evaluation. Please bring the following items with you to this meeting

portfolio of work.
transcription monthly log reports.
attendance record.
list of questions or concerns.

Your immediate supervisor can give you the log and attendants reports. You may chose to postpone this review if you can not obtain these documents by the deadline, but you cannot postpone the review for more than three weeks. This is because we are on a very very tight schedule to discuss preformance reviews for one hundred and fifty employees.

Could you please notify your supervisor if a conflict exists with prior commitments that you may have made for next Tuesday that cannot be changed.

Sincerely,

Peggy Jones

lm

VOCABULARY PREVIEW

adjustable rate mortgage (ARM)	A type of mortgage where the interest rate can float up or down and the monthly payments can change accordingly; pronounced as the word arm
affiliate	Associate, colleague
appraisal	An estimation of property value by a competent person
beltway	A road system that connects various parts of a county or state
deed recordings	Record of a legal document by which one person transfers property to another
earnest money	A sum, which, if a contract is executed, is applied against the down payment
eminent domain	The constitutional right given to a unit of government to take private property involuntarily if taken for public use and a fair price is paid to the owner
employ	Apply, use
escrow account	An account in a bank, title company, or trust company having trust powers, which may not be used for deposit of personal funds by any person
estate	Tenancy; the interest one holds in real property; the total of one's property and possessions
executrix	A female appointed to perform the terms of a will
feasibility	Probability, possibility that something will succeed
foreclosure	A court process to transfer title to real property used as security for a debt as a means of paying the debt by involuntary sale of property
in conjunction with	Together with
lien	A claim on property for payment of some obligation or debt
mortgage	A contractual obligation in which one party (the mortgagor) owes a sum of money to a second party (the mortgagee)
multiple listing service (MLS)	An arrangement among members of a real estate board or exchange, which allows each member broker to share his or her listings with other members so that greater exposure is obtained, and greater chance of sale will result
negotiating	Conferring with another to arrange a settlement
penalty clause	A provision in a mortgage that requires the borrower to pay a penalty if the mortgage payments are made in advance of the normal due date, or if the mortgage is paid in full ahead of schedule
plat	A plan of a tract of land subdivided into lots and showing required or planned amenities
power of attorney	Designation of another person to act in and for a principal as though he or she were present

4

points, mortgage discount	A charge of an established percent of the mortgage value; assessment by a lender to increase the interest yield to compare with the interest yield from other types of investments
real estate	Property that consists of land or buildings
residency	Dwelling, home; place where people live
rezoning	Changing the purpose for which a given land parcel may be used; most urban and suburban property is located in zones that are restricted for certain uses: commercial, residential, high-density multiple dwellings, and so on
sales associate	An individual engaged in selling, renting, purchasing, and managing real estate
stay	Delay temporarily, stop for a limited time
subdivision	A development of homes
title search	A search to prove the rights which represent ownership of real property and the quality of the estate owned; evidence of ownership of property
township	A square tract of land measuring six miles on each side and including 36 sections (formed by the crossing of range and township lines)
variance	An exception to zoning regulations or ordinances granted to relieve a hardship

TRANSCRIPTION PREVIEW: SELF-CHECK

Directions: Insert punctuation marks in the following sentences. Check your answers in Appendix C.

1. Teresa Puglisi who designed our Web site is no longer with our firm she is presently operating her own Internet service in Houston.

2. As marketing manager I recommend that we become part of Realtor.com which is the official site of the National Association of Realtors.

3. Hoping to save their homes several neighbors and your mother hired a lawyer to fight the location of the beltway.

4. Since your mother gave you power of attorney during her illness and named you as executrix of her estate in her will you should be able to sell her property consisting of the house she lived in and several rental properties if you so choose.

5. At the conclusion of a six-month listing agreement with Monery Real Estate in North Carolina she decided not to sell the property and it has not been on the market since.

6. Through legal pressure this group of citizens was able to obtain a stay on the building of the beltway while alternate routes are reviewed.

4

7. In view of the owner's arrangements with the current tenants I cannot believe that the home will be put on the market.

8. This couple Mr. and Mrs. Edward Elsman qualified for a loan on the house at a local bank but the money that they would have to pay in mortgage discount points was high.

9. The state could employ the eminent domain rights at a future time so it is important that you discuss the status of this real estate problem with your mothers attorney.

10. In order to capitalize on maximizing your capital investment you can not delay the sale of this real estate.

Directions: If an item below is correct, write "C" in the blank at the right; if the item is not correct, write the correct form in the blank.

1. six month lease _____
2. $450,000 _____
3. 3 bedroom, 2 bath home _____
4. $575.00 _____
5. Township 36-C _____

FORMATTING PREVIEW

Document 17: Memorandum

This memorandum concerns becoming part of Realtor.com, which is an Internet site linked to homestore.com.

SPELLING OF NAMES: LUCI HENSON, TERESA PUGLISI

Document 18: Block-Style Letter with Subject Line and Enumerated Items

This letter contains an enumerated list of four items. If available, use the numbering feature of your word processing software to create this list. Review DF 9 (Enumerated Lists) and the rule about periods used with lists (GP 1.2).

Document 19: Two-Page Block-Style Letter with Subject Line and Indented Text

Review second-page headings in DF 2 in *The Office Guide.*

SPELLING OF NAMES: GERTRUDE ORTIZ, ELIZABETH ESQUIROZ

This letter contains a paragraph-style list. The paragraphs should be indented five spaces from the left and right margins. Single space the "listed" paragraphs and double space between them. Example:

4

Below is an overview of the status of the various properties owned by your mother at the time of her death:

Windermere Resort. This resort consists of four cabins located in Township 36-C Section 541 of Montreat, North Carolina. A real estate affiliate of ours . . .

Document 20: Block-Style Letter with Subject Line

This subject line includes an address. Type the subject line as *one* line. You may have to indent part of the subject line if it wraps to a second line.

SHORT COURSE:	**STANDARD COURSE:**
Transcribe documents 17, 18, 19	Transcribe the four documents from Rocky Mountain High Realty.

You may want to use the block-style letter template in your word processing software rather than formatting the letters yourself.

Refer to DF 6 and DF 20 in *The Office Guide* for information on placement of subject lines if you do not use the template.

TAPE: LESSON 6: ROCKY MOUNTAIN HIGH REALTY

Tape Counter: Start _175_ Stop _214_ Doc. 17
Start _215_ Stop _254_ Doc. 18
Start _256_ Stop _348_ Doc. 19
Start _350_ Stop _390_ Doc. 20

4

7 THE CITY OF GENEVA

P.O. Box 765
Geneva, MI 36595
Phone: 524-290-7783
Fax: 524-299-7894
E-mail: GenevaM@laser-net.com
Internet:
www.genevacity.org

Mandrella Smith, mayor of the City of Geneva for the last six years, has seen much growth in the city. Geneva originally was a citrus and agricultural center. Growth in these and other industries such as electronics, manufacturing, distribution, and tourism has helped Geneva to become one of the fastest growing communities in the United States. To accommodate ever-increasing roadway traffic, $950 million was spent for road improvements and a computerized traffic signalization system. The population of the region is projected to increase as much as 550,000 within the next ten years. A city of this size affords employees the opportunity to work in every aspect of business, such as transportation, zoning, accounting, document processing, personnel, advertising, desktop publishing, printing, data processing, computer programming, real estate, law, health, and law enforcement.

PERSONNEL FOR WHOM YOU WILL BE TRANSCRIBING

You will be transcribing dictation from:

Walter Pepper, Benefits Officer
- Establishes, maintains, and administers the employee benefits programs.

Mary Robbins, Assistant Training Director
- Schedules training programs; performs research to determine the nature of programs needed to upgrade the skills or knowledge of employees.

Frank Ruddy, Vice President, Personnel
- Responsible for managing the Personnel Department and determining that all line and staff functions are performed efficiently.

YOUR JOB

You will be working in the Personnel Department for the City of Geneva. As one of several transcriptionists in the Document Processing Department, you transcribe dictation from the personnel manager and administrators. Often the information processed is confidential in nature, and you are expected to maintain the confidentiality.

This department uses simplified letter style. The activities in this department include:

4

Recruitment
Establishing jobs, titles, descriptions, specifications, and classifications; recruiting; reviewing applications; testing, and interviewing applicants.

Labor-management relations
Assessing attitudes; determining disciplinary action; counseling; handling grievances; establishing bargaining procedures; and complying with legislation such as the Equal Employment Opportunity Act.

Compensation
Developing job evaluation systems, incentive plans and supplementary plans; profit sharing and stock purchase.

Training
Establishing, conducting, and evaluating training programs for preparing supervisory, management, and executive personnel.

Benefits
Establishing safety programs and benefits (retirement and insurance plans); complying with legislation such as the Occupational Health and Safety Act and the Pension Reform Act.

JOB PREPARATION

Before you begin this lesson, access the simplified letter template format if it is available in your word processing software program. See how closely it resembles the simplified letter format outlined in DF 1 and shown as an example in DF 20 in *The Office Guide*.

WORD USAGE REVIEW 7

CONFUSING WORDS

Review GR 1 Confusing Words in the General Reference section of *The Office Guide*. Study words *conscience* through *detract*.

Directions: Circle the correct word choice in each of the following sentences. Check your answers in Appendix C. Review the rule in *The Office Guide* again for each incorrect answer.

1. Not knowing the specific software did not (distract, detract) from his ability to figure out the solution.
2. Mary was very (conscience, conscious) of her foreign accent.
3. The news (correspondence, correspondents) experienced fatigue after many nights of work in the field.
4. Several advisory (councils, consuls) were formed.
5. The (conservation, conversation) was very limited since they did not speak the same language.

6. She gave him a (cue, queue) so that he would know when to begin the program.

7. Out of (deference, difference) to the new manager, he did not request to be transferred.

8. The (dairy, diary) was sold for $250,000 when the storm destroyed the farm.

9. The (correspondence, correspondents) was found in a "dead letter" file.

10. Jill's (conscience, conscious) bothered her if she was absent without being sick.

11. The (core, corps) of the training program focused on developing computer skills.

12. Because the cost of paper is so high, (conservation, conversation) is recommended in purchasing and using letterhead and other paper supplies.

13. The rapport among the drum (core, corps) members was special.

14. The embassy (council, consul, counsel) helped him find his relatives.

15. The printer documents were (cued, queued) according to job order.

16. His (decent, descent, dissent) from president to manager was quick.

17. The main (deference, difference) between their leadership styles was delegation of duties.

18. The writer's identity was not revealed in the (dairy, diary).

19. There was much (decent, descent, dissent) about the new policy.

20. Was he given any (council, consul, counsel) before he was fired?

21. We should (defer, differ) purchasing a computer until after the first of the year since the new models will be out then.

22. The Macintosh operating system (defers, differs) from the Windows operating system in several ways.

23. The (deposition, disposition) was taken last March and a trial is scheduled in October.

24. Ginny's happy (deposition, disposition) made it easier to ignore Charlie's negative attitude.

LANGUAGE REVIEW 7

Review GP 10.3, GP 10.8, GP 17.1, GP 17.2, and GP 17.3 in the Grammar and Punctuation section of *The Office Guide*.

4

Directions: Review the rules below in *The Office Guide* and then complete the following exercises. Check your answers in Appendix C. Review the rule again for each incorrect answer.

GP 10.3 **Capitalize a job or position title when it is used preceding a name. Do *not* capitalize occupational titles such as "author," "surgeon," "publisher," and "lawyer." Do not capitalize job titles when they stand alone.**

Write a sentence that includes job titles. Use the examples in *The Office Guide* as a help.

1) _____

_____

_____

GP 10.8   Compass points are capitalized when they are used as adjectives to identify specific geographical areas of cities, states, countries, or the world. Some commonly recognized proper nouns and adjectives are: the South Side (Chicago), the East Side (New York), Southern California, West Texas, the East, the Pacific Northwest, the Eastern Seaboard, the Far East, and Western Europe.

Write a sentence that includes a compass point. Use the examples shown in *The Office Guide* as a help.

1) _____

_____

_____

GP 17.1   When *each, every, any, many a,* and *many an* are used as adjectives, the subjects that are modified require a singular verb.

Write a sentence to demonstrate this rule. Use the examples given in *The Office Guide* as a help.

1) _____

_____

_____

GP 17.2   Whether or not a verb is singular or plural in sentences with compound subjects joined by "or" or "nor" is determined by the subject closest to the verb.

Write a sentence using either/or and use the correct singular or plural verb. Use the examples in *The Office Guide* as a help.

1) _____

_____

_____

GP 17.3   The subject is never part of a phrase.

Write a sentence that contains a phrase. Circle the subject. Use the examples in *The Office Guide* as a help.

1) _____

_____

_____

Directions: Punctuate and correct the following sentences if needed. Check your answers in Appendix C. Review the rule in *The Office Guide* again for each incorrect answer.

1. Some of the heavy equipment is going to the middle east.

2. Each one of the transcription operators have been late.

3. Either the new department chairman or the old department chairman have the book.

4. Neither Molly nor her replacement know where to get their checks signed.

5. One of his many duties are to train the supervisors.

6. The East Coast is beautiful but it can be dangerous during hurricane season.

7. Only one of the boxes are small enough to store the files.

8. Neither the new counselor nor his many assistants are eligible for a promotion.

9. She lived in west Texas for a short time before she moved to the Midwest.

10. The marketing manager only learned yesterday that she was transferred.

11. We had to wait until President Anderson gave her approval.

12. When the companies merged the President from our company became President of the new firm.

13. Either our Engineering Division will sponsor the event or the advertising department will.

14. Ginger did not know council representative Juan Perez's extension.

FORMAT REVIEW 7

Review DF 1 (Simplified Letter Style), DF 7 (Confidential Notation), DF 16 (Itinerary), and DF 20 in the Document Format section of *The Office Guide*.

Directions: Write a T in front of the statement if it is true or an F if it is false. Check your answers in Appendix C. Review the rule in *The Office Guide* again for each incorrect answer.

_____ 1. In the simplified letter style, the date is not included in the letter.

_____ 2. In the simplified letter style, the writer's name is typed at the end of the letter in initial capitals.

_____ 3. There is no salutation included in the simplified letter style.

_____ 4. There is no complimentary close in the simplified letter style.

_____ 5. Only open punctuation is used in the simplified letter style.

_____ 6. All lines in a simplified letter are typed at the left margin.

_____ 7. The word *confidential* is typed after the inside address in a letter that is confidential.

_____ 8. The word *confidential* is typed at the left margin in initial caps to show that only the person to whom the letter is addressed should read the letter.

_____ 9. The word *subject* is included before the subject in a simplified letter.

_____ 10. The main headings in an itinerary are dates.

_____ 11. A two-column format is usually used in an itinerary.

_____ 12. The information in the body of an itinerary is double spaced.

PROOFREADING EXERCISE 7

This proofreading exercise covers the rules identified and reviewed in *The Office Guide* for this lesson and previous lessons. This is a simplified letter.

Directions: Use proofreader's marks shown in GR 4 of *The Office Guide* to indicate needed corrections. There are **17** errors. Check your answers in Appendix C.

Current Date

Confidential

Ms. Terry Carter
278 5th Ave. SW
Decatur, GT 37891

COUNSEL ADVISORY BOARD

This is to notify you, confidently, that you have been selected to serve on the Council Advisory Board. Since the announcement will not me made until next week we are asking that you not share this news until the public announcement is made.

It is an honor to be selected to serve on this board, and I can assure you that you will find serving on the board to be a very rewarding experience. We are hoping that this letter will give you enough advance notice to schedule time to fly to southern California for the installation ceremony next month. I will send you correspondents with more details regarding the installation ceremony next week.

The members of our council advisory board have a diverse breath of knowledge and experience which aides us in deciding company policy. We can not thank our board members enough for sharing their expertise.

Jane McAlpine

lm

VOCABULARY PREVIEW

accrue	Accumulate, increase
adhere	Stick to, follow
aspects	Characteristics
derived	Obtained
eligible	Qualified
ensure	Guarantee, assure

enunciate	Pronounce clearly, articulate
flextime	A work arrangement in which employees may choose to work eight hours a day, four hours a day, or four ten-hour days during a week; usually certain restrictions apply such as that a large percentage of employees must work during the busiest part of the day
flexible	Adaptable, easily changed
generated	Created, made
implemented	Putting a procedure or plan into practice
intangible	Hypothetical, incapable of being touched, abstract
modes	Manner, styles, methods, way of doing things
necessitated	Made necessary, demanded, required
negotiated	Bargained, settled
overhead costs	The operating expenses of a business including the costs of rent, utilities, interior decorators, and taxes, but excluding labor and materials
productivity	Effectiveness, ability to produce
stood out	Drew attention, display characteristics that set apart
tangible	Capable of being appraised at a value, touchable, material
turnaround time	The amount of time it takes for a document to be typed, revised, or transcribed
verify	Confirm, validate
violated	Broken, disregarded
workflow	The continuity or pace with which work proceeds from one phase or person to another

TRANSCRIPTION PREVIEW: SELF-CHECK

Directions: Punctuate and correct the following sentences if needed. Check your answers in Appendix C.

1. Every one of the candidates possesses the qualities needed however three candidates stood out.

2. Operators on the 7 am to 3 pm shift have requested a meeting.

3. I will keep you informed of any type of flextime plan settled upon.

4. We believe this expense is justified because the City would benefit by an improvement in the quality of communications labor material and overhead costs would decrease and the morale of dictators and transcription operators would improve.

5. Scheduling conflicts exist because of the limited number of computers the workflow requirement and the need to retain the 3 pm to 5 pm part time people on those hours for which they were hired.

6. (1) we already have qualified individuals on our staff (2) payment of moving and transfer costs are expensive and (3) promoting from within promotes good morale.

4

7. Tangible savings would accrue in the categories of labor material and overhead and intangible benefits in the area of personnel satisfaction should also bring about savings necessitated by hiring employees to replace those who quit due to stress from conflicts arising between supervisors and transcription operators.

Directions: If an item below is correct, write "C" in the blank at the right; if the item is not correct, write the correct form in the blank.

1. eighty percent of the employees _____
2. Could you please verify the attached information? _____
3. north central area _____
4. twenty-four hour schedule _____
5. two-hour course _____
6. select the Purchasing Manager _____

FORMATTING PREVIEW

Document 21: Memorandum with Confidential Notation

Review DF 6, DF 11, and DF 18. Use memo format from template in word processing software, if available. The word *city* is capitalized in this memorandum and in the other letters in this lesson because it is referring specifically to the City of Geneva.

Document 22: Two-Page Simplified Letter with Bulleted Items

Use a simplified letter format from your template formats in your word processing software if one is available. Make this a two-page letter.

Document 23: Simplified Letter with Enumerated Items

Use a simplified letter format from your template formats in your word processing software if one is available.

Document 24: Travel Itinerary

This is the format for the heading information:

THE CITY OF GENEVA

TRAVEL ITINERARY FOR FRANK RUDDY
SAN DIEGO, CALIFORNIA
REGENCY POINT RESORT
MAY 15-MAY 19

The example below is for the first entry in the itinerary.

MONDAY, MAY 15

11:30 a.m.   Delta Flight 979. Ticketless reservation.

2:15 p.m.   Arrive San Diego. Take shuttle to Regency Point Resort.

6:30 p.m.   Dinner with Stephen Morton from the City of Orlando.

SHORT COURSE:

Transcribe documents
21, 23, 24

STANDARD COURSE:

Transcribe the four documents for the
City of Geneva.

TAPE: LESSON 7: CITY OF GENEVA

Tape Counter: Start __3__ Stop __26__ Doc. 21
Start __28__ Stop __65__ Doc. 22
Start __66__ Stop __107__ Doc. 23
Start __108__ Stop __132__ Doc. 24

4

8   TRL TESTING & RESEARCH

TRL Testing & Research is one of several independent companies that perform testing on products for pharmaceutical companies or individuals wishing to market a product. The research portion of their business also includes long-term follow-up and studies. When testing a new drug, the company may be involved in tracking performance or effects of usage for several years. A large part of their research is to monitor study results and report patterns in statistics or problems.

187 E. Orange Blvd.
Green Bay, WI 54307
Phone: 250-666-8312
Fax: 250-656-9122
E-mail: MasonT@tr.com
Internet:
www.TRLTesting.com

PERSONNEL FOR WHOM YOU WILL BE TRANSCRIBING

You will be transcribing dictation from:

Mason Timmons, Vice President Developmental Control

Bruce Benjamin, Research and Testing Supervisor

YOUR JOB

As one of several transcriptionists in the Research and Development Department, you transcribe dictation from the researchers and supervisors. Dictation usually involves the results of testing and product development.

JOB PREPARATION

TRL Testing & Research uses the simplified letter format. Review *The Office Guide* if you are uncertain of this letter style. Complete the word usage and other exercises prior to transcribing.

WORD USAGE REVIEW 8

CONFUSING WORDS

Review GR 1 Confusing Words in the General Reference section of *The Office Guide*. Study words *device* through *farther.*

Directions: Circle the correct word choice in each of the following sentences. Check your answers in Appendix C. Review the rule in *The Office Guide* again for each incorrect answer.

1. They worked very hard to (elicit, illicit) the formula from the employee without resorting to (elicit, illicit) behavior.

2. She used the wrong size (envelop, envelope) and the printer got jammed.

3. The new manager was not (fair, fare) in her treatment of older employees.

4. Making (every one, everyone) happy in their jobs (every day, everyday) is an impossible task.

5. Mr. Thompson (ensured, insured, assured) his car with the same company for the last ten years.

6. We developed a product to (envelop, envelope) the camera in a protective case.

7. The managers, left to ponder the (eminent, imminent) effects of the downsizing caused by the merger, tried to (device, devise) a "lay off" policy that was (fair, fare).

8. How much (farther, further) did Jane go in the race than Polly?

9. A few hours after the voting polls closed, it was apparent that he would (emerge, immerge) as the winner.

10. The (fair, fare) for the ferry increased several hundred dollars.

11. The signature on the (dairy, diary) was (eligible, illegible).

12. If you (emerge, immerge) or immerse the eggs in water immediately after boiling them, they should be easier to peel.

13. (Elicit, Illicit) drug use was an (every day, everyday) occurrence, and it was all the police could (do, due) to (ensure, insure, assure) the parents that the neighborhood was safe.

14. He contacted a patent attorney to see if the (device, devise) could be patented.

15. News of the (eminent, imminent) journalist's visit brought about (farther, further) political debate disrupting the (everyday, every day) routine.

16. How much money (do, due) you owe in (dos, dues)?

17. Practicing good transcription skills (everyday, every day) will (ensure, insure, assure) that your skills are strong, making you more (eligible, illegible) for a promotion.

18. He was so (discreet, discrete) in paying her tuition that (everyone, every one) thought that her scholarship paid for all her schooling.

19. The fans waiting in line began to (disburse, disperse) when it was announced that Madonna had (already, all ready) left the theater.

20. The (dual, duel) controls on the bed (aloud, allowed) Mary to keep her side of the bed warm and her husband to keep his side cooler.

21. The (elusive, illusive) butterfly managed to escape capturing no matter how hard Mary tried to catch it with the net.

22. The (dual, duel) between the police and the thief resulted in a child getting injured.

4

23. There were six (discreet, discrete) parts to the puzzle.

24. The treasurer will (disburse, disperse) the funds when the work is (done, dun).

25. The (elusive, illusive) advertisement made (a lot, allot) of people angry.

26. The accountant will (done, dun) each department for the supplies used.

27. The company will (expand, expend) a great deal of time and money to (expand, expend) the office complex.

28. (Everyone, Every one) of the transcriptionists received a bonus.

29. More people will (emigrate, immigrate) to the region if the entry regulations are relaxed.

30. With all (do, due, dew) respect, you should pay the library fine that is (do, due, dew) since you made Tony late in returning the book.

LANGUAGE REVIEW 8

Review GP 3.13, GP 6.1, GP 6.5, GP 17.5A, GP 17.6, and GP 18.1 in the Grammar and Punctuation section of *The Office Guide*.

Directions: Review the rules below in *The Office Guide* and then complete the following exercises. Check your answers in Appendix C. Review the rule in *The Office Guide* again for each incorrect answer.

GP 6.1 **Use quotation marks to enclose a direct quotation. Words such as** *said, remarked, stated,* **and** *replied* **frequently indicate a direct quotation.**

Write a sentence that includes a direct quote. Check the pitfall shown in *The Office Guide* to make sure you are not writing an indirect quote.

1) _____

_____

_____

GP 3.13 and GP 6.5 **Place commas and periods inside the end quotation mark. Periods and commas also go inside the single quotation mark. If a direct quotation is interrupted by expressions such as "he said" or "she replied," a comma and quotation mark precede the interrupting expression and a comma follows it. The continued expression is preceded by a quotation mark.**

Write a sentence that contains a direct quotation with an interrupted expression. Use the examples given in *The Office Guide* as a guide.

1) _____

_____

_____

4

GP 17.5A **Indefinite pronouns** (*anybody, another, anyone, anything, each, each one, either, neither, everybody, everyone, everything, much, nobody, on one, nothing, somebody, someone, something*) **always require a singular verb. This rule also applies when there are two subjects in the sentences joined by** *and.*

Write a sentence using an indefinite pronoun. Use the examples given in *The Office Guide* as a help.

1) _____

_____

_____

GP 17.6 **The pronoun** *you* **always requires a plural verb.**

Write a sentence using the pronoun *you.*

1) _____

_____

_____

GP 18.1 **A pronoun must agree in number with its antecedent (the noun to which the pronoun refers).**

Write a sentence that contains a pronoun other than the pronoun *you* and make sure the antecedent and pronoun agree in terms of being singular or plural. Refer to *The Office Guide* for examples of this rule.

1) _____

_____

_____

Directions: Punctuate and correct the following sentences if needed. Check your answers in Appendix C. Review the rule in *The Office Guide* again for each incorrect answer.

1. When discussing the new contract he commented, "The 4% pay increase is not acceptable".
2. "I will attend the training session on Monday night," reported Martha, but Alice will go on Tuesday after work.
3. Anyone can attend the classes if they sign up in advance.
4. You and Martha should go to the class.
5. Either the instructor or his assistant have been given the test forms.
6. You is not going to graduate if you don't get better grades.
7. The Vice President reported that he had many chances to be promoted but, in his words, didn't take them because, "I didn't want to transfer change positions or work longer hours for little extra pay".
8. Something has to be done and done soon about the network problems, complained the transcription operator.
9. No one on the committee were informed about the meeting.
10. "Did you go to the orientation" asked Mary?

4

11. Mr. Harper reported that "the merger is imminent."

12. Every employee should bring their report.

13. Your main responsibility the supervisor instructed the new employee is to answer the phone."

14. We did not get the information in time to make the deadline consequently, we did not submit the grant."

FORMAT REVIEW 8

Review information about the simplified letter style in sections DF 10 and DF 20 in the Document Format section and GR 5 and GR 7 in the General Reference section of *The Office Guide*.

Directions: Write a T in front of the statement if it is true or an F if it is false. Check your answers in Appendix C. Review the rule in *The Office Guide* again for each incorrect answer.

_____ 1. The copy notation is typed underneath the enclosure notation or reference initials.

_____ 2. The notation "bbc" is used when the writer does not want the addressee to know that someone else will also receive a copy of the letter.

_____ 3. A colon is always used after the copy notation.

_____ 4. Either one or two c's may be used in the copy notation.

_____ 5. If there is room, the copy notation is typed a double space below the enclosure notation or reference initials.

_____ 6. It is correct to divide this word as shown: *extra-ordinary.*

_____ 7. Dates may be divided between the day and year.

_____ 8. It is correct to divide this word as shown: *estima-tion.*

_____ 9. It is correct to divide this word as shown: *em-pty.*

_____ 10. It is acceptable to divide the last word on a page.

_____ 11. Names may be divided between the first name and the middle initial.

_____ 12. If you do not know the sex of the person to whom you are writing, it is acceptable not to use Ms. or Mr. in the inside address.

_____ 13. If you know the addressee is a woman but do not know if she is married, use Ms. as a title.

_____ 14. Use figures instead of spelling out words for building and house numbers in the address unless the number is 1.

_____ 15. This is the correct form to use in an address: Ms. Paula Anderson, M.D.

_____ 16. If you were addressing a letter to an organization with both male and female members, the salutation would be "Ladies and Gentlemen."

4

____ **17.** This is the correct form to use in addressing a letter to a husband and wife: Mr. & Mrs. Tom Royal.

____ **18.** The newer trend in addressing a letter to a husband and wife is to not use titles such as Mr. and Mrs. and to only use the husband's and wife's first and last names.

PROOFREADING EXERCISE 8

This proofreading exercise covers the rules identified and reviewed in *The Office Guide* for this lesson and previous lessons.

Directions: Use proofreader's marks shown in GR 4 of *The Office Guide* to indicate needed corrections. There are **9** errors. Check your answers in Appendix C.

Current Date

Mr. & Mrs. Jon Andersen
Four Glendale Blvd.
Sarasota, FL 37871

Dear Mr. & Mrs. Anderson

Some of the information on the form you completed regarding your availability to volunteer to register voters at the mall was eligible due to water stains from rainy weather. We need to insure that the information we have deciphered is correct. Please review the enclosed card to see if the information is correct so that we may process your application correctly.

According to policy guidelines, everyone who is eligible to work will receive information about the proper procedures to follow and farther information will be sent closer to the actual volunteer day. We try to be fare in our assignments and try to assign you to a mall close to your house. Our supervisor has asked us to inform you that "volunteers will be treated to an appreciation dinner in June."

Sincerely,

Jane McAlpine

Ref. Initials

Enclosure

cc Mr. Tony Peterson

VOCABULARY PREVIEW

ailment	Illness
immobilized	Unmoving, paralyzed
insidious	Entrapping, deceitful, subtle corruption, quietly spreading harm
melded	United, fused
monitoring	Observing
orthopedic	Correction or prevention of skeletal deformities
osteoporosis	Loss of bone mass
pervasive	Everywhere
porous	Spongy, absorbent
precautions	Take care of in advance, foresight
scaffolding	Structural support
sensitivity	Compassion
spur	Induce, goad
synthetic	Artificial
trauma	Shock
virtually	Essentially

TRANSCRIPTION PREVIEW: SELF-CHECK

Directions: Insert punctuation marks in the following sentences and make corrections if needed. Check your answers in Appendix C.

1. So far this therapy of using coral and cloned proteins to rebuild crushed brittle and broken bones appears to be positive in one hundred percent of the cases we have been monitoring for five years.

2. In his presentation three years ago the imminent orthopedic trauma surgeon Dr. Cole Ricks predicted By using coral orthopedic trauma surgeons nationwide will create walking miracles among people injured in sports and near death accidents

3. The new bone melded with the implant and a limb lengthening device stretched the limb to match the length of her other leg.

4. The every day contact with latex products ranging from disposable diapers to buttons on calculators and TV remotes is making the problem of latex allergies very widespread.

5. We have had success with a topical cream that treats the rash but the only relief we have found so far for severe sensitivity is a self-injected dose of epinephrine.

6. With regard to the No Sugar Added product I can inform you that in fact to our surprise it has reacted differently to market storage conditions than our pre released studies indicated and we are already taking steps to remedy the situation.

4

Directions: If an item below is correct, write "C" in the blank at the right; if the item is not correct, write the correct form in the blank.

1. for 5 years _____
2. Foxley's no sugar Added Ice Cream _____
3. pre-released studies _____
4. deep sea coral implant _____
5. career ending ailment _____

FORMATTING PREVIEW

Document 25: Simplified Letter

Use the simplified letter-style template if one is available in your software program. Review DF 1, DF 9, and DF 18.

Document 26: Simplified Letter

Use a simplified letter format from your template formats in your word processing software if one is available.

Document 27: Simplified Letter

Use a simplified letter format from your template formats in your word processing software if one is available.

Document 28: Memorandum

Use a simplified memo format from your template formats in your word processing software if one is available.

SHORT COURSE:	STANDARD COURSE:
Transcribe documents 25, 26, 28	Transcribe the four documents for TRL Testing & Research.

TAPE: LESSON 8: TRL TESTING & RESEARCH

Tape Counter: Start _133_ Stop _171_ Doc. 25
             Start _173_ Stop _206_ Doc. 26
             Start _208_ Stop _231_ Doc. 27
             Start _233_ Stop _262_ Doc. 28

TEST TIME

After your instructor has graded your transcribed letters for Lesson 8, review the confusing words and language rules presented in lessons 1 through 8. Ask your instructor for the second written test covering confusing words, punctuation, grammar, and proofreading. Then ask your instructor for the tape for Transcription Test 2.

INTRODUCTION TO TEST 2

You should be familiar with these terms and vocabulary words prior to taking Test 2. Make sure you review the names of the individuals who dictated in lessons 5 through 8.

pen-based PC	Equipment with technology that allows for computerlike applications to be made by using an instrument similar to a pen
metaphor	Allegory, figure of speech, or story
schedulers	Software application used to schedule events
intrusive	Irritating, annoying, presumptuous
pharmaceutical	Related to pharmacy or medical areas
externally	Outside
parallel	Corresponding, equal to
private sector	A part of the business community that is not related to government
locality	Area, district, community
legion	Division, large group
core	Center such as the cardboard around which foil is wrapped

Test 2 Doc. 1: Block-Style Letter

Test 2 Doc. 2: Modified Block-Style Letter

Test 2 Doc. 3: Memo

Test 2 Doc. 4: Simplified Letter

4

9   ECHO FAMILY INSURANCE

189 Tower Plaza
Warren, MI 48092
Phone: 734-982-8554
Fax: 734-982-5448
Internet: www.echo.com
E-mail: Echofi@net.com

Echo Family Insurance has been in business for ten years and is affiliated with a large insurance network. The company has offices in metropolitan areas throughout the country, as well as regional and state administrative offices and local sales offices. Specialized groups of employees perform these duties: (1) sell policies and services, (2) process the paperwork resulting from these transactions, (3) invest the income to obtain a maximum return for the insured and the company, and (4) administer the activities to achieve company goals. As a full-service insurance company, Echo provides its customers with coverage in the following areas: health, disability, life, automobile, mortgage, home, and tenants' insurance. Other services include annuities and endowments. A large portion of the insurance Echo sells relates to homeowners', auto, and life insurance.

PERSONNEL FOR WHOM YOU WILL BE TRANSCRIBING

This agency is growing rapidly and serves over 500 customers. The founder of this agency's branch, Mr. Martin Boyd, began the operation with only himself and a secretary. Since then, four more underwriters specializing in specific insurance areas have been added to the staff. You will be transcribing dictation from:

Martin Boyd, Manager/Owner
- Oversees staff training for all agents, supervises office functions, handles all types of insurance coverage for the 500 customers who have been covered by Echo Insurance during the last eight to ten years.

Sally Bankowetz, Automobile Insurance Agent

Karen Kogut-Tift, Homeowner Insurance Agent

Edward Weidenheimer, Claim Specialist

Marion Prinse, Life Insurance Agent

YOUR JOB

You are one of three office staff members who support Mr. Boyd and the other agents.

4

JOB PREPARATION

Echo uses full block letter style. Complete the word usage and other exercises prior to transcribing.

WORD USAGE REVIEW 9

CONFUSING WORDS

Review GR 1 Confusing Words in the General Reference section of *The Office Guide.* Study words *flair* through *libel.*

Directions: Circle the correct word choice in each of the following sentences. Check your answers in Appendix C. Review the rule in *The Office Guide* again for each incorrect answer.

1. We will meet the Andersons (later, latter) in the day.

2. She was involved in several fraudulent (incidences, incidents) that lead to her being (indicted, indited) for embezzlement.

3. The famous actor sued the magazine for (liable, libel) because of the false story.

4. (Its, It's) a good idea to (formerly, formally) go through the proper personnel channels when (higher, hiring) employees.

5. The (legislator, legislature) was (liable, libel) for not getting the report to the press on time in several (instants, instances).

6. The defense attorney told the jury about her suspected child abuse and gambling, the (later, latter) of which was (implied, inferred) to have caused her to file for bankruptcy.

7. He was (formally, formerly) employed by Johnson Motors, Inc.

8. We were insulted when she (implied, inferred) that we should take a course in English.

9. He was (formally, formerly) recognized for his many years of service as a (legislator, legislature) in the (legislator, legislature).

10. Jon was able to reach the (higher, hire) typing speed required for a promotion.

11. The dictator dictated in quick (instants, instance) that caused the operators to (later, latter) ask him to slow down when dictating.

12. The manager was given credit for (indicting, inditing) the new guidelines, but Betty was the one who actually did the work.

13. There is an unusually low (incidence, incidents) of safety violations at the firm.

14. (It's, its) about time that Sally helped decorate the cake by sprinkling chocolate bits on (it's, its) top.

15. We (implied, inferred) from her remarks that neither one of us would be (indicted, indited) for (liable, libel) for (formerly, formally) being employed by the company found guilty of tax fraud.

4

16. Marty had a (flair, flare) for decorating.

17. Terry had to (forgo, forego) the opportunity to meet Mr. Reynolds because he promised his children he would attend their ball game.

18. We should (here, hear) soon if the (lead, led) pipe in the (leased, least) apartment was the cause of the water leak.

19. Peter and Juan were (here, hear) earlier and hid their (horde, hoard) of old coins in the (hall, haul) closet.

20. It took a long time to (heard, herd) the chickens into the pen.

21. The Bible is considered to be a (holy, holey, wholly) book.

22. At (least, leased) Pete can (hall, haul) the trash out since he was (holy, holey, wholly) responsible for the mess.

23. The bones they found were (human, humane).

24. There is no guarantee that the (flair, flare) will work.

25. The (horde, hoard) of holiday shoppers made it hard to walk in the mall.

26. Did Peter (incinerate, insinuate) that the (correspondence, correspondents) was forged?

27. She will (forward, foreword) the (lessen, lesson) plans to him.

28. Do not (lay, lie) the book on the counter because it is wet.

29. She was not (allowed, aloud) to wear the (holy, holey, wholly) shirt outside of the house.

30. The (forward, foreword) of the book told about how (human, humane) the village residents were because they refused to harm the thief.

31. Lester was supportive of the protest to (incinerate, insinuate) the old books because not (everyone, every one) realized their value.

LANGUAGE REVIEW 9

Review GP 3.3B, GP 7.2, GP 7.4, GP 8.3, GP 8.4, and GP 13.3 in the Grammar and Punctuation section of *The Office Guide*.

Directions: Review the rules below in *The Office Guide* and then complete the following exercises.

GP 3.3C **Use commas to set off contrasting expressions (phrases that often begin with *but only, not,* and *rather than*) that are not essential to the meaning of the sentence.**

Write a sentence that includes a contrasting expression. Refer to *The Office Guide* for an example if you need assistance.

1) _____

_____

_____

GP 7.2   **Hyphenate commonly used word parts such as *re, self, co,* or *pre* when confusion may result without the hyphen.**

Write a sentence using one of the word parts shown above in which a hyphen is needed to facilitate understanding. Refer to *The Office Guide* if you need to see an example of this rule.

1) _____

   _____

   _____

GP 7.4   **Use a hyphen when consecutive numbers are used or with time.**

Write a sentence with consecutive numbers or periods of time. Use the examples in *The Office Guide* if you need more guidance in order to write the sentence.

1) _____

   _____

   _____

GP 8.3   **Add only an apostrophe to plural nouns ending in *s*. Review the hint, too, given about this rule in *The Office Guide* before writing your sentence.**

Write a sentence using a plural noun that ends in *s*.

1) _____

   _____

   _____

GP 8.4   **Use the possessive form of the word preceding a gerund (a verb form ending in *ing* that is used as a noun).**

Write a sentence that contains a gerund. Refer to *The Office Guide* for examples of this rule.

1) _____

   _____

   _____

GP 13.3   **Write even amounts of a million or more with a figure followed by the word *million, billion,* etc.**

Write a sentence that contains an amount over 1 million. Refer to *The Office Guide* for examples of this rule.

1) _____

   _____

   _____

Directions: Punctuate and correct the following sentences if needed. Check your answers in Appendix C. Review the rule in *The Office Guide* again for each incorrect answer.

4

1. The auditors findings showed that the accounting procedures were being followed.

2. The new employees started on the first of the month rather than beginning work in the middle of a pay period.

3. We will not be able to have the meetings in conference rooms 301 308 because they don't have teleconferencing capabilities.

4. The supervisor changed the arrangement of the reception area not the work area in order to make it more convenient for individuals to pick up completed work.

5. He was asked to re-evaluate his position on refusing to accept payroll turned in late from self employed contractors.

6. Marys typing was so good it earned her a promotion.

7. Please return the forms in the self addressed envelope.

8. Please arrange your schedule so that you have time to attend the meeting that will take place in Room 4C between 8 a.m. and 10:30 a.m.

9. Rather than transfer to our company she stayed in the Finance Department at her company where her job was secure.

10. All of the department managers received a pay increase.

11. He understanding of the project enabled them to complete the job on time.

12. Mr. Williams was willing to transfer to another state but only if the company would pay moving costs.

13. Two years experience is required before employees can be considered for a promotion.

14. She was given a salary increase but only after she questioned her evaluation.

15. Before employees can be considered for a promotion they must work for the company for two years.

16. All of the department managers salaries were increased.

FORMAT REVIEW 9

Review sections GR 7 (Apartment Building, ZIP codes, and Job Titles), in the General Reference section and DF 8, DF 10, and DF 11 in the Document Format section of *The Office Guide.*

Directions: Write a T in front of the statement if it is true or an F if it is false. Check your answers in Appendix C. Review the rule in *The Office Guide* again for each incorrect answer.

4

_____ 1. The U.S. Post Office prefers that two spaces be left between the two-letter state abbreviation and the ZIP code.

_____ **2.** This inside address is correctly formatted:

Ms. Nancy Abteron, Research and Development Manager
Regional Sales
376 South Avenue
Salem, NC 78432

_____ **3.** This inside address is correctly formatted:

Ms. Janie Thompson, Coordinator
Medical International Laboratories
6 Park Lane
St. Petersburg, FL 33710

_____ **4.** Addition notations are used to add information that was thought of after the letter was composed.

_____ **5.** The information below is correctly formatted:

ps: We have the items needed for your next shipment. Please call our Order Department immediately to have the order shipped.

_____ **6.** If the letter is block style, the postscript is not indented.

_____ **7.** If the letter style uses indented paragraphs, the postscript should be indented.

_____ **8.** If the writer wants the receiver of the letter to know that it is his or her personal views reflected in the letter, he or she would use the company name in the letter's closing.

_____ **9.** If a modified block-style letter is used and the company name is requested to be included in the closing, it is typed at the left margin.

_____ **10.** The company name is typed in initial capitals on the second line below the closing.

_____ **11.** If an apartment building or number is used in the address and is put on a separate line, it should be typed on the line after the street address.

_____ **12.** This address is formatted correctly:

Dr. Paul Smith
765 East Street, Apt. 87E
Cleveland, OH 86409

_____ **13.** This address is formatted correctly:

Peter and Elaine Smith
301 West Amelia Street
Apartment 86B
Orlando, FL 32801

4

PROOFREADING EXERCISE 9

This proofreading exercise covers the rules identified and reviewed in *The Office Guide* for this lesson and previous lessons.

Directions: Use proofreader's marks shown in GR 4 of *The Office Guide* to indicate needed corrections. There are **16** errors. Check your answers in Appendix C.

Current Date

Ms. Mary Halloran, Southeastern District Conference Coordinator
MS Office Products
878 23rd Avenue North
Building 83B
Decater, GA 50812

Dear Mr. Holloran:

Putting on a conference can be a major headache as well as an major accomplishment. A subscription to our magazine Conferences & Conventions can help you take some of the "headache" out of the sometimes overwhelming planning involved in setting up a conference.

Rather than spending hours trying to pull together all the elements of putting on a good conference; let *Conferences & Conventions* do all the networking and information gathering for you. This versatile monthly magazine covers everything form destination guides, free information, planing portfolios, hot ideas, and important news to convention managers and planners. Not only are issues such as cancelation clauses and political concerns associated with conference planning covered but also topics such as international updates are covered.

We are sending you a complimentary issue of *Conferences & Conventions*. Return the enclosed subscription form to commence having a monthly issue delivered to your doorstep. We are certain that you will see the tremendous value from this complimentary issue.

Sincerely,

Ted Liberman

CONFERENCES & CONVENTIONS

lm

Ps: If you return the enclosed subscription form between May tenth and May twentieth, you will have the option of accessing *Conferences & Conventions* online.

4

VOCABULARY PREVIEW

affidavit	Sworn statement
agent	A representative of an insurance company who sells insurance, sometimes called an "underwriter"
beneficiary	After the death of the insured
commercial	Business
deductible	The amount of out-of-pocket expenses the insured agrees to pay before the benefits begin
facsimile (fax) electronically	Information transmitted electronically; (fax-verb) transmit information
grace period	The amount of time immediately following the premium due date during which payment can still be made to keep the policy in force
imperative	Essential
incurred	Became liable for
insured	The person, group, or organization whose life or property is covered by an insurance policy
notarized	Verifying that the person signing a document is the person required to do so; legalizing a signature
premium	The amount a policyholder pays to keep an insurance policy in force
rider	Special features or clauses added to an insurance policy
witnessed	Observed; testified as to the validity of a signature or event

TRANSCRIPTION PREVIEW: SELF-CHECK

Directions: Insert punctuation marks and make corrections if necessary in the following sentences. Check your answers in Appendix C.

1. To provide prompt payment of your claim please submit the following information as soon as possible.

2. We can not process this claim however without your assistance.

3. Therefore the damage to the paint or waterproofing material applied to the exterior of your residence is not covered.

4. Although there is a short grace period I suggest that we meet prior to this renewal deadline to help you select the option most appropriate to cover your commercial needs.

5. Each question must be answered and the affidavit must be signed witnessed and notarized.

6. Since you have changed the conditions under which the policy was originally issued I believe that you should consider updating the coverage under this policy.

4

Directions: If an item below is correct, write "C" in the blank at the right; if the item is not correct, write the correct form in the blank.

1. from June fifth through June tenth _____
2. the Commercial Liability Umbrella Policy _____
3. $1,000,000 _____
4. re-newability _____
5. self addressed _____

FORMATTING PREVIEW

Document 29: Block Letter with Subject Line, Job Title and Company Name in Closing, Enclosure, and Postscript

Use block style for this letter. The subject for this letter includes three parts that should be typed on separate lines:

> RE: Claim Number: 10-5185-634
> Date of Loss: March 23, 20—
> Our Insured: Edward Long

This letter also includes enclosures. Instead of typing the number of enclosures, type the name of the enclosed items. Example:

> Enclosures   Affidavit
> Return Envelope
> Form

Document 30: Block Letter with Subject Line

The subject line is one line:

> In Re: Policy No. 689-32-4033

Document 31: Short Block Letter

Arrange this letter attractively on the page.

Document 32: Block Letter with Enumerated Items, Job Title in Closing, Enclosure, and Postscript

Double space between the enumerated items and type a line after the question:

1. Was the accident work related? _____

2. Where did the accident happen? _____

_____

This letter also contains an enclosure. Include the name of the enclosed item in the enclosure notation.

SHORT COURSE:

Transcribe the following documents: 29, 31, 32

STANDARD COURSE:

Transcribe the four documents for Echo Family Insurance.

TAPE: LESSON 9: ECHO FAMILY INSURANCE

Tape Counter: Start ___3___ Stop ___30___ Doc. 29
Start ___31___ Stop ___57___ Doc. 30
Start ___60___ Stop ___75___ Doc. 31
Start ___78___ Stop ___107___ Doc. 32

4

10 POTOMAC NATIONAL BANK

POTOMAC NATIONAL BANK

Security You Can Trust
1825 Pennsylvania Ave., NW
Washington, DC 24209
Phone: 289-874-5433
Fax: 289-866-7342
Internet:
www.PotomacNB.net
E-mail: BidwellL@neb.com

Potomac National Bank was First National Bank until the bank merged with Potomac National two years ago. The merger enabled the bank to provide various services to its commercial and noncommercial customers. In addition to the bank, located in downtown Washington, Potomac National has branches throughout the area and offers 24-hour automated banking services at convenient locations. As well as offering the conventional banking services (savings and checking accounts, bank box rentals, loans, identification, debit and credit cards, and special Christmas Club and line-of-credit accounts), Potomac provides financial management services such as investment advice, trust supervision, and travel services, which range from foreign currency exchange to traveler's checks. Also offered are online banking services, which allow customers to make transactions from home.

PERSONNEL FOR WHOM YOU WILL BE TRANSCRIBING

Robert Barnes, Personal Loan Officer
- Approves noncommercial customers' loans based on their credit records.

Lloyd Bidwell, Vice President, Marketing
- Directs the activities that inform potential and current customers of the bank's services, thereby increasing the volume of deposits, savings, loans, and trusts.

Imogene Duckett, Vice President, Investment Department
- Directs the activities of the investment department including certificate of deposit and retirement account services.

YOUR JOB

The Potomac National Bank still has a large centralized information processing center. Within the next few months, the center will become decentralized and smaller centers will be established within each of the bank's departments. You will transcribe dictation from the executives, managers, supervisors, and administrators at the main bank building.

The bank is controlled by a Board of Directors and managed by a president who implements the Board's policies. The authority over each department is vested in a vice president (for example, Vice President in charge of Personal Loans). Under the vice presidents are department managers, officers who direct the activities of each department. Supervisors, administrators, and clerical personnel complete the workforce. Following is a description of the bank's organization:

4

- **Board of Directors:** Potomac National's Board of Directors is composed of business executives, professional people, and members of the community. These people are usually selected for their expertise in a specific area, their position in local business or industrial firms, or their prestige in the community.

- **Bank Departments:** These departments perform specific functions, such as managing trusts or approving commercial loans.

- **Branch Banks:** Divisions of the main bank are located in various sections of Washington, D.C. These branches provide services comparable to but less extensive than the main bank's services; each is managed by a branch manager who is responsible to the Vice President of Bank Operations.

JOB PREPARATION

Complete the word usage and other exercises prior to transcribing.

WORD USAGE REVIEW 10

CONFUSING WORDS

Review GR 1 Confusing Words in the General Reference section of *The Office Guide*. Study words *loose* through *quiet*.

Directions: Circle the correct word choice in each of the following sentences. Check your answers in Appendix C. Review the rule in *The Office Guide* for each incorrect answer.

1. Some of the (patience, patients) did not want to leave the hospital because the (personal, personnel) attention they received was superior to their (every day, everyday) attention at home.

2. He took the test this (past, passed) week and was pleased when he finally (past, passed).

3. From the supervisor's (perspective, prospective) we (maybe, may be) considered (quiet, quite) (confidant, confident), but we really need some (assistance, assistants) in learning the software.

4. The (loose, lose, loss) of the (annual, annul) fundraiser resulted in a deficit that required monitoring expenses (everyday, every day).

5. The marketing manager is the (principal, principle) (perspective, prospective) candidate for the new position according to (personal, personnel) staff.

6. The new employees were (quite, quiet) during the orientation and were intimidated by the president's (presence, presents) at the meeting.

7. Did you (peruse, pursue) the new employee handbook so that you are ready for the meeting?

8. Esther donated (a lot, allot) of (personal, personnel) time to work at the school (bizarre, bazaar) to raise money for (presence, presents) to give the (patience, patients) at the children's home.

9. They would not (precede, proceed) with the ceremony until (everyone, every one) was (quiet, quite).

10. The store did not (persecute, prosecute) the young shoplifter, but the manager gave him (quiet, quite) a lecture.

11. Tom did not (peruse, pursue) the opportunity to run for political office because he was afraid that he may (loose, lose, loss) the election.

12. In the (past, passed), the supervisors were (loose, lose, loss) with their criticism of employees until the new management sent them for training on how (personal, personnel) should be treated.

13. The managers learned several (principals, principles) about (complementing, complimenting) employees.

14. Marty's presentation about the budget will (precede, proceed) the voting on the issue.

15. The handle on the file cabinet drawer was (loose, lose, loss) so access to the files (maybe, may be) unprotected allowing unauthorized (personnel, personal) to (peruse, pursue) confidential material.

16. If you (loose, lose, loss) your company identification card, you need to get a new one as quickly as possible.

17. The (moral, morale) of the story is to follow the Golden Rule if you want (peace, piece) to prevail.

18. If you take the medication in the (morning, mourning) be sure to eat breakfast.

19. The (peace, piece) of the (plane, plain) that was found on the (peak, peek, pique) of the old building (peaked, peeked, piqued) the interest of several (analyst, annalist).

20. The employees' (moral, morale) was low (do, due) to (morning, mourning) for the CEO who appeared to have been in excellent (physical, fiscal) condition, but who died suddenly of a heart attack.

21. The director's dictation took (precedence, precedents) over the general manager's.

22. Mark was fired because he would (prophecy, prophesy) about the company going bankrupt.

23. The Web site was very (plane, plain).

24. If you are (perfect, prefect), there is nothing to (perfect, prefect).

25. The (physical, fiscal) year for the budget is from July 1 to June 31.

26. The (peer, pier) was a popular place for lovers to meet.

27. If you (peer, pier) into the glass, you will see a (peace, piece) of wood that was taken from an old window frame.

28. Hopefully the recent high-tech mergers will not start a (precedence, precedent) because they often (lead, led) to layoffs.

29. The (prophecy, prophesy) about the world ending has led to much discussion.

30. It was (plane, plain) to see that the (plane, plain) was in trouble from its fast descent.

31. Long ago the land was a great (plane, plain) where buffalo roamed and carpenters used simple tools, such as (planes, plains) and chisels to build log homes.

4

Directions: Review the rules below in *The Office Guide* and then complete the following exercises.

GP 6.6 **Place question marks and exclamation points inside the closing quotation mark when they apply to only the quoted material. Place question marks or exclamation points outside the closing quotation mark when they apply to the entire sentence.**

Write a sentence with a quotation that includes a question related only to the quotation. Refer to *The Office Guide* for an example if you need assistance.

1) _____

_____

_____

Write a sentence that includes a quotation and a question related to the entire sentence and not just to the quoted text. Refer to *The Office Guide* for an example if you need assistance.

1) _____

_____

_____

GP 6.7 **The semicolon and colon are always placed outside the end quotation mark.**

Write a sentence that requires use of a semicolon or colon and includes a quotation. Refer to *The Office Guide* if you need to see an example of this rule.

1) _____

_____

_____

GP 8.5 **Add an apostrophe and an *s* to form the possessives of proper names with only one syllable and add only an apostrophe to proper names with more than one syllable.**

Write a sentence using the proper names Puglisi and Holtz.

1) _____

_____

_____

GP 8.8 **Add an apostrophe and an *s* to form the plurals of most figures, symbols, letters, and words.**

4

Write a sentence that contains the plural form of figures, symbols, letters, or words. Use the examples in The *Office Guide* if you need more guidance in order to write the sentence.

1) _____

_____

_____

GP 10.5   **Capitalize trade names, product brands, and words that identify specific services offered by an organization.**

Write a sentence that includes a trade name. Refer to *The Office Guide* if you need to see an example of this rule.

1) _____

_____

_____

Directions: Punctuate and correct the following sentences if needed. Check your answers in Appendix C. Review the rule in *The Office Guide* for each incorrect answer.

1. The Ss did not print on the hard copy although they showed on the screen.

2. The question the new employees wanted answered was When will we be eligible for a raise

3. Hilary Thompson salary was $8.50 an hour—or was it $9.50 an hour.

4. During the last committee meeting he was asked to bring the auditors final report in which the question, Did any employees violate accounting procedural rules was answered.

5. Sally shrieked with delight when told that she had won the contest and shouted I can't believe I won!

6. We attended Vernita Holtz engagement party and the host of the party predicted Vernita you will have a long and happy marriage

7. The department manager asked the vice president the following question If we went on a flextime schedule would all departments have the option of choosing their schedules.

8. At the orientation did the vice president say all new employees are eligible immediately for health care benefits

9. We will see if Tom can watch the Prez dog when they are vacationing.

10. All the students attending school in the 90 took part in technical preparation training.

11. The new ice cream minneapolis delight will be available in June.

12. We won't know if many people will take advantage of the circle of friends long distance telephone service.

13. When you select our fixed rate option you can finance up to 95 percent loan-to-value on owner occupied purchases at a 9 percent interest rate.

4

FORMAT REVIEW 10

Review section GR 7 (Department Identification, Compass Points Appearing before the Street Name, and Compass Points Appearing after the Street Name) in the Document Formats section of *The Office Guide*.

Directions: Write a T in front of the statement if it is true or an F if it is false. Check your answers in Appendix C. Review the rule in *The Office Guide* again for each incorrect answer.

_____ **1.** If the word *Southeast* is used before the street name in the address, it should be abbreviated.

_____ **2.** The name of the department should be put on the line after the company's name.

_____ **3.** If the word *Northwest* is used in the street address and appears after the street name, it should not be abbreviated.

_____ **4.** If the word *West* is used after the street name, a comma is placed before it.

_____ **5.** Compound directions (Northeast, Northwest, Southeast, and Southwest) should be abbreviated when they appear after a street name.

_____ **6.** If a compound direction is used in the street address after the street name, a comma is placed before the compound direction.

_____ **7.** The correct abbreviation for Southwest is S.W.

_____ **8.** The following address is formatted correctly:

Mr. Paul Anderson
Research and Development Department
Research Director
769 East Rochester Drive
Warren, MI 39812

_____ **9.** The following address is formatted correctly:

Mr. Paul Anderson
Vice President Production
Research and Production Division
8700 30th Street S.
Warren, MI 39812

_____ **10.** The following address is formatted correctly:

Mr. Paul Anderson
Vice President Production
Emerging Technologies Department
6200 SW Oakridge Road
Warren, MI 39812

4

PROOFREADING EXERCISE 10

This proofreading exercise covers the rules identified and reviewed in *The Office Guide* for this lesson and previous lessons.

Directions: Use proofreader's marks shown in GR 4 of *The Office Guide* to indicate needed corrections. There are **24** errors. Check your answers in Appendix C.

June 31, 20—

Mrs. Robert L. Morrison, Manager
Purchasing Department
Capital Manufacturing Company
2199 Essex Knoll Drive
Stone Harbor, NJ 03247

Dear Mr. Morrison:

Many firms spend thousands of dollars annually to purchase find letterhead which will carry the the image of there company to its readers. Many companies insist on expensive paper and print that is eligible and up-to-date. Some require a letterhead into colors of a highly artistic nature. This touch of individuality, they feel, will create a lasting impression on their customers and leave an feeling of confidence about there firm. We understand this need to set yourself apart in order to establish a strong client base. For this reason we offer our customers that individualized touch.

Our company just moved in to a knew building adjacent to the Winterside Mall. This new location allowed us to expend our inventory, and we now have a complete line of office supply. Because passed experience has shown us that many customers need to shop after they have finished working, we are open from 9 a.m. in the morning until 9 p.m. in the evening.

We invite you to take advantage of our expert, courteous staff, and quality merchandise. The enclosed coupon will give you a ten percent discount on your first purchase.

Very truley yours,

Mr. Don Patterson

lm

VOCABULARY PREVIEW

APR	Abbreviation for Annual Percentage Rate
competitive	Several firms trying to secure business; contests between rivals
consolidating	Centralizing; unifying
earned interest	Money that is received on capital investments or savings
substantial	Considerable in quantity, large
escalating	Increasing
maintenance	Upkeep
matures	Becomes due
maturity date	The date when a loan or certificate is due
mortgage	A conditional conveyance of rights to a piece of property with security for the payment of a loan or debt
prevailing	Current
promissory note	Surety; obligation or promise to pay an established amount
proportionally	Having the same or constant ratio

TRANSCRIPTION PREVIEW: SELF-CHECK

Directions: Correct and insert punctuation marks in the following sentences if needed. Check your answers in Appendix C.

1. As a valued Potomac Bank customer you've earned special recognition and we're saying Thank You by offering you a pre-approved Potomac Gold MasterCard with no annual fee a low fixed 7.9% APR and a credit limit of $8,000

2. For instance All-In-One customers can write any number of checks without a service charge and the interest on MasterCard balances is 13% which is lower than competitive cards with 15% to 20% interest rates.

3. You may however pay the $5,000 at any time before the due date and reduce the amount of interest proportionately.

4. You will receive a statement prior to that date which will show the term maturity date current balance interest rate and earned interest on this certificate.

5. For current rate information please call our 24 hour rate line (919-468-7889) on the day your certificate matures.

6. Many banks offer online computer banking services but our service allows you to choose how you access your accounts such as from America Online Microsoft Money Quicken or from Potomac National Bank's Cyberbanking.

4

Directions: If an item below is correct, write "C" in the blank at the right; if the item is not correct, write the correct form in the blank.

1. on-the-spot savings _____

2. Acceptance certificate _____

3. $5.00 service charge _____

4. All-In-One Account _____

5. post card _____

6. 360-day promissory note _____

7. customer service representative _____

FORMATTING PREVIEW

Document 33: Block Letter with Enclosures and Job Title Used in Closing

The percents used in this letter and in the other letters for this lesson are considered to be of a more technical nature; therefore, use the % sign instead of writing out the word *percent* in most instances. Example:

$$7.9\% \text{ APR}$$

This letter also contains enclosures. Instead of typing the number of enclosures, type what the items are. Example:

Enclosures: Acceptance Certificate
Return Envelope

Document 34: Block Form Letter with Variable Information, Enclosure, and Job Title Used in Closing

The dictator will say the word *variable* to indicate where you should put merge codes in the letter. After the letter has been dictated, the dictator will dictate the names and addresses of two individuals to whom the letter should be sent.

Document 35: Short Block Letter with Enclosures and Job Title Used in Closing

Arrange this letter so that it is centered vertically on the page. List the three items enclosed in the Enclosure Notation.

Document 36: Average Length Block Letter with Job Title Used in Closing

4

SHORT COURSE:

Transcribe documents 34, 35, 36

STANDARD COURSE:

Transcribe the four documents from Potomac National Bank.

TAPE: LESSON 10: POTOMAC NATIONAL BANK

Tape Counter: Start __109__ Stop __132__ Doc. 33
Start __134__ Stop __170__ Doc. 34
Start __172__ Stop __199__ Doc. 35
Start __201__ Stop __229__ Doc. 36

4

11   AUNT DEE'S KIDS KAMPUS

407 West Oakridge Road
Chattanooga, TN 59823
Phone: 287-694-8655
E-mail: DeeKids@net.com
Internet:
www.auntdeeskids.com

Dee Showalter started watching children in her home ten years ago. The demand for her services grew; and in order to meet the childcare needs of more parents, she opened her own childcare business. She took classes to become certified and became a licensed childcare provider. Currently 120 children are enrolled in Aunt Dee's Kids Kampus, and the center has been recognized by the state and district for its creative, excellent programs.

PERSONNEL FOR WHOM YOU WILL BE TRANSCRIBING

You will be transcribing dictation from:

Dee Showalter, Owner

YOUR JOB

Your job title is Office Assistant, and one of your responsibilities is to transcribe letters dictated by Dee Showalter. Because the office is small and everyone knows each other, Dee does not use "operator" when dictating to alert you to when she is giving you instructions. Instead she uses your first name, Karen. Dee usually dictates between the time the last staff member leaves and the time the cleaning crew arrives. She used to draft letters for you to type, but found this time-consuming; and only recently did she begin dictating. As a novice dictator, she makes changes and corrections in her dictation.

JOB PREPARATION

Before you begin transcribing the documents for this lesson, complete the following exercises. Make certain that you review the rules identified in *The Office Guide* first. Your instructor may want to see these completed exercises before you transcribe the letters for this lesson.

4

WORD USAGE REVIEW 11

CONFUSING WORDS

Review GR 1 Confusing Words in the General Reference section of *The Office Guide*. Study words *respectably* through *they're*.

Directions: Circle the correct word choice in each of the following sentences. Check your answers in Appendix C. Review the rule in *The Office Guide* again for each incorrect answer.

1. The new employee (respectably, respectfully) asked his supervisor if he could serve as his assistant on the project.

2. She did not play a very big (role, roll) in the company's reorganization.

3. They watched the banner (sore, soar) overhead as it trailed behind the plane.

4. The seniors were given certain (rights, rites, writes) that made the juniors envious.

5. The senior told the freshman: "(Someday, Some day) you will have senior privileges and (everyone, every one) will treat you (respectably, respectfully)."

6. Her jaw was swollen and (soar, sore).

7. Who will (right, rite, write) the last (scene, seen) in the play?

8. The computer log did not match the instructor's (role, roll).

9. The new letterhead (stationary, stationery) was more expensive (than, then) the old one because of the new logo.

10. Mary dressed (respectably, respectfully) for the interview.

11. The announcement of who the new supervisor is will be made on (someday, some day) next week.

12. Some of the fraternity's initiation (rights, rites, writes) were dangerous.

13. The new employee was (scene, seen) making copies of (their, there, they're) reports.

14. Joan tried to (loose, lose, loss) weight by riding a (stationary, stationery) bike.

15. (Sometime, Sometimes) we have to ask questions to make sure we understand the procedures.

16. She worked (their, there, they're) for five years before she (perused, pursued) her dream of starting her own business.

17. We checked the price of the (stationary, stationery) at six stores, and (their, there, they're) the least expensive.

18. Which (route, root) did you take to get here?

19. The (statue, stature, statute) of limitations for claiming the prize had run out, and he was (to, too, two) depressed to go to the party.

20. The (to, too, two) students scrubbed the dirt from the (statue, stature, statute) until it gleamed.

21. Her craving for (suites, sweets) caused her to gain weight, which was the (route, root) of her health problems.

22. His (statue, stature, statute) was diminished when he tripped on a tree (route, root) trying (to, too, two) get to the stage.

23. The (suite, sweet) was large enough for (to, too, two) families.

LANGUAGE REVIEW 11

Review GP 7.3, GP 8.6, and GP 8.7 in the Grammar and Punctuation section of *The Office Guide.*

Directions: Review the rules below in *The Office Guide* and then complete the following exercises.

GP 7.3 **Use a hyphen after each word or figure in a series that modifies the same noun.**

Write a sentence that includes a series of adjectives modifying a noun. Refer to *The Office Guide* to see an example of this rule.

1) _____

_____

GP 8.6 **Add an apostrophe and *s* (*'s*) to the final syllable of a possessive compound word.**

Write a sentence that includes a possessive compound word. Refer to *The Office Guide* if you need to see an example of this rule.

1) _____

_____

GP 8.7 **Add an apostrophe or an apostrophe and *s* (*'s*) to the last name in joint ownership when a possessive is needed.**

Write a sentence that requires the possessive form of joint ownership. Use the example in *The Office Guide* if you need help in writing the sentence.

1) _____

_____

_____

Directions: Punctuate and correct the following sentences if needed. Check your answers in Appendix C. Review the rule in *The Office Guide* for each incorrect answer.

1. The Purchasing Departments Personnel Departments and Production Departments reports were all turned in on time.

2. The new form was changed to include categories for high medium and low priority ratings.

3. The new assistant only met Mary when they both attended the reception for his son in laws graduation.

4. Andersons Smiths and Johnsons report on the new surgery procedure was printed in the latest journal.

5. Hotels in the AAA book receive a one two three four or five diamond rating.

6. Marys Susans and Tims typing speeds were all more than 55 wpm.

7. The six word processing operators and four transcriptionists productivity logs showed that the majority of the work processed was for the Accounting Department.

8. The notary publics seal was missing from her desk.

9. The do it yourself books format made it easy to follow.

10. Over 50 people attended the parents and teachers reception at the beginning of the school year.

11. The teams red white and blue banner could be seen from a distance.

FORMAT REVIEW 11

Review section DF 13 (Press Releases) in the Document Format section of *The Office Guide*.

Directions: Write a T in front of the statement if it is true or an F if it is false. Check your answers in Appendix C. Review the rule in *The Office Guide* again for each incorrect answer.

_____ **1.** A press release is lengthy and usually is sent at the time of the event.

_____ **2.** The body of a press release is usually single spaced.

_____ **3.** A press release should have a 2-inch top margin.

_____ **4.** Either "End" or "###" is typed a double space after the message to signify the end of the press release.

_____ **5.** The 1-inch default side-and-bottom margins are used for a press release.

_____ **6.** The heading lines of a press release are double spaced.

_____ **7.** A triple space should be used after the heading in a press release.

PROOFREADING EXERCISE 11

This proofreading exercise covers the rules identified and reviewed in *The Office Guide* for this lesson and previous lessons.

Directions: Use proofreader's marks shown in GR 4 of the General Reference section of *The Office Guide* to indicate needed corrections. There are **11** errors. Check your answers in Appendix C.

Current Date

Paul and Teresa Roderberg
East 3rd Street
Banger, ME 86329

Dear Paul and Theresa:

It has been sometime since we met to discuss you're financial planning. I am not sure if I should precede with the changes we agreed upon. Please let me know your wishes on this matter as soon as possible so I can determine what the current APR is in order to quote you new rates.

I look foreward to hearing from you.

Respectably,

Laura Ashley

VOCABULARY PREVIEW

academic	Scholastic, related to education
advantageous	Worthwhile, beneficial
apprenticeship	Work agreement where skills are learned on the job
bewildered	Confused
charges	Individuals that someone is responsible for taking care of or watching; cost of purchases made
confrontational	Aggressive behavior; fighting or disagreeable attitude
demeanor	Attitude; behavior
escalate	Increase; expand; make worse
hors d'oeuvres	Appetizers; canapé (Note: The "h" is not pronounced—begins with the sound of the word "or.")
internship	Apprenticeship
logo	Trademark; heading
motto	Saying; slogan
nonparticipative	Not participating; not involved
promote	Advance; encourage
receptive	Open to ideas, suggestions; agreeable
reside	Lives

4

TRANSCRIPTION PREVIEW: SELF-CHECK

Directions: Insert punctuation marks and make corrections in the following sentences if needed. Check your answers in Appendix C.

1. Please contact me or my office assistant Karen Smith to arrange a time when we can meet.

2. If a cake in this design is too complicated perhaps cupcakes with wrappers that have teddy bear stickers could be used.

3. Some students although they have excelled in different child development courses have difficulty applying what they have learned in regard to teaching and nurturing young children in a formal setting.

4. The date you noted in your letter October 25 does not present a conflict with my schedule.

5. Aunt Dee's offers a secure loving environment where children develop socially emotionally physically and intellectually.

6. Refreshments will be served and information about our age appropriate learning activities will be available.

7. I would like to design a coupon with our teddy bear logo and motto Where Creativity and Children Flourish.

Directions: If an item below is correct, write "C" in the blank at the right; if the item is not correct, write the correct form in the blank.

1. Clip 'N' Save _____
2. 1 and 7 _____
3. zip codes _____
4. *Chattanooga Express* _____
5. state-of-the-art center _____
6. Murray the Clown _____
7. sign up roll _____
8. E-mail _____

FORMATTING PREVIEW

4

Document 37: One-Page Block-Style Letter

Dee Showalter needs to take lessons on how to use her dictation unit so she can make corrections electronically instead of dictating corrections. This letter contains "office style" dictation, so keep alert.

Document 38: One-Page Block-Style Letter

This letter contains more "office style" dictation and includes nontranscription assignments that you do not have to complete.

Document 39: One-Page Block-Style Letter

Document 40: Press Release and Short Block Letter with Enclosure

In addition to the press release, Dee dictates a short letter to an old friend that should be mailed with a copy of the press release. Use the format below for the heading information for the press release.

FOR IMMEDIATE RELEASE

FROM:	Aunt Dee's Kids Kampus	**CONTACT**:
	407 West Oakridge Road	
	Chattanooga, TN 59823	

CONTACT: Dee Showalter
Phone: (287) 694-8655
E-mail: *DeeKids@net.com*

SHORT COURSE:

Transcribe documents 37, 38, 40

STANDARD COURSE:

Transcribe the four documents for Aunt Dee's Kids Kampus.

TAPE: LESSON 11: AUNT DEE'S KIDS KAMPUS

Tape Counter: Start __3__ Stop __31__ Doc. 37
Start __32__ Stop __67__ Doc. 38
Start __68__ Stop __105__ Doc. 39
Start __107__ Stop __143__ Doc. 40

4

12 SNAPSHOTS, INC.

Snapshots, Inc. is a camera store that provides a full-service line of camera equipment and accessories. The store also conducts photography classes for novice and experienced photographers. One-hour film development is available as well as specialized film processing for black and white film and enlargements.

6200 East Fangorn Road
St. Petersburg, FL 32817
Phone: 273-769-0072
Internet:
www.SnapshotsRU.com
Email:
MiddendorfR@jet. com
E-mail: VecseyR@jet.com

PERSONNEL FOR WHOM YOU WILL BE TRANSCRIBING

You will be transcribing dictation from:

Rita Vecsey, Store Manager

Richard Middendorf, Photographer/Instructor

YOUR JOB

Most of the correspondence you will transcribe is related to classes and the general operation and management of the store.

JOB PREPARATION

Before you begin transcribing the documents for this lesson, complete the following exercises. Make certain that you first review the rules identified in *The Office Guide.* Your instructor may want to see these completed exercises before you transcribe the letters for this lesson.

WORD USAGE REVIEW 12

CONFUSING WORDS

Review GR 1 Confusing Words in the General Reference Section of *The Office Guide.* Study words *thorough* through *your.*

Directions: Circle the correct word choice in each of the following sentences. Check your answers in Appendix C. Review the rule in *The Office Guide* again for each incorrect answer.

1. She (thorough, through, threw) the keys to him.
2. We did not know (whose, who's) keys were left on the desk.
3. It was difficult to know (weather, whether) or not she would make a good transcription operator because she did not know the software.
4. Timothy didn't know if he wanted the responsibility of being (vice, vise) chairperson.
5. Do you know (were, where) they (were, where) last night?
6. The (weather, whether) should be good for hiking.
7. (Whose, Who's) the owner of the car parked in the tow-away zone?
8. Sally did not know that (their, there, they're) was a meeting at 3 p.m.
9. The supervisor went (thorough, through, threw) the 50 applications and (thorough, through, threw) out any that were incomplete or hard to read.
10. The employee left a (trail, trial) of toner from the copier to the trash can when he added toner to the machine.
11. The marketing director did a (thorough, through, threw) analysis of the area in terms of services, schools, and businesses before designing a campaign slogan.
12. The new employee shook hands with his supervisor and was surprised at her (vise-, vice-) like handshake.
13. Not many employees know that (your, you're) the youngest manager in the company's history.
14. Did she (undo, undue) the knots in the rope or did Paul?
15. She did not (waiver, waver) under pressure from her parents to change her major from education to physics.
16. (Whether, Weather) or not you agree that Pedro is (vain, vane, vein), you have to admit that he spends an (undo, undue) amount of time on his appearance.
17. It took us one (weak, week) to make the journey because the (whether, weather) was so bad.
18. Her parents signed a (waiver, waver) allowing her to participate in the camp activities.
19. It took the nurse a long time to find a (vain, vane, vein) that could be used to insert the IV.
20. The (whether, weather) (vain, vane, vein) was old and (weak, week), and Jon tried in (vain, vane, vein) to repair it.

LANGUAGE REVIEW 12

Review GP 10.7, GP 11.1, GP 11.2, GP 11.3, and GP 11.4 in the Grammar and Punctuation section of *The Office Guide.*

4

Directions: Review the rules below in *The Office Guide* and then complete the following exercises.

GP 10.7 **Capitalize each word in the title of a book, magazine, article, speech with the exception of (1) articles (*a, an, the*) and (2) prepositions containing not more than three letters (e.g., *for, of,* or *but*).**

Write a sentence that includes the title of a book, magazine, or article. Use the example in *The Office Guide* if you need assistance.

1) _____

_____

_____

GP 11.1 **When the words *all*, *these*, and *they* are used as subjects that summarize preceding lists, use a dash in front of them. Note the dash is used only when there is no verb used.**

Write a sentence similar to the example in *The Office Guide* using *all, these,* or *they* as a subject that summarizes a list that precedes it.

1) _____

_____

_____

GP 11.2 **Dashes can be used in place of commas, semicolons, colons, and parentheses. Generally, dashes are used in place of other punctuation when more emphasis is desired.**

Write a sentence similar to the examples shown in *The Office Guide* that uses dashes in place of a comma, semicolon, or colon.

1) _____

_____

_____

GP 11.3 **Use a dash to stress single words.**

Write a sentence using a dash to emphasize a word. Refer to the examples shown in *The Office Guide* if you need more assistance.

1) _____

_____

_____

GP 11.4 **Use a dash with repetitions and restatements.**

Write and punctuate a sentence with dashes that includes repetitions or restatements. Refer to the examples shown in *The Office Guide* if you need assistance.

1) _____

_____

_____

Directions: Punctuate and correct the following sentences if needed. Check your answers in Appendix C. Review the rule in *The Office Guide* for each incorrect answer.

1. Here is the perfect solution how could we have missed it for so long.

2. He waited for his turn to interview nervous apprehensive and well-prepared ready to sell himself as the best candidate for the job.

3. The United Way Drive was successful because all the employees support staff supervisors and divisional representatives contributed.

4. Strong grammar typing punctuation and word processing skills all of these are essential for success as a transcriptionist.

5. The managers old office the tiny room in the back of the building has been turned into a storage area.

6. The company offers several services consulting purchasing typing and remodeling.

7. Do the newly employed transcription operators have strong communication skills listening speaking and writing?

8. The new all-in-one account only costs $25.00 more a month.

9. The new medicine proctramle will go on sale next week.

10. We went fishing last week at eagle run and caught 5 fish.

FORMAT REVIEW 12

Review sections GR 7 (Post Box Numbers and Mail Stop Codes) in the General Reference section of *The Office Guide.*

Mail stop codes are used in large organizations where mail is delivered to specific points for distribution.

Directions: Write a T in front of the statement if it is true or an F if it is false. Check your answers in Appendix C. Review the rule in *The Office Guide* again for each incorrect answer.

_____ 1. If you know the street address and the post box number, it is best to use both in the address to make sure the letter gets to its destination.

_____ 2. The United States Post Office prefers the all-capital abbreviation PO BOX to be used on the envelope.

_____ 3. The abbreviation for mail stop code used in the envelope address is msc.

_____ 4. For Express mail, the post office box should be used.

_____ 5. The mail stop code goes on the first line of the address.

_____ 6. This is a correct address format:

Mail Stop Code 705
Ms. Beverly Fain, Director
Watson Health Department
1897 Anderson Place
Atlanta, GA 73298

_____ 7. It is correct to include both the mail stop code and street address in the address.

PROOFREADING EXERCISE 12

This proofreading exercise covers the rules identified and reviewed in *The Office Guide* for this lesson and previous lessons.

Directions: Use proofreader's marks shown in GR 4 of the General Reference section of *The Office Guide* to indicate needed corrections. There are **16** errors. Check your answers in Appendix C.

Ms. Luz Castiblanco   April 22, 20—   Page 2

conference schedule will be to our advantage.

The flight leaves at 6 am so we will have to pick up DR. Thomas before 5:00 a.m. in order to get to the airport in time. This airline does not use tickets and seats are assigned on a first come first served basis.

If we get their early enough, we may be able to get an isle seat. I have all ready encouraged Dr. Thomas to only take carry on luggage so we can save allot of time by not checking baggage. If for some reason our luggage gets lost, Nancy should be notified at the following address:

Post Box 95
Ms. Nancy Drew
MSC 543
Orlando, FL 32891

Sincerely,

Gene Atkinson

lm

VOCABULARY PREVIEW

4

accessories	Items not essential that add convenience or effectiveness
amateur	Not professional
brochure	Printed pamphlet
courtesy	As a favor
deviate	Change from an established standard
digital	Using electronic means to generate and store text and numbers
exposure	To be seen or viewed
hotbed	Environment that favors rapid growth or development (activity)

incorporation	To combine with something already in existence
intuitive	Instinctive, innate, unconscious
modem	A communications device using phone lines
novices	Beginners
optional	Not mandatory, permitted by choice
photojournalism	Journalism in which photography dominates the storytelling
stills	Pictures, drawings, or photographs predominately of inanimate (lifeless) objects
stock photography	Photographs that have been sold to a company to be resold as royalty-free images
transmission	Sending material by electronic means
versatile	Flexible
via	Through, by way of

TRANSCRIPTION PREVIEW: SELF-CHECK

Directions: Insert punctuation marks and make corrections in the following sentences if needed. Check your answers in Appendix C.

1. If you have any questions regarding the photos payment policy or if you would like to have the photos of the building please let me know.

2. Many of the slide show programs have TWAIN support so you can import images directly from the scanner without switching to another imaging program.

3. Photo processing software such as Corel's Photo-Paint Digital Camera Edition includes a slide show utility that allows the creation of basic slide shows.

4. Another option if video editing software is used is to output the project to VHS or DVD for playback on television.

5. In addition to the photo contest award-winning photos by local professional photographers will be on exhibit and a workshop on digital cameras and digital photography will be offered at no cost between 10 a.m. and noon.

6. If you are able to position yourself ahead of time the action will come to you rather than you having to run around trying to follow it.

7. I don't know what model point and shoot camera you own but many have an "action" feature that selects a fast shutter speed.

Directions: If an item below is correct, write "C" in the blank at the right; if the item is not correct, write the correct form in the blank.

1. drag-and-drop workspace _____

2. award winning photos _____

3. five percent _____

4. Major Boulevard _____

5. 2 p.m. to 4:30 p.m. _____

6. Recordable CD's _____

4

FORMATTING PREVIEW

Document 41: Block-Style Letter with Mail Stop Code and Enclosure Notation

Document 42: Two-Page Block-Style Letter with Post Office Box in Address

Check your second-page heading rules (DF 2 in *The Office Guide*) if you have forgotten this format.

Document 43: Two-Page Report

Review Figure 11 for an example of report format.

These are some terms and names of software programs used in this report:

PhotoCD
Picture CD
TWAIN
Corel's Photo-Paint Digital Camera Edition
ScanSoft PhotoFactory
Camcorders
Ulead VideoStudio
Adobe Premier
SmartSound

Document 44: Press Release

SHORT COURSE:	**STANDARD COURSE:**
Transcribe documents 41, 43, 44	Transcribe the four documents for Snapshots, Inc.

FOR IMMEDIATE RELEASE

FROM:	SNAPSHOTS, INC. 6200 East Fangorn Road St. Petersburg, FL 32817	**CONTACT:**	Rita Vecsey Phone: 273-769-0072 E-mail: *VecseyR@Jet.com*

SHORT COURSE:	**STANDARD COURSE:**
Transcribe documents 41, 43, 44	Transcribe the four documents for Snapshots, Inc.

4

TAPE: LESSON 12: SNAPSHOTS, INC.

Tape Counter: Start __145__ Stop __171__ Doc. 41
Start __173__ Stop __214__ Doc. 42
Start __216__ Stop __274__ Doc. 43
Start __276__ Stop __303__ Doc. 44

TEST TIME

After your instructor has graded your transcribed letters for Lesson 12, review the confusing words and language rules presented in the lessons 1 through 12. Ask your instructor for the third written test covering confusing words, punctuation, grammar, and proofreading. Then ask your instructor for the tape for Transcription Test 3.

The test dictation includes a merge document.

INTRODUCTION TO TEST 3

Before you begin transcribing the documents for Test 3 make sure you have reviewed all the confusing words in GR 1 and have reviewed lessons 8 through 12. The following are a few terms that may help you accurately transcribe the test dictation.

wage-earner	A person who is a paid employee
term insurance	Temporary insurance purchased for a specific period of time
cash-value	Monetary value of a policy in terms of payment
hindering	Impeding, holding back
photojournalism	Photography that tells a story
portraiture	Photography that centers around family or people as the only or main focus in the photo
portfolio	A collection of art, photography, or samples of work

4

Test 3 Doc. 1: Block-Style Letter

Test 3 Doc. 2: Block-Style Form/Merged Letters with Enumerated Items

Test 3 Doc. 3: Block-Style Letter

Test 3 Doc. 4: Two-Page Block-Style Letter

13   NOVA TRAVEL

NOVA TRAVEL
287 Garland Dr.
Conyers, GA 85432
(943) 321-7542
Internet:
www.NovaTravel.com
E-mail: Ntgo@jet.com

Nova Travel has 45 branches in the United States and 3 branches overseas. You will be working in the Conyers, Georgia, branch, which employs eight travel agents who assist individuals and firms with domestic and international travel arrangements. Nova Travel is a full-service agency that books cruises for vacations as well as flights for corporate travel.

PERSONNEL FOR WHOM YOU WILL BE TRANSCRIBING

You will be transcribing dictation from:

Martha Mitchell, Manager
- Works closely with headquarters' staff.
- Determines employees' work schedules, arranges and conducts training for agents.
- Works with local advertising agencies.

Don Cassidy, Assistant Manager Domestic Travel
- Oversees all tours related to domestic travel.
- Works closely with large hotel chains to secure promotional travel packages to be used in sales campaigns.

Carol Lynn Bertoncini, Assistant Manager, International Travel
- Oversees all tours related to international travel.
- Works closely with universities and corporations to provide exchange-training programs.

Dominique Wren, Assistant Manager, Educational Programs
- Establishes educational programs for students, teachers, tourists, and business personnel traveling overseas. These programs include short courses in various foreign languages, customs, and procedures for traveling abroad.

4   YOUR JOB

Since this company is part of an international network, the majority of its advertising is done through the company's home office which is headquartered in Atlanta. Although the headquarters' staff designs major travel campaigns, each branch has the freedom to implement local travel promotions. The primary service provided by Nova Travel is to arrange domestic and international travel and excursions for corporate executives, businesspersons, tourists, students, and promotion/contest award vacations for large corporations.

As one of three transcriptionists, you will type a variety of documents. The letter style the company uses is modified block.

JOB PREPARATION

Before you begin transcribing the documents for this lesson, complete the following exercises. Make certain that you first review the rules identified in *The Office Guide.*

WORD USAGE REVIEW 13

CONFUSING WORDS

Review GR 2 Troublesome Words in the General Reference section of *The Office Guide.* Study words *A* through *good.*

Directions: Circle the correct word choice in each of the following sentences. Check your answers in Appendix C. Review the rule in *The Office Guide* again for each incorrect answer.

1. "Mary, please (bring, take) me a fresh cup of coffee and (bring, take) these empty cans to the kitchen."
2. We will (defer, differ) selecting the new supervisor until the merger is finalized.
3. The new employee (may, can) take his break at 9:30 a.m.
4. Did Mary (bring, take) her purse when she left?
5. The prize money was divided (between, among) the two salesmen.
6. The new employee and his supervisor (defer, differ) concerning the number of overtime hours he worked.
7. His supervisor, Mary, (may, can) give him a raise, but she (may, can) decide not to.
8. The governor approved the (interstate, intrastate) gasoline tax increase.
9. The people were very fickle and treated him (bad, badly) when he was no longer in power.
10. The (desert, dessert) heat made him very thirsty.
11. The farmers in the United States (import, export) goods to Canada and all parts of the world.
12. Ms. Anderson did not feel very (good, well) so the nurse told her to (lay, lie) down.

4

13. We (import, export) the fruit from Canada.

14. There was much fighting (between, among) the six children over their parents' money since no will was left.

15. Three employees offered to (bring, take) (desert, dessert) to the party.

16. Did she think her (good, well) looks would get her the job?

17. How (good, well) the candidates did on the test determined their eligibility for a promotion.

18. Jon did (bad, badly) on the test.

19. Mary feels (bad, badly) because she did not do (good, well) on her last job evaluation.

20. The lottery prize was split (between, among) five winners.

21. Since Tom had just started driving, his mother was (anxious, eager) when he did not return home on time.

22. The (trail, trial) was a difficult one for the jury to decide, but in the end they agreed with the insanity plea based upon the doctor's testimony that the defendant was (angry, mad) at the time of the crime.

23. Dana was (anxious, eager) to open her boyfriend's gift because she thought it was tickets to the Madonna concert but was (angry, mad) when she saw that the gift was only movie tickets.

LANGUAGE REVIEW 13

Review GP 9.1, GP 9.2, GP 9.3, and GP 17.13 in the Grammar and Punctuation section of *The Office Guide.*

Directions: Review the rules below in *The Office Guide* and then complete the following exercises.

GP 9.1 **Enclose figures or letters that are used as enumerated items in a paragraph with parentheses.**

Write a sentence that includes enumerated items that are part of a sentence and not in a list.

1) _____

_____

_____

GP 9.2 **Enclose figures with parentheses when they verify numbers that are written in words.**

Write a sentence similar to the examples in *The Office Guide* using either figures or amounts that appear in parentheses to "verify" them.

1) _____

_____

_____

GP 9.3   **Place the ending punctuation mark before the closing parenthesis in a parenthetical sentence.**

Write a sentence similar to the examples shown in *The Office Guide* that uses parentheses.

1) _____

_____

_____

GP 17.13   **Use a plural verb when *number* is preceded by *a*. Use a singular verb when *number* is preceded by *the*.**

Write a sentence using the word *number* making sure that the correct form of the verb (singular or plural) is used. Refer to *The Office Guide* for examples of this rule.

1) _____

_____

_____

Directions: Punctuate and correct the following sentences if needed. Check your answers in Appendix C. Review the rule in *The Office Guide* for each incorrect answer.

1. The proposed contract contained the following 1 one more paid vacation day 2 a 5 percent pay increase and 3 a 45-minute lunch.

2. Sometimes in legal documents monetary amounts are written in words and then in figures enclosed with parenthesis such as one hundred dollars $100.

3. Between the two companies, one thousand dollars $1000 was raised for the United Way.

4. She had no indication that she was to be transferred (neither did any of us for that matter)

5. Did Edward Allen receive a pay increase (If so this should cause a demand for a pay increase from every employee in his department)

6. The managers of the Legal Department Finance Department and Personnel Department stayed within their budgets. (The Production Department failed to do so)

7. The tour includes (1) one week of sightseeing (2) air transportation and (3) five dinners three lunches and six breakfasts.

8. The supervisor said she was busy. (How busy could she really have been though if she read a novel for an hour)

9. Who should conduct the orientation for the new employees? (Should it be the new manager or the previous manager who already is familiar with the organization)

10. She gave the message to Larry (or was it Sally)

11. There is a number of students who qualified for the new grant.

12. The number of students passing their board tests are increasing.

FORMAT REVIEW 13

Review DF 16 in the Document Format section of *The Office Guide.*

Directions: Write a T in front of the statement if it is true or an F if it is false. Check your answers in Appendix C. Review the rule in *The Office Guide* again for each incorrect answer.

_____ **1.** An itinerary is a schedule of activities used by individuals when traveling.

_____ **2.** Usually an itinerary is typed in three columns: person's name, activity, and event.

_____ **3.** Itineraries are typed double spaced.

_____ **4.** An itinerary usually includes travel directions.

_____ **5.** An easy way to format an itinerary is to use columns or tables without lines.

_____ **6.** Except on the first page of an itinerary there should be a heading that includes the name of the person the itinerary is for, page number, and date.

PROOFREADING EXERCISE 13

This proofreading exercise covers the rules identified and reviewed in *The Office Guide* for this lesson and previous lessons.

Directions: Use proofreader's marks shown in GR 4 of the General Reference section of *The Office Guide* to indicate needed corrections. There are **17** errors. Check your answers in Appendix C.

Current Date

MEMORANDUM

TO: Art Dallas

FROM: Dorothy Lynch

SUBJECT: Required Training for new employees

You are required to attend an orientation session next Monday, August 10, at 10:00 a.m. in room 7B on the second floor of the Professional Development Center. The meeting should last 3 hrs. Please take the following to the meeting: (1) social security card (2) insurance card and (3) fingerprint clearance.

Prior to the meeting you should view the viedo at your worksite concerning company benefits. You can check the video out but be sure to return it to your supervisor within a one day period since there is a limited number of copies to share between several departments.

VOCABULARY PREVIEW

canoeists	Individuals traveling by canoe
concierge	Multilingual hotel staff member who handles special guest requests and problems
consulate	The office of an official appointed by a government to reside in a foreign country to represent the interests of the citizens of the appointing country
encompass	Surround or include, envelop
expedition	Journey; excursion
host country	The country that guests are visiting
immunization	Vaccinations to protect against cholera, yellow fever, and other diseases
inoculated	The process of immunization from a disease by the introduction of a pathogen or antigen to stimulate the production of antibodies
isolated	Separate; all alone
itinerary	A written outline of travel and appointment schedules
kayaking	Paddling down a river in a small Eskimo-designed canoe that has a small opening in the center and is propelled by a double-bladed paddle
levied	Assessed; taxed
nationalization	Citizenship
nominal	Inexpensive, small
passport	A travel document, given to a citizen by his or her own government, granting permission to leave the country and to travel in certain specified foreign countries
rations	Food; provisions
redeemed	Used; bought back
shuttle	Transportation available to take travelers to hotels from the airport and from the main terminal to departing gates at airports
spanning	Extending across
tactics	Strategies; procedures
tributaries	Streams feeding into a larger stream or lake
videotex service	Electronic network guides providing information about restaurant, airline, entertainment, electronic mail, and Dow Jones activities
visa	An official document granted by a foreign country permitting a nonresident to enter that country for a specified purpose for a given length of time

4

TRANSCRIPTION PREVIEW: SELF-CHECK

Directions: Punctuate and correct the following sentences if needed. Check your answers in Appendix C.

1. Do you think it would be possible to put together a full scale expedition along the trail from Dyea Alaska to Bennett British Columbia?

2. Since most of the major tributaries on the Yukon have roadside access trips can vary depending on which roadside access points are used.

3. Since you work with our clients most directly you know their needs and I value your evaluation of the courses and their content.

4. For instance Don if you design a wilderness hiking tour we could offer a course on survival tactics such as how to endure unpredictable weather conditions (such as snow sleet fog and thunderstorms) and what emergency rations should be packed.

5. It is also important that a traveler who has diabetes or a physical condition which might require emergency care wear a medical card, tag, or bracelet.

6. Take shuttle transportation to Marriot International Hotel International Drive Orlando, Florida. Phone (407) 354-2778.

7. Nova tour escorts in Europe will assist you in exchanging United States money into foreign currency during your European visit but it is a good idea for you to obtain European currency before leaving the United States.

8. Unless travelers are aware of these restrictions they may unknowingly violate laws such as taking unauthorized pictures and items as souvenirs.

Directions: If an item below is correct, write "C" in the blank at the right; if the item is not correct, write the correct form in the blank.

1. Canada's Yukon _____

2. pre-packaged _____

3. short-term courses _____

4. companies headquarters' staff _____

5. six months away _____

6. travelers checks _____

4

FORMATTING PREVIEW

Document 45: Modified Block-Style Letter with Subject Line and Enclosures

This is a long letter but make margin adjustments so that it fits on one page. Pay attention to the spelling of places that are dictated. Review subject line information in *The Office Guide* if you have forgotten where to place this feature.

Document 46: Memorandum

This memorandum is going to two individuals: Don Cassidy and Carol Lynn Bertoncini.

Document 47: Two-Page Letter with Enumerated Items, Subject Line, and Attachment

Most of the letters you will transcribe are not very lengthy. Occasionally, as in this case, you will be asked to transcribe a long two-page letter. Use paragraph format for the enumerated items in this letter.

Document 48: Travel Itinerary

The easiest way to format an itinerary is to use the table feature of your word processing software. Two columns are used: one for the date and time and the other for the corresponding activity information. (Hint: All date and time information is typed in the first column.) The example below shows how the information is arranged in each column. There are at least five spaces between the information in the first column and the information in the second column. Refer to **DF 16** and **Figure 10** in *The Office Guide*.

MONDAY, APRIL 15

8 a.m.	Leave Atlanta Airport on Delta Flight #278.
10:15 a.m.	Arrive Orlando International Airport. Take shuttle transportation to Marriot International Hotel, International Drive . . .
12:30 p.m.	Lunch with Anita Anderson . . .

SHORT COURSE:	**STANDARD COURSE:**
Transcribe documents 45, 46, 48	Transcribe the four documents for Nova Travel.

TAPE: LESSON 13: NOVA TRAVEL

Tape Counter: Start __3__ Stop __34__ Doc. 45
Start __36__ Stop __63__ Doc. 46
Start __65__ Stop __118__ Doc. 47
Start __119__ Stop __154__ Doc. 48

4

14   AMERICAN PUBLISHING CO.

28 Academic Excellence Dr.
Hammond, LA 70402
Phone: 790-341-6700
Fax: 790-318-67002
E-mail: AMP@laser.com
Internet:
www.AmericanPub.com

American Publishing Co. is one of seven divisions of Petersen International Publishing. American was a fairly well-known independent publishing company prior to its acquisition by Petersen three years ago and has retained its niche in textbook publishing. The publishing field is highly competitive, and American employs a top-notch sales team to assist in marketing its books. The individuals involved with the production and development divisions of the company are experienced personnel who have been with the company for several years.

PERSONNEL FOR WHOM YOU WILL BE TRANSCRIBING

You will be transcribing dictation from:

Nancy Maurin, Project Manager

Andre Jakubowski, Senior Editor Office Technology

Jose Gutierrez, Developmental Editor

Carla Milunski, Acquistions Editor

YOUR JOB

Your job is a constant challenge to meet deadlines, but you enjoy the fast-paced nature of the publishing field. You enjoy being part of the team responsible for the developmental process of "birthing" books. As a five-year employee of American Publishing, you have gotten to know many of the authors and consulting editors.

Nancy Maurin is new to American. She worked for a rival publishing company until a few months ago; and although she has made a smooth transition, she is not used to dictating. As a matter of fact, her dictation frequently contains changes. You understand her inexperience since at her last job she drafted the majority of her work instead of dictating.

JOB PREPARATION

Before you begin transcribing the documents for this lesson, complete the following exercises. Make certain that you first review the rules identified in *The Office Guide.* Your instructor may want to see these completed exercises before you transcribe the letters for this lesson.

WORD USAGE REVIEW 14

CONFUSING WORDS

Review GR 2 Troublesome Words in the General Reference section of *The Office Guide*. Study words *in depth* through *which, that, who*. This exercise also includes a few confusing words from other lessons.

Directions: Circle the correct word choice in each of the following sentences. Check your answers in Appendix C. Review the rule in *The Office Guide* again for each incorrect answer.

1. Sara stayed up to early (mourning, morning) waiting for the election results to be announced so that she would know if her candidate won and had a hard time (raising, rising) in order to (leave, let) for work on time.

2. The (piece, peace) (between, among) the farmers and animal rights group did not last very long.

3. The (leased, least) popular course is English 101.

4. We need to (set, sit) close to the front so we can hear the speaker.

5. The (mourning, morning) paper, (which, that, who) carried the news of the fire, had photos of many residents (morning, mourning) the loss of property and loved ones.

6. The (leased, least) car did not perform (good, well) on the road (which, that, who) was covered with ice.

7. Where did Anne (sit, set) the (lease, least) agreement?

8. You should (leave, let) the new employee alone if you want him to get any work done.

9. Did the dough (raise, rise) enough? If not, we should (let, leave) it out a little longer before baking.

10. We (shall, will) (let, leave) the new manager (set, sit) the schedule.

11. Do you know (who's, whose) keys were left on the desk?

12. The (peace, piece) of ribbon (which, that, who) was left on the counter (shall, will) be used to make a bow on the basket.

13. (Which, That, Who) will volunteer to (bring, take) the speakers to the hotel from the airport?

14. (Whose, Who's) going to the store?

15. At (least, lease) her parents could (leave, let) her stay out until midnight.

16. The report was an (in depth, in-depth) analysis of the murder.

17. You must (teach, learn) the formulas for the new system before you will be allowed to input the data.

18. She was determined to finish the race (in spite, in spite of) the fact that she injured her ankle the day before.

19. You can make extra money if you (learn, teach) the new employees how to operate the new computer program.

20. Jean was furious that the new manager was hired instead of her; and (in spite, in spite of) her supervisor's request that she give the new manager a ticket to go to the conference, she tore the ticket up (in spite, in spite of).

21. The state lottery drew a lot of attention from neighboring states, and it was decided to develop (a, an) (intrastate, interstate) lottery with four states participating.

22. The (intrastate, interstate) toll for the all seven counties in the state did not increase.

23. (Less, Fewer) than six employees received the bonus.

24. (Less, Fewer) discipline was needed to keep the students on task when they used the computer.

LANGUAGE REVIEW 14

Review, **GP 10.11, GP 12.3, GP 12.5,** and **GP 12.7** in the Grammar and Punctuation section of *The Office Guide.*

Directions: Review the rules below in *The Office Guide* and then complete the following exercises.

GP 10.11   Capitalize names of specific course titles. Capitalize academic degrees only if they are used after a person's name.

Write two sentences: one that includes specific course titles and another that includes an academic degree used with a person's name.

1) _____

_____

_____

2) _____

_____

_____

GP 12.3   Always spell out numbers at the beginning of a sentence.

Write a sentence that begins with a number.

1) _____

_____

_____

GP 12.5   Express ordinal numbers (first, fifteenth, twenty-second, etc.) in words. If the ordinals cannot be written in one or two words, express them in figures with one of these endings: st, nd, rd, th.

Write a sentence that uses an ordinal.

1) _____

_____

_____

GP 12.7   **When two numbers appear consecutively in a sentence and one is used as an adjective, express the first number in words and the second number in figures. However, if the second number is much shorter, express it in words and the first number in figures.**

Review the examples for this rule in *The Office Guide* and then write a sentence that includes two consecutive numbers.

1) _____

_____

_____

Directions: Punctuate and correct the following sentences if needed. Check your answers in Appendix C. Review the rule in *The Office Guide* for each incorrect answer.

1. No. 653 was the first number to be called.
2. The advertising campaign was going into its 5th season.
3. The supply order showed that the 5 twenty-pound trays were ordered.
4. All the transcription operators were required to take a course in machine transcription.
5. His master of arts degree helped him get the supervisor job.
6. 350 people attended the conference.
7. The report was dated May 5th but he received it on May 10th.
8. The new employees had to take a course called customer relations in the workplace.
9. The purchase order showed that 6 five ounce tubes of ointment were ordered.
10. Did Mae say she wanted 4 15 pound hams for the Thanksgiving party, or did she say she wanted ten 15 pound turkeys?
11. The author of the article Rose Episton RN was not able to be the keynote speaker.
12. The tenth caller received the 10-day cruise.
13. Her parents celebrated their 50th wedding anniversary with a party attended by one hundred and fifty guests.
14. The conference was held on the tenth floor of the Harley Hotel.
15. Did everyone know that he had his bachelor of arts degree before his eighteenth birthday?

FORMAT REVIEW 14

Review sections **GR 9** in the Document Format section of *The Office Guide.*

Directions: Write a *C* in front of the abbreviation if it is correct or write an *I* in front of the abbreviation if it is incorrect. Check your answers in Appendix C. Review the rule in *The Office Guide* again for each incorrect answer.

_____ **1.** LN (Lane)

_____ **2.** ST (Station)

_____ **3.** VW (View)

_____ **4.** ANNX (Annex)

_____ **5.** RR (Rural Route)

_____ **6.** TR (Terrace)

_____ **7.** JUN (Junction)

_____ **8.** LK (Lake)

_____ **9.** ST (Street)

_____ **10.** MTN (Mountain)

PROOFREADING EXERCISE 14

This proofreading exercise covers the rules identified and reviewed in *The Office Guide* for this lesson and previous lessons.

Directions: Use proofreader's marks shown in GR 4 of *The Office Guide* to indicate needed corrections. There are **21** errors. Check your answers in Appendix C.

Current Date

Ms. alice Jones
MSC 769
Anderson University
PO Box 87
23 East Bayshore St.
Dayton, OH 67307

Dear Ms. Jones

I feel badly that I haven't written sooner. This is a very busy time of year for are company so it has been very difficult for me to respond to your request to serve on your School Advisory Board. I will be honored to serve in this capacity for a second term, however, I will not be able to participate until the 1st of the year when things have calmed down.

I have had an opportunity to prusue the comprehensive, indexed catalog and am impressed with the variety of programs offered at the university. I am glad to see that humanities 509 was added as we recommended last year.

In regards to your request to be a guest speaker for the graduating business students in the bachelor of science environmental engineering program, I will have to decline do to a conflict with a previous engagement, however, I will be able to attend the university's 50th anniversary celebration on August tenth. Please give my administrative assistant Doug Peterson the details on this event so that I can plan accordingly.

Sincerely,

Ronda Perez, PHD

VOCABULARY PREVIEW

acetate	A plastic made from cellulose acetic acid similar to a transparency
affiliations	Associations, connections
camera copy (also called camera-ready copy)	Type or illustrative copy that is ready to be photographed to produce a negative. The negative is then used to make a printing plate.
color separation	The photographic process of separating type or illustrations into parts that will print in different colors
compositor	A person who typesets or compiles manuscript for printing
copy editor	A person who edits the manuscript for spelling, punctuation, sentence structure, consistency, and organization
cover mechanical	The technical design of a book cover including mechanical aspects of production
debut	First appearance, view; introductory event
dummy	A page-by-page pasteup of galley proofs on printed layout sheets of type and illustrations as they will appear in the printed book
duotone	A two-color halftone reproduction; one image is usually printed in black ink and the other in color
entrepreneurs	Individuals who take initiative and risk to start and organize businesses
envision	Picture, predict, imagine
four-color process printing	A method of reproducing all colors of the spectrum with printing plates of yellow, red, blue, and black ink

4

freelancing	Performing work not on a regular salary basis for any one employer, organization, or business
galley proofs (galleys)	Proofs of copy that have been set in type but not yet divided into pages
offset printing	Copy is photographically transferred to a thin metal plate; the ink image from the plate is transferred to an intermediate surface and paper is pressed against it to form an impression
outsourcing	The process of companies to "hire out" work that could have been done "inhouse" by employees in an effort to cut employment costs
page proof	Proof made after the type and illustrations have been assembled into the page lengths that will appear in the published work
perforated	Lined with tiny holes to make separation easy
spiralbound	Book that is bound with wire or plastic "rings" at the side or top
trim size	The dimensions of a text
typeface	A design for the letters of the alphabet, figures, and symbols that uses the same style and weight of type
typesetting	The process of converting characters in manuscript into words, lines, and paragraphs of text for reproduction by printing

TRANSCRIPTION PREVIEW: SELF-CHECK

Directions: Punctuate and correct the following sentences if needed. Check your answers in Appendix C.

1. They will be wrapped for long term storage and I ask only that you keep them in a warm dry place.
2. A fax machine is also available and I leave the fax and answering machine on at all time so please feel free to leave a message or send a fax 24 hours a day.
3. Depending on manufacturing costs, it will cost between $2.00 and $5.00 more to purchase the student CD with the simulation.
4. If the contract looks all right to you please sign and initial all copies and return them directly to Charlotte at our home office in Hammond Louisiana.
5. If this is not possible please send the original camera copy page along with the marked copy and we will try to match the corrections to the original typeface.
6. The target audience for this magazine is self employed individuals entrepreneurs and freelance employees who are hired on an outsourcing or consulting basis.
7. The project has many innovative features and sales handles and will be a lot of fun to sell.

Directions: If an item below is correct, write "C" in the blank at the right; if the item is not correct, write the correct form in the blank.

1. *WordPerfect for Windows Quick and Easy* _____
2. one hundred sheets _____
3. our Production Supervisor Cheryl Jimenez _____
4. former in-house _____
5. FAX machine _____
6. model 15 camera copy paper _____
7. form entitled what to submit and how _____

FORMATTING PREVIEW

Document 49: Block-Style Letter with Enclosure and Post Script. Dictated corrections.

Document 50: Block-Style Letter with Enclosure

Document 51: Long Block-Style Letter with Enclosure

Document 52: Two-Page Block-Style Letter with Enumerated Items, Enclosures and Copy Notations.

Ms. Milunski dictates "paragraph" at the end of each item in the first enumerated list to indicate the start of the next item. Example:

1. Student kit

2. Instructor's Resource Package . . .

Some of these documents contain numerous dictation changes

SHORT COURSE:	**STANDARD COURSE:**
Transcribe Documents 49 and 52	Transcribe the four documents for American Publishing.

TAPE: LESSON 14: AMERICAN PUBLISHING

Tape Counter: Start __155__ Stop __201__ Doc. 49
Start __203__ Stop __239__ Doc. 50
Start __241__ Stop __291__ Doc. 51
Start __293__ Stop __375__ Doc. 52

4

15 METROPOLITAN COUNTY PUBLIC SCHOOLS

PO Box 376
Orange City, FL 22787
Phone: 905-634-6597
Fax: 601-765-3298
E-mail:MetroCPS@cp.com
Internet:
www.metro.loc.gov

The Metropolitan (Metro) County Public School system is the twenty-second largest in the nation and the fifth largest in the state. All the public schools and vocational centers in the system are accredited. The enrollment for the current school year is 116,045 students. There are 122 schools in this public school system: 83 elementary schools, 20 middle schools, 11 high schools; 4 exceptional education centers, and 4 vocational centers. The student population is diverse and consists of various ethnic groups. Encompassing 1,003 square miles, the Metro County Public School system operates the largest public transportation system. School buses travel more than 11 million miles annually, transporting 54,000 students through a fleet of 755 buses. The school system has recently adopted year-round school, and several elementary schools in the system are on a year-round education schedule.

PERSONNEL FOR WHOM YOU WILL BE TRANSCRIBING

You will be transcribing dictation from:

Jacqueline McGee, Senior Manager, Benefits Administration
- Handles personnel benefits.

Denise Johnson, Senior Administrator, Pupil Assignment
- Responsible for student placement and transfers.

Sonia Romaguera, Program Assistant, Bilingual Education Program
- Responsible for the testing and curriculum for students who speak English as a second language.

Trudie McNamara, Manager, Personnel Services
- Responsible for personnel verification, orientation, and interviewing.

Samuel Zegel, Assistant to the Associate Superintendent, Vocational/Adult Data Systems
- Responsible for processing student data to produce reports and validation of student enrollment for state and federal funding purposes.

YOUR JOB

The Metro County Public School system uses a system of planning and budgeting that emphasizes school-based management, which means that most decisions affecting the education of children are made at the local and school level. Certain district procedures, however, unify and strengthen individual school instructional and extracurricular activities.

The six word processing centers are housed in the Metro County Public School system's nine-story administration building. Generally, you work in the word processing center on the fifth floor, which supports personnel and student placement; however, because many operators are taking vacations this month, you will float to their centers as needed. This means that you will be transcribing a wide variety of dictation.

Although the document processing division has a procedures manual that unifies many policies and procedures, individual departments may select the letter style they want to use. The following shows the letter styles preferred by the administrators for whom you will transcribe.

Jacqueline McGee: Full Block

Denise Johnson: Modified Block

Sonia Romaguera: Modified Block with paragraph indention

Trudie McNamara: Full Block

Samuel Zegel: Modified Block

JOB PREPARATION:

Before you begin transcribing the documents for this lesson, complete the following exercises. Make certain that you first review the rules identified in *The Office Guide*. Your instructor may want to see these completed exercises before you transcribe the letters for this lesson.

WORD USAGE REVIEW 15

FOREIGN WORDS

Review GR 3, Foreign Words in the General Reference section of *The Office Guide*. Study foreign words *ad hoc* through *in toto*.

Directions: Use the words below to fill in the blank with the foreign word that completes the sentence. Check your answers in Appendix C. Review the information in *The Office Guide* for each incorrect answer.

ad hoc	circa (c. or ca.)	fait accompli
ad valorem	confer (cf.)	faux pas
a la carte	connoisseur	finesse
a la mode	coup d'état	hors d'oeuvres
aplomb	debut	ibidem (ibid.)
apropos	encore	id est (i.e.)
au jus	esprit de corps	idem
avant-garde	et alii (et al.)	infra
bona fide	et cetera (etc.)	instans (inst.)
carpe diem	exempli gratia (e.g.)	in toto
carte blanche	ex post facto	
cause celebre	facade	

4

1. The _____ of the building was cracked and mildewed.

2. They ordered pie _____ as a celebration dessert.

3. The band was well received and the audience demanded an _____.

4. She was a _____ of Greek art, but he knew nothing of art so he sat around and ate _____ while she discussed art _____ 1800.

5. The terrorist pulled a _____ that made the war-torn country even more vulnerable to violence.

6. Because he was unfamiliar with the customs of the country, he made a _____. The host, realizing his embarrassment, handled the problem with _____; and his _____ "saved the day."

7. The _____ committee presented the report at the meeting.

8. She put on a _____ that hid her unhappiness.

9. The new perfume will make its _____ on the market in March.

10. They found out about the contest _____ and were disappointed that they were too late to enter.

11. The new supervisor gave his employees _____ in deciding their schedules resulting in _____ that boosted morale.

12. The items on the menu were listed _____, and the roast beef _____ entree with a salad, vegetable, and drink cost $35, which was _____ "cash wise" what he had in his wallet.

13. An _____ tax was voted upon to help fund the _____ redesign of the city's transportation system.

The Office Guide

LANGUAGE REVIEW 15

Review GP 12.8, GP 13.2, GP 14.2, GP 14.3, GP 16.1, and GP 16.2 in the Grammar and Punctuation section of *The Office Guide.*

Directions: Review the rules below in *The Office Guide* and then complete the following exercises.

GP 12.8 **Express general ages in words unless they have contractual or statistical significance or if exact ages (years, months, days).**

Write a sentence to illustrate this rule.

1) _____

_____

_____

GP 13.2 **Express amounts under $1 in figures followed by the word *cents*. When amounts under and over $1 appear in a series, write all amounts with dollar signs and decimal points for consistency.**

Write two sentences. One sentence should include an amount under a dollar, and the other sentence should include amounts over and under a dollar.

1) _____

   _____

   _____

2) _____

   _____

   _____

GP 14.2   **Express decimals in figures.**

Write a sentence that includes decimals. Refer to *The Office Guide* to see examples of this rule.

1) _____

   _____

   _____

GP 14.3   **Express fractions in words with a hyphen between the two parts unless the fractions are combined with whole numbers or cannot be written in one or two words.**

Review the examples for this rule in *The Office Guide* and then write a sentence using fractions.

1) _____

   _____

   _____

GP 16.1   **Do not abbreviate professional, military, and civil titles when used with surnames only. The abbreviation *Dr.* may be used, however, for *Doctor.***

Review the examples for this rule in *The Office Guide* and write a sentence that includes titles.

1) _____

   _____

   _____

GP 16.2   **Abbreviate academic degrees and professional designations.**

Review the examples for this rule in *The Office Guide* and write a sentence that includes either an academic degree or professional title.

1) _____

   _____

   _____

Directions: Punctuate and correct the following sentences if needed. Check your answers in Appendix C. Review the rule in *The Office Guide* for each incorrect answer.

1. Because she was such a good employee she was given a $50 a month raise but he only received a 25 cents an hour raise.

2. The pay increase was about a 4.2 percent raise.

3. Only 3/4 of the employees voted to change their hours.

4. Col. Anderson won a medal for his bravery.

5. Mary contributed $5; Suzie, 50 cents; and Joan, $8.50.

6. In order to change the bylaws a two thirds membership majority had to be present.

7. We couldn't remember if Mrs. Thompson paid her $.50 donation.

8. The assistant dean asked his colleagues to support Prof. Roders' research.

9. The average age of the students attending the community college was 30.

10. The 15-pound laptop cost $944.50 but the battery cost $15.00.

11. There are eight months and 5 days before the holidays.

12. The bookstore had to start charging .60 for bookmarks.

13. Martha couldn't wait until she turned 21.

14. The book was given to Doctor Johnson to review.

15. She did not have the .35 needed for the toll so she took the long way home.

FORMAT REVIEW 15

Review sections GR 11.1 and GR 11.4 in the Document Formats section of *The Office Guide*.

Directions: Write a T in front of the sentence if it is correct or write an F in front of the sentence if it is incorrect. Check your answers in Appendix C. Review the rule in *The Office Guide* for each incorrect answer.

_____ 1. If correspondence originating in the United States is sent to China, this is the correct address format:

Dr. Paulette Parkway
870 East Robinson
Taipei, Taiwan
Republic of China

_____ 2. If someone in Tallahassee, Florida, sent a letter to someone in Buffalo, New York, the words, "United States of America" should be typed in all capitals on the last line of the address.

_____ 3. There are 16 provinces in Canada.

_____ 4. The abbreviation YK in Canadian mail stands for Yukon Territory.

_____ 5. New Brunswick is a city in the United States and a province in Canada.

_____ 6. The country's name should be typed in all capitals as the last line of an address for correspondence coming from the United States to another country.

PROOFREADING EXERCISE 15

This proofreading exercise covers the rules identified and reviewed in *The Office Guide* for this lesson and previous lessons.

Directions: Use proofreader's marks shown in GR 4 of *The Office Guide* to indicate needed corrections. There are **12** errors. Check your answers in Appendix C.

Current Date

Dr. Paul Anderson, M.D.
Tri-County Medical
2867 Eastwood Dr.
Ft. Lauderdale, FL 32851

Dear Doctor Anderson:

Ms. Dorothy DeChant has applied for a position at our medical lab. Her application shows that you were her last employer and we would like to have you're input in regards to the following:

1. Ms. DeChant's attendance
2. Work performance
3. Job Responsibilities
4. Initiative

We understand the legal issues in giving us this information and ensure you that your response will be strictly confidential. You may wish not to comment on the above requests. If so, please just drop us a note to this affect. Mrs. DeChant's application shows that she has the skills we are looking for, but we must check her credentials to make sure that she is a bona fid physician's assistant and that all her references are accurate. Being in the medical profession, I am sure you can understand our need to screen employees.

Please respond as soon as possible as we have a deadline of filling this position. Because our practice is growing and we take care of such a diverse group of individuals, we need individuals who are team oriented. Please comment on Ms. Dechant's attitude in these areas.

Sincerely,

Charlotte Morgan, M.D.

xx
Enclosures

4

VOCABULARY PREVIEW

amnesty	The act of a government to pardon a large group of individuals.
naturalization	The process of acquiring citizenship
vested	Eligibility to a retirement plan after making continuous contributions for 10 years to the system.
FTE	The Florida Education Finance Program provides a prorated amount for capital outlay of local and state participation based on full-time equivalent (FTE) students.
sick leave bank	The pooling of a group of employees' sick leave days to provide coverage for missed work when an employee exceeds his or her number of sick days.

TRANSCRIPTION PREVIEW: SELF-CHECK

Directions: Insert punctuation marks or make corrections in the following sentences if needed. Check your answers in Appendix C.

1. We further realize that inconveniences are created as a result of the court order and we regret our inability to assist you at this time.
2. Your child Amanda Andrews has been scheduled to take a test designed to measure her knowledge of English and Spanish.
3. Attached are two copies of the Initial FTE report for the February survey period.
4. Since the Intermediate FTE report will be scheduled the evening of February 8 all corrections and additions should be entered by that afternoon.

Directions: If an item below is correct, write "C" in the blank at the right; if the item is not correct, write the correct form in the blank.

1. re-apply _____
2. on-line system _____
3. payroll department (within the company) _____
4. 24-hour job vacancy hotline _____
5. (407) 995-2667 extension 2856 _____

4 FORMATTING PREVIEW

Document 53:

Block-Style Letter with Merge Variables. Two merged letters.

This letter contains dictated changes.

Document 54:

Modified Block-Style Letter with Merge Variables, Subject Line, and Copy Notation. One merged letter.

This letter contains a copy notation that should be formatted in the following style:

c   School assigned
School denied

In this letter *committee* is used to refer to a specific committee, therefore, capitalize the "C."

Document 55: Indented Modified Block-Style Letter with Merge Variables. Three merged letters.

This merge letter includes indented information that should be typed in the following format: a ☐ indicates merged text.

DATE: ☐

TIME: ☐

PLACE: 586 North Dixie Ave. . . .

TELEPHONE: ☐

Sometimes more than one individual will sign a letter. When two names will appear in the closing, either of the formats below is appropriate. The closing (Sincerely, Cordially, Yours truly, etc.) is typed in position according to the letter style used (full block, modified block, etc.). Because this is a modified block-style letter, use the following format.

Sincerely,

Sonia Romaguera   Maria Ferguson
Program Assistant   Program Assistant
Bilingual Ed. Program   Bilingual Ed. Program

Document 56: Memorandum with Attachment and Copies

SHORT COURSE:	STANDARD COURSE:
Transcribe Documents 53, 54, and 56	Transcribe the four documents for Metro County Public Schools.

TAPE: LESSON 15: METRO COUNTY PUBLIC SCHOOLS

Tape Counter: Start __2__ Stop __28__ Doc. 53
Start __29__ Stop __54__ Doc. 54
Start __55__ Stop __99__ Doc. 55
Start __101__ Stop __124__ Doc. 56

4

16 BED AND BREAKFAST AROUND THE WORLD

125 Rue Lefort
CH-1201
Geneva, Switzerland
Phone: 1-800-464-9224
Fax: 1-800-420-6544
E-mail: BB@world.com
Internet:
www.BedBrekworld.com

Bed and Breakfast Around the World is an international company only a few years old. The company originally handled reservations for bed and breakfasts in the United States and Canada, but through Internet activity it expanded service beyond these boundaries and now offers this unique service around the world. A great deal of inquiries and reservations are handled through the company's Internet site. Bed and Breakfast Around the World has been very successful in filling a niche in a competitive global market.

PERSONNEL FOR WHOM YOU WILL BE TRANSCRIBING

You will be transcribing dictation from:

Mr. Yu-ching Wu, Reservation Specialist

Mr. Paul van Zutphen, Reservation Specialist

Birgitta Svensson, Reservation Specialist

Abigail Turner, Vice-President

YOUR JOB

Most of the company's communications are done through E-mail, faxing, and voice mail. As a transcription operator working in this global setting, you have learned to listen carefully to the dictation because several of the dictators have foreign accents. You also have to be familiar with some of the requirements for international mail.

JOB PREPARATION

Complete the word usage and other exercises prior to transcribing. Make certain that you first review the rules identified in *The Office Guide*. Your instructor may want to see these completed exercises before you transcribe the letters for this lesson.

WORD USAGE REVIEW 16

FOREIGN WORDS

Review GR 3, Foreign Words in the General Reference section of *The Office Guide*. Study foreign words *ipso facto* through *vis-à-vis*.

Directions: Use the words below to fill in the blank with the foreign word that completes the sentence. Check your answers in Appendix C. Review the information in *The Office Guide* for each incorrect answer.

ipso facto	proximo (prox.)
joie de vivre	Q.E.D.
laissez faire	quod vide (q.v.)
loco citato (loc. cit.)	R.S.V.P.
modus operandi (M.O.)	re (in re)
motif	rendezvous
noblesse oblige	sans
nolle prosequi (nol. pros.)	savoir faire
non sequitur (non seq.)	status quo
nota bene (N.B.)	supra
opere citato (op cit.)	tete-a-tete
passé	ultimo (ult.)
per annum	verbatim
per capita	vice versa
per diem	videlicet (viz.)
per se	vis-à-vis
pro tempore (pro tem.)	

1. What is the _____ of the department's furniture and equipment?

2. The hat she wore was very chick, but the dress she wore was _____.

3. Are you interested in the new health plan, _____, or just the insurance coverage?

4. The arrangement in the waiting room forced the job applicants to sit _____ each other.

5. Her shorthand was so good that she could repeat _____ what he said.

6. Until we can get money for new equipment, we will have to operate _____ with the status quo hardware.

7. The income _____ is much lower in the southern part of the state than the northern part.

8. The new manager resented the older manager and _____.

9. The sales representatives were reimbursed $50 _____.

10. She forgot that the invitation had a _____ notation and did not respond.

11. The new supervisor's leadership style was _____.

12. They met in France for their _____ and were unaware that he saw them enjoying a _____ at an outdoor cafe.

13. The _____ used to decorate the renovated house was Victorian.

14. We had to attend the party _____ the VIP escort because the governor rode in a different car.

15. His reasoning about who was responsible for the crime did not make sense especially when he threw in the _____ about hors d'oeuvres leading to esprit de corps and murder.

LANGUAGE REVIEW 16

Review GP 10.6, GP 16.6, GP 17.4, GP 17.5A, GP 17.5B, GP 17.5C, GP 17.11, GP 17.12, GP 17.7, and GP 17.8 in the Grammar and Punctuation section of *The Office Guide*.

Directions: Review the rules below in *The Office Guide* and then complete the following exercises.

GP 10.6   **Capitalize titles of business forms, legal documents, and laws.**

Write a sentence to illustrate this rule.

1) _____

_____

_____

GP 16.6   **Commonly abbreviated business terms are expressed in capital letters, without periods. The common abbreviations *c.o.d., f.o.b., a.m.,* and *p.m.* are generally expressed in lowercase letters separated by periods.**

Write a sentence that includes a business term.

1) _____

_____

_____

GP 17.4   **When sentences are inverted, the subject comes after the verb.**

Write a sentence that is arranged so that it begins with a verb. Refer to *The Office Guide* for examples of this rule.

1) _____

_____

_____

GP 17.5A **Singular indefinite pronouns (*another, any, either, neither, somebody, someone, each, every,* etc.) always require a singular verb.**

Review this rule in *The Office Guide* for a more comprehensive list of indefinite pronouns. Write a sentence using a singular indefinite pronoun.

1) _____

_____

_____

GP 17.5B **Plural indefinite pronouns (*both, few, many, others, several*) always require a plural verb.**

Write a sentence using a plural indefinite pronoun.

1) _____

_____

_____

4

GP 17.7   **Collective nouns usually take singular verbs; however, members of group acting individually take plural verbs.**

Review the examples for this rule in *The Office Guide* and then write a sentence to illustrate the rule where a plural verb is required.

1) _____

_____

_____

GP 17.8   **When a noun ending in *-ics* refers to one topic or body, use a singular verb. When it refers to a plural meaning, use a plural verb.**

Review the examples for this rule in *The Office Guide* and then write a sentence to illustrate the rule when the *-ics* word refers to one topic.

1) _____

_____

_____

GP 17.5C   **Indefinite pronouns (*some, most, none,* and *all*) take either singular or plural verbs. If these words tell how much, the verb is singular. If these words tell how many, the verb is plural.**

Review the examples for this rule in *The Office Guide* and then write a sentence that uses an indefinite pronoun.

1) _____

_____

_____

GP 17.11   **Certain words ending in *s* such as *scissors, pliers, glasses, pants,* and *trousers* are plural unless "pair of" is in front.**

Review the examples for this rule in *The Office Guide* and then write a sentence that uses one of these words in plural form.

1) _____

_____

_____

GP 17.12   **Fractions and portional amounts such as *half, one-fourth, none, part of, majority of,* and *a portion of* take singular or plural verbs according to the modified noun. Hint: If the word following "of" is plural, use a plural verb. If it is singular, use a singular verb.**

Review the examples for this rule in *The Office Guide* and then write a sentence that includes a proportional amount.

1) _____

_____

_____

4

Directions: Punctuate and correct the following sentences if needed. Check your answers in Appendix C. Review the rule in *The Office Guide* for each incorrect answer.

1. The bylaws had to be changed because they were not in keeping with the articles of incorporation.

2. The school advisory council is responsible for the school improvement plan therefore the members take their duties seriously.

3. The new employee received a vip welcome.

4. The box was shipped ups but the letter was mailed federal express.

5. The merchandise was shipped COD but he didn't have money to pay the bill when it arrived.

6. Half of the employees has passed their examination for certification.

7. Have the instructor's information been given to the students?

8. Most of the employees has attended the required workshop.

9. The curriculum review committee which was composed of members from thirty states are independently evaluating sixteen courses.

10. In addition to the new medical coverage is new insurance plans that include new benefits for all employees.

FORMAT REVIEW 16

Review section DF 16 in the Document Formats section of *The Office Guide.*

Directions: Write a T in front of the sentence if it is correct or write an F in front of the sentence if it is incorrect. Check your answers in Appendix C. Review the rule in *The Office Guide* for each incorrect answer.

_____ 1. Most reports include a table of contents and title page.

_____ 2. Many word processing software programs include report templates.

_____ 3. If side headings are used in a *traditional* report style, a double space is placed before and after the side heading.

_____ 4. Every page in a report should have a page number on it.

_____ 5. The body of the report should be double spaced.

_____ 6. The first page of the report should have a 1-inch top margin.

_____ 7. Usually the default margins are used for typing a report.

_____ 8. Enumerated items are single spaced but not indented.

_____ 9. The title of the report may be used as a header on all pages.

_____ 10. If the title is used as a header, it should be typed in all lowercase letters.

_____ 11. Footnotes or endnotes are used to show referenced text in the report.

_____ 12. Long quotations are double spaced and indented.

_____ **13.** The title should be centered in all capital letters on the first page of the report.

_____ **14.** The top margin on the second page of the report is 2 inches.

PROOFREADING EXERCISE 16

This proofreading exercise covers the rules identified and reviewed in *The Office Guide* for this lesson and previous lessons. In addition, you should review GP 17.9, GP 17.10, GP 18.1, GP 18.2, GP 19.1, GP 19.2, GP 19.3, GP 19.4, GP 19.5, and GP 19.6

Directions: Use proofreader's marks shown in GR 4 of *The Office Guide* to indicate needed corrections. There are **12** errors. Check your answers in Appendix C.

Before you do this proofreading exercise, complete the following exercise as a review of agreement rules.

SELF-CHECK: SUBJECT/VERB AGREEMENT

Directions:

1. Underline the subject and verb in each of the following sentences.

2. In the blank next to each sentence, write a "C" if the subject and verb agree or "I" if the subject and verb do not agree. If you have any wrong answers, refer to the rule that applies and write the number of the rule in front of the letter by the sentence.

(1) _____ The computer components are in the storage room.

(2) _____ You, as well as Andy, has been chosen to serve on the Advisory Council.

(3) _____ Somebody on one of the swim teams is going to give him a ride home.

(4) _____ Neither the band director nor his students is responsible for the missing money.

(5) _____ One of the students receive a monthly check to cover school expenses.

(6) _____ The band members are in disagreement over who should be their captain.

(7) _____ Everything stored using computers are easy to retrieve.

(8) _____ The report about the word processing operators was sent to the supervisor for review.

(9) _____ The number of transcription operators working in medical records determine the speed of document turn around.

(10) _____ The band plans to rehearse for the concert.

(11) _____ Each of the new jobs pay a higher salary.

(12) _____ The number of software spreadsheet programs have increased.

(13) _____ Either the judge or his staff members was responsible for the breakdown in communication.

(14) _____ Was the facsimile machine with the computers that were stolen?

(15) _____ One of the fields were deleted when Jon entered the data.

(16) _____ Answers to the student survey shows that many students leave home by the time they are 18.

(17) _____ Where is the secretary for the two men?

(18) _____ Does Mary and Jane likes their class?

(19) _____ Each department branch and home office division were audited for compliance with software copyright laws.

(20) _____ Neither a reporting delay nor several power failures is reason for the manuscript not being completed on time.

(21) _____ Either of those dresses are appropriate.

(22) _____ Most of the report contains information we already know.

(23) _____ There's several types of word processing software available.

(24) _____ Many of the company's 500 employees are at a sales conference.

(25) _____ Mathematics are not her favorite subject.

SELF-CHECK: PRONOUN/ANTECEDENT AGREEMENT

Directions: Review the following sentences for agreement errors. If the sentence is correct, write a C in the blank next to the sentence. If the sentence is incorrect, write an I in the blank next to the sentence.

(1) _____ The collaborative consultation process requires training on both the speech and consumer education teacher's parts.

(2) _____ "The key determinant of the quality of an early childhood program," she further states, "are trained staff who have knowledge and ability to implement developmentally appropriate curriculum."

(3) _____ It was his hat.

(4) _____ As principal, he or she must choose the kind of leader they want to be—no one else can make the choice.

(5) _____ The child is an individual, and we need to help them to be successful.

(6) _____ Many students didn't bring their books.

(7) _____ The style of leadership chosen by a principal will have a great influence on the kind of person he or she will become.

(8) _____ Teachers must design their programs so that each child can gain confidence in their own ability.

SELF-CHECK: VERB/TENSE AGREEMENT

This self-check exercise will help you refine your skill in using the correct verb tense. Pay particular attention to verbs that end in *d* or *ed*. Fill in the correct tense of the verbs shown below the blank lines in the following text.

Many beginning transcription students have problems _____ with verbs
                                                        associate

ending in *d* or *ed*. Students must master the art of listening carefully for these

verbs. _____ problems with verb tenses can be _____ with hard
          Repeat   eliminate

work. If past tense verbs give you trouble, you must analyze the problem and be

_____ enough to practice correct verb usage in speaking as well as in writ-
   commit

ing. The more _____ you are, the quicker the problem will be _____.
                 determine   eliminate

Machine transcription operators are _____ to produce work that is error
                                       require

free. Therefore, verb tense usage must be _____.
                                            master

FINAL AGREEMENT SELF-CHECK

Directions: Circle the agreement errors in the following sentences. These agreement errors were made by machine transcription students who knew less than you about subject/verb, pronoun/antecedent, and verb/tense agreement.

1. There are many advantages offered by Telex. The messages usually get immediate attentions and response. They can be cleared for security through sender and receiver codes. Detailed monthly billing as well as multiple polling is also offered by Telex. Another feature being offer is a 57-page memory for sequential broadcasting.

   One of the benefits are the ability to leave a message without conversing with the recipient, transmitting messages to one or more recipients, and adding comments to messages. These benefits integrates with a wide range of E-mail services.

2. Computer-based messaging systems and services (CBMS) provides the base for E-mail. During recent years, E-mail has prove a cost-effective way of

communicating. It is used by all type of organizations and millions of consumers who have PCs.

3. It will be beneficial for you to review the mortgage insurance on your home. You told me that you have not change the beneficiary on the policy since your divorce.

4. Susan Jones will retire after working with our firm for 40 years. She started as a part-time clerk when she was a college student. She have always been a person who is loyal and hard working.

5. The enclose report, as well as the appropriate tables, may give you a simply written bit of information that you could use with the students in your next presentation.

6. Insurance companies classifies the value of an automobile through a process whereby a symbol is assigned to the various makes and models of cars. The enclosed chart provide a clear picture of how value and age of automobile are figured.

7. Both of these women will be rechecked in six months. Further violations will mean the end of their coverage. We are willing to reinsure, but only on our terms. Coverage for these drivers are high price; and only they, not you, can act to lower the cost. Only the absence of hazards incur in their driving will warrant a reduction in premiums.

VOCABULARY PREVIEW

amenities	Features; comforts
connoisseur	Expert, a discerning judge of the best in any field
endeavor	Attempt; efforts
fending	Ward off; fight off
gregarious	Congenial; friendly
homey	Cozy; comfortable
intimacy	Warmth; emotional closeness
melds	Blends; mixes
mulled cider	Sweetened and heated cider
nestled	Snuggled; burrowed
oozes	Exudes; emits
pizzazz	Showy display; flashy
prestigious	Distinguished
refurbished	Renovated; restored
renowned	Prominent; acclaimed; famous

4

TRANSCRIPTION PREVIEW: SELF-CHECK

Directions: Punctuate and correct the following sentences if needed. Check your answers in Appendix C.

1. We have connoisseurs individuals who have experience in evaluating inns and hotels visiting several bed and breakfasts that have been nominated for selection as one of our best 150.
2. She was impressed with Kathy the gregarious hostess. She reported that each of the four guest rooms is decorated with colorful motifs that have transformed the rooms into portraits of Victoriana.
3. During this same time period 55 clients did not renew their contracts.
4. We have retained all our reservation specialists and have hired only one new staff member Marie Fierro from California.
5. As part of your contract obligations we would like you to develop a B & B bonus package for the 150 B & B's selected.

Directions: If an item below is correct, write "C" in the blank at the right; if the item is not correct, write the correct form in the blank.

1. world-renowned advertising agency _____
2. best 150 B & B's _____
3. one minute videos _____
4. Greek revival home _____
5. our family of Bed and Breakfast sites _____

FORMATTING PREVIEW

Document 57: Block-Style Letter

The following foreign words are used in this letter: *motifs, bona fide, au jus, a la mode,* and *facade.*

The letter will be sent to:

Monsieur Jacques Lenoir	Monsieur means Mr. followed by first name and family name.
Rue de la Muse	Rue is the most common word for "street."
Case Postale	Case Postale means P.O. Box—not always followed by a number.
1211 GENEVE 11	Required four-digit postal code, city not usually capitalized in domestic use, and postal district number.

4

This letter also contains a description that should be indented from the left and right margins. Appositions are also used in this letter. Instead of using commas for the appositions, use parentheses. Example:

Host (an architect), hostess (a furniture designer and interior decorator)

Document 58: Block-Style Letter with Enclosures

This letter includes the following foreign words: *carte blanche, avant-garde, status quo, debut, sans, verbatim, per se, carpe diem,* and *connoisseurs.*

This letter will be sent to:

Frau Gisela Bauer	Frau means Ms., first given name and family name.
International Web AG	AG = Aktiengesellschaft, signifying a corporation.
Birchstrasse 185	Street name—the suffix "strasse" means street.
Postfach	Postfach means P.O. Box, not always followed by a #.
8050 Zürich 12	Four-digit postcode, city, postal district number.

Document 59: Block-Style Letter

This letter contains dictated changes.

Document 60: Short Report

This report includes a list that should be typed in columns (or use the table feature). The list should be indented from the left margin so that it is centered between the margins. Example:

United States 35

This report includes several side headings that should be typed at the left margin and underlined.

SHORT COURSE:	STANDARD COURSE:
Transcribe Documents 58 and 60.	Transcribe the four documents for Bed and Breakfast Around the World.

TAPE: LESSON 16: BED AND BREAKFAST AROUND THE WORLD

Tape Counter: Start __125__ Stop __154__ Doc. 57
             Start __156__ Stop __181__ Doc. 58
             Start __183__ Stop __220__ Doc. 59
             Start __222__ Stop __280__ Doc. 60

TEST TIME

After your instructor has graded your transcribed letters for Lesson 16, review the confusing words and language rules presented in lessons 1 through 16. Ask your instructor for the fourth written test covering confusing words, punctuation, grammar, and proofreading. Then ask your instructor for the tape for Transcription Test 4.

The test dictation includes a merge document.

INTRODUCTION TO TEST 4

Below are some words and terms that may help you transcribe the letters in Test 4. In addition to this preview, review lessons 13 through 16 in your text prior to taking the transcription test.

The following are one word:

- flatwater
- riverboat
- mountainsides
- breathtaking
- snowmobiling
- whitewater

adrenaline	Energizer, chemical stimulus
arctic	Frozen, icy cold
cascading	Going down, such as in a waterfall
craggy	Jagged, irregular
cyberspace	Computer-related term associated with the Internet
domestic	Home; household

4

majestic	Magnificent, splendid
pristine	Pure, natural
randomly	Selected hazardously
snowmobiling	Using automotive vehicles to travel in the snow
torrents	Streams, flood
wanderlust	Impulse to wander or explore

Make sure you review the foreign terms in *The Office Guide* before you take Test 4. Some of the letters in this test will be dictated in office style dictation with corrections.

Test 4 Doc. 1: Block-Style Letter with Paragraph Lists and Minor Dictation Changes

Test 4 Doc. 2: Block-Style Letter with Bulleted List

Test 4 Doc. 3: Block-Style Form/Merge Letter

Test 4 Doc. 4: Long Block-Style Letter with Subject

4

APPENDIX A
Machine Transcription Student Progress Record

Use this form to help pace yourself through the language exercises and transcription assignments in this text. This form will also help you keep track of your progress and allow you to see how well you are doing and how many of the exercises and assignments you have completed.

SECTION 2: MACHINE TRANSCRIPTION OVERVIEW

_____Machine Transcription Terms Self-Test (pp. 26)
_____Introductory Tape and Self-Check (pp. 32)

SECTION 3: WRITTEN COMMUNICATION ASSESSMENT

_____Score on Language Arts Pretest

Depending upon your grade on the Language Arts Pretest or the structure of your course, your instructor will direct you to follow one of these options.

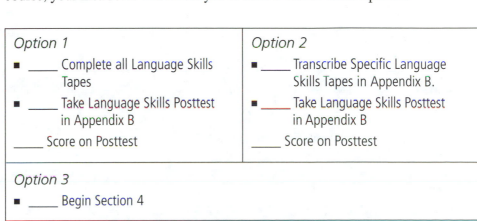

Option 1	Option 2
■ ____ Complete all Language Skills Tapes	■ ____ Transcribe Specific Language Skills Tapes in Appendix B.
■ ____ Take Language Skills Posttest in Appendix B	■ ____ Take Language Skills Posttest in Appendix B
____ Score on Posttest	____ Score on Posttest

Option 3
■ ____ Begin Section 4

SECTION 4: EASY CORRESPONDENCE: BLOCK-, MODIFIED-, AND SIMPLIFIED-STYLE LETTERS

A

Lesson 1 (Lightning Catering)
Complete:
- ____Word Usage Review 1
- ____Language Review 1
- ____Format Review 1
- ____Proofreading Exercise 1
- ____Transcription Preview Self-Check

- Transcribe Documents
  - ____Doc. 1
  - ____Doc. 2
  - ____Doc. 3

____Practice Pts. on Transcription

Lesson 2 (The Camberley Anderson Resort)
Complete:
- ____Word Usage Review 2
- ____Language Review 2
- ____Format Review 2
- ____Proofreading Exercise 2
- ____Transcription Preview Self-Check

- Transcribe Documents
  - ____Doc. 4
  - ____Doc. 5
  - ____Doc. 6

____Practice Pts. on Transcription

Lesson 3 (Sweet Hollow Landscaping)
Complete:
- ____Word Usage Review 3
- ____Language Review 3
- ____Format Review 3
- ____Proofreading Exercise 3
- ____Transcription Preview Self-Check

- Transcribe Documents
  - ____Doc. 7
  - ____Doc. 8
  - ____Doc. 9

____Practice Pts. on Transcription

Lesson 4 (Evergreen Products, Inc.)
Complete:
- ____Word Usage Review 4
- ____Language Review 4
- ____Format Review 4
- ____Proofreading Exercise 4
- ____Transcription Preview Self-Check

- Transcribe Documents
  - ____Doc. 10
  - ____Doc. 11
  - ____Doc. 12

____Practice Pts. on Transcription

____**Grade Transcription Test 1**
____**Grade on Language Arts/Proofreading Test 1**

SECTION 4: MODERATE COMPLEXITY: MEMORANDUMS, TWO-PAGE LETTERS AND LETTERS WITH SPECIAL NOTATIONS AND PARTS, DOCUMENTS WITH ENUMERATED ITEMS

Lesson 5 (PC Answers)	Lesson 6 (Rocky Mountain High Realty)
Complete:	Complete:
■ ____Word Usage Review 5	■ ____Word Usage Review 6
■ ____Language Review 5	■ ____Language Review 6
■ ____Format Review 5	■ ____Format Review 6
■ ____Proofreading Exercise 5	■ ____Proofreading Exercise 6
■ ____Transcription Preview Self-Check	■ ____Transcription Preview Self-Check
■ Transcribe Documents	■ Transcribe Documents
____Doc. 13	____Doc. 17
____Doc. 14	____Doc. 18
____Doc. 15	____Doc. 19
____Doc. 16	____Doc. 20
____Practice Pts. on Transcription	____Practice Pts. on Transcription
Lesson 7 (The City of Geneva)	**Lesson 8 (TRL Testing & Research)**
Complete:	Complete:
■ ____Word Usage Review 7	■ ____Word Usage Review
■ ____Language Usage Review 7	■ ____Language Review 8
■ ____Format Usage Review 7	■ ____Format Review 8
■ ____Proofreading Exercise 7	■ ____Proofreading Exercise 8
■ ____Transcription Preview Self-Check	■ ____Transcription Preview Self-Check
■ Transcribe Documents	■ Transcribe Documents
____Doc. 21	____Doc. 25
____Doc. 22	____Doc. 26
____Doc. 23	____Doc. 27
____Doc. 24	____Doc. 28
____Practice Pts. on Transcription	____Practice Pts. on Transcription
	____**Grade Transcription Test 2**
	____**Grade on Language Arts/Proofreading Test 2**

SECTION 4: MODERATE COMPLEXITY: INTRODUCTION OF CORRECTIONS TO DICTATION, INTRODUCTION OF MERGED ITEMS, DOCUMENTS WITH ENUMERATED ITEMS

A

Lesson 9 (Echo Family Insurance)
Complete:
- ____Word Review 9
- ____Language Usage Review 9
- ____Format Review 9
- ____Proofreading Exercise 9
- ____Transcription Preview Self-Check

- Transcribe Documents
  ____Doc. 29
  ____Doc. 30
  ____Doc. 31
  ____Doc. 32

____Practice Pts. on Transcription

Lesson 10 (Potomac National Bank)
Complete:
- ____Word Usage Review 10
- ____Language Review 10
- ____Format Review 10
- ____Proofreading Exercise 10
- ____Transcription Preview Self-Check

- Transcribe Documents
  ____Doc. 33
  ____Doc. 34
  ____Doc. 35
  ____Doc. 36

____Practice Pts. on Transcription

Lesson 11 (Aunt Dee's Kids Kampus)
Complete:
- ____Word Review 11
- ____Language Usage Review 11
- ____Format Review 11
- ____Proofreading Exercise 11
- ____Transcription Preview Self-Check

- Transcribe Documents
  ____Doc. 37
  ____Doc. 38
  ____Doc. 39
  ____Doc. 40

____Practice Pts. on Transcription

Lesson 12 (Snapshots, Inc.)
Complete:
- ____Word Usage Review 12
- ____Language Review 12
- ____Format Review 12
- ____Proofreading Exercise 12
- ____Transcription Preview Self-Check

- Transcribe Documents
  ____Doc. 41
  ____Doc. 42
  ____Doc. 43
  ____Doc. 44

____Practice Pts. on Transcription

____**Grade Transcription Test 3**
____**Grade on Language Arts/Proofreading Test 3**

SECTION 4: ADVANCED COMPLEXITY: MERGING, REPORTS, FOREIGN ACCENTS, FOREIGN ADDRESSES

Lesson 13 (Nova Travel)
Complete:
- ■ ____Word Usage Review 13
- ■ ____Language Review 13
- ■ ____Format Review 13
- ■ ____Proofreading Exercise 13
- ■ ____Transcription Preview Self-Check

- ■ Transcribe Documents
  - ____Doc. 45
  - ____Doc. 46
  - ____Doc. 47
  - ____Doc. 48

____Practice Pts. on Transcription

Lesson 14 (American Publishing Co.)
Complete:
- ■ ____Word Usage Review 14
- ■ ____Language Review 14
- ■ ____Format Review 14
- ■ ____Proofreading Exercise 14
- ■ ____Transcription Preview Self-Check

- ■ Transcribe Documents
  - ____Doc. 49
  - ____Doc. 50
  - ____Doc. 51
  - ____Doc. 52

____Practice Pts. on Transcription

Lesson 15 (Metropolitan County Public Schools)
Complete:
- ■ ____Word Usage Review 15
- ■ ____Language Review 15
- ■ ____Format Review 15
- ■ ____Proofreading Exercise 15
- ■ ____Transcription Preview Self-Check

- ■ Transcribe Documents
  - ____Doc. 53
  - ____Doc. 54
  - ____Doc. 55
  - ____Doc. 56

____Practice Pts. on Transcription

Lesson 16 (Bed and Breakfast Around the World)
Complete:
- ■ ____Word Usage Review 16
- ■ ____Language Review 16
- ■ ____Format Review 16
- ■ ____Proofreading Exercise 16
- ■ ____Transcription Preview Self-Check

- ■ Transcribe Documents
  - ____Doc. 57
  - ____Doc. 58
  - ____Doc. 59
  - ____Doc. 60

____Practice Pts. on Transcription

____**Grade Transcription Test 4**
____**Grade on Language Arts/Proofreading Test 4**

APPENDIX B

Language Arts Skill Review with Language Tapes B

Punctuation: Language Tape 1

	Rule	Reference Handbook	Assigned	Completed
Rule 1.1	Period	GP 1.1		
2.1	Question Mark	GP 2.1		
3.1	Comma: Compound Sentence	GP 3.1		
3.2	Comma: Introductory Phrases and Clauses	GP 3.2A GP 3.2B GP 3.2C GP 3.2D		
3.3	Comma: Parenthetical Expressions	GP 3.3a, GP 3.3b		
3.4	Comma: Elements in Apposition	GP 3.4		
3.5	Comma: Direct Address	GP 3.5		
3.6	Comma: Consecutive Adjectives	GP 3.6		
3.7	Comma: Series	GP 3.8		

Punctuation: Language Tape 2

	Rule	Reference Handbook	Assigned	Completed
Rule 4.1	Semicolon: Independent Clauses without a Connective	GP 4.1		
4.2	Semicolon: Transitional Expressions	GP 4.3		
4.3	Semicolon: Series with Internal Punctuation	GP 4.2		
5.1	Colon	GP 5.1		
6.1	Quotation Marks: In relation to commas and periods	GP 6.5		
6.2	Quotation Marks: In relation to the question mark and exclamation point	GP 6.6		
6.3	Quotation Marks: In relation to the semicolon and colon	GP 6.6		
6.4	Underscore and quotation marks for reference sources	GP 6.3		

Punctuation: Language Tape 3

		Rule	Reference Handbook	Assigned	Completed
Rule	7.1	Hyphen	GP 7.1		
	8.1	Apostrophe: Contractions	GP 8.1		
	8.2	Apostrophe: Possessives not ending in "s"	GP 8.2		
	8.3	Apostrophe: Possessives ending in "s"	GP 8.3		
	8.4	Apostrophe: Possessives general	GP 8.4		
	9.1	Parentheses: In a sentence	GP 9.2		
	9.2	Parentheses: End of sentence	GP 9.2		
	9.3	Parentheses: With a separate sentence	GP 9.3		

Capitalization: Language Tape 4

		Rule	Reference Handbook	Assigned	Completed
Rule	10.1	Organizations: Business, government, & other	GP 10.1		
	10.2	Subdivisions of organizations	GP 10.2		
	10.3	Job titles	GP 10.3		
	10.4	Rooms and buildings	GP 10.4		
	10.5	Trade names	GP 10.5		
	10.6	Documents	GP 10.6		
	10.7	Publications	GP 10.7		
	11.1	Compass points: Proper nouns & adjectives	GP 10.8		
	12.1	Identifying elements: Numbers	GP 10.10		
	12.2	Identifying elements: Letters	GP 10.10		
Numbers: Language Tape 4					
	13.1	Above and below ten	GP 12.1		
	13.2	Related numbers	GP 12.2		
	13.3	Beginning of sentence	GP 12.3		
	13.4	Dates	GP 12.4		
	13.5	Ordinals	GP 12.5		
	13.6	Measurements	GP 12.6		
	13.7	Combination numbers	GP 12.7		

Numbers: Language Tape 5

Rule			Reference Handbook	Assigned	Completed
Rule	14.1	Money: Amounts of $1 or more	GP 13.1		
	14.2	Money: Amounts under $1	GP 13.2		
	14.3	Money: Amounts of a million or more	GP 13.3		
	15.1	Percentages	GP 14.1		
	15.2	Decimals	GP 14.2		
	15.3	Fractions	GP 14.3		
	16.1	Time: A.M., P.M., and o'clock	GP 15.1		
	16.2	Time: Periods of time	GP 15.2		
	16.3	Time: Ages	GP 12.8		
	17.1	Identification: Serial numbers	GP 12.2		
	17.2	Identification: House and building numbers	GR 7		
	17.3	Identification: Street numbers	GR7		
Abbreviations: Language Tape 5					
	18.1	Titles	GP 16.1		
	18.2	Academic degrees	GP 16.2		
	18.3	Organizations	GP 16.3		
	18.4	Business names	GP 16.4		
	18.5	Communications systems	GP 16.5		
	18.6	Business terms	GP 16.6		

APPENDIX C
Answers to Lesson Exercises

ANSWERS TO MACHINE TRANSCRIPTION TERMS
SELF-TEST, SECTION 2

1. His foreign accent makes his <u>enunciation</u> unclear, and it is difficult to transcribe his work.

2. Prior to digital technology, the nonremovable media used to record dictation called <u>endless loop</u> was commonly used in large organizations.

3. The dictator used the <u>verbal insertion</u> feature on her transcription unit to automatically insert a change in the dictation.

4. Another name for the person dictating besides originator or dictator is <u>principal.</u>

5. The transcription operator used the <u>search</u> feature on her transcriber to locate and preview instructions before transcribing.

6. The <u>turnaround time</u> was improved when the dictators and transcription operators learned how to use 70 <u>trigger phrases,</u> which eliminated a great deal of typing.

7. The <u>tank</u> for the endless loop tape system took up one corner of the room.

8. Metro-Plex will install a <u>centralized system</u> that will allow all its employees to dictate 24 hours a day from <u>remote</u> locations.

9. By monitoring the <u>supervisor's console,</u> the supervisor can tell how much work each transcription operator has been assigned.

10. You have to know <u>syllabication</u> in order to correctly divide words.

11. <u>Portable dictation units</u> are used by many individuals in sales because they can easily be carried while working in the field.

12. An <u>adaptor</u> is needed in order to allow the transcriber to interface with the computer.

13. The direction machine transcription technology is taking is <u>digital,</u> which allows software to randomly access dictated text without media handling.

14. The <u>LCD window display</u> on the transcription unit shows the location and length of each document as well as the dictator's location on the tape.

15. Many new transcription units have <u>voice-activated (VOR)</u> capabilities that automatically stop the dictation when the dictator stops speaking.

ANSWERS TO INTRODUCTORY TAPE SELF-CHECK

1. volume, tone, speed
2. tone
3. right
4. speed
5. operator
6. RR
7. left and right brackets
8. b
9. MN
10. A double space below the salutation
11. On the first line of the inside address
12. Double spaced usually
13. Ms. Linda C./ Anderson
14. b
15. Simplified
16. any way
17. accent
18. roll
19. assistants
20. capital
21. chronicle
22. confidant
23. principal
24. Whose
25. complement

LESSON 1: LIGHTNING CATERING

Word Usage Review 1

1. add
2. access
3. exceed
4. adopt
5. except
6. ascent
7. adverse
8. advise
9. adherents
10. adept
11. accent
12. ad
13. adapt
14. accede
15. excess
16. advice
17. adherence
18. accept
19. averse
20. accept
21. edition
22. addition

Language Review 1

1. Region Five placed first in sales, and every employee in that region will receive a bonus. (GP 3.1)
2. Mr. Runnels, former chairman of the committee, resigned last month. (GP 3.4)
3. Mr. Smith and Ms. Anderson both are candidates for the position, and they will be interviewed next week. (GP 3.1)
4. You, too, are qualified and should apply for the position. (GP 3.8)
5. The new director believes that ergonomic concerns, such as eyestrain and wrist pain, can be alleviated with better equipment and peripheral selection. (GP 3.3A, GP 3.4)
6. The deadline was last week, and at that time there were 57 applicants. (GP 3.1)

7. Should we open another branch in Ohio too? Correct (GP 3.8)

8. The no-smoking policy, which is not popular with employees, takes effect on Monday. (GP 3.3A, GP 3.4)

9. Correct (GP 3.1)

10. Ms. Smith, the vice president, will remodel his old office, which was once the conference room. (GP 3.3A, GP 3.4)

11. The association's dues will increase this year in order to cover the cost of hiring an administrative assistant. (GP 8.2)

12. The Leatherwood Manufacturing Company will hold its convention in August. (GP 10.1)

13. We only have six chairs and nine people are coming. (GP 3.1 [one independent clause has only four words], GP 12.1)

14. The new concert hall can hold 1000 people, which should be adequate seating for each of the 30 scheduled shows. (GP 3.3A, GP 3.4, GP 12.1)

15. Sally made a last-minute attempt to finish before 5 p.m. (GP 7.1, GP 15.1)

16. The new transcriptionist had to learn the software, transcription equipment, and office rules. (GP 3.7)

17. As soon as the new president took over, employee morale improved. (GP 3.2A)

18. We could not locate the reference manual, ZIP code book, style guide, or thesaurus. (GP 3.7)

19. When Juan and Nancy volunteered to do Mary's work while she was on vacation, they didn't know that they were expected to take over her responsibilities for the mail too. (GP 3.2D and GP 3.8)

20. Unless someone tells Ms. Henson to slow down when she dictates, we will continue to have difficulty transcribing her dictation. (GP 3.2D)

21. The cost of the item was $2, and he made $2000 selling it. (GP 3.1, GP 12.1, GP 13.1)

22. The transcription operator transcribed **5** memos, **6** reports, and 15 letters. (GP 12.2)

23. She will not be home until **8** p.m. (GP 15.1)

24. Mr. Adams, who was the last manager transferred, will be available to assist the new employees at **3** o'clock. (GP 3.4, GP 15.1)

25. The business started with **80** employees. (GP 12.1)

Format Review 1

T   1. All letters except simplified should include a return address, date, inside address, salutation, closing, and writer's identification.

F   2. All letters regardless of their style should be **single** spaced.

F   3. The letter style that uses indented paragraphs is **modified block with paragraph indention.**

T   4. Block-style letters have the date and closing starting at the left margin.

F   5. "Dear Ms. Anderson" is the **salutation.**

T **6.** The inside address is the same address used on the envelope.

F **7.** If the letter style uses indented paragraphs, you **should** double space between paragraphs.

F **8.** The two-letter state abbreviation for Alaska is **AK.**

F **9.** Reference initials are the **typist's** initials.

T **10.** Reference initials are typed in lower case.

T **11.** Reference initials are typed a double space below the typed signature (name of the writer).

Proofreading Exercise 1

Current Date   *(There should be more than one return between date and inside address.)*

Mr. Thomas Whitney
2976 West Street
Orlando, **FL** 3870   *(Missing digit in ZIP code)*

Dear Mr. Thomas:

We are sorry that we couldn't respond to your earlier request faster. Our **ad exceeded** our expectations in reaching new customers, and we didn't have enough parts on hand to fill orders quickly. We have since resolved the problem **(no comma)** and can now **accept** and fill orders in a timely manner. We are pleased to announce that, due to an **excess** of parts in stock, we can repair the six printers and two monitors too.   *(no comma before too)*

We do not have the part needed to repair the switch on the surge protector, but we can **adapt** a lever from an older model to repair the switch. Let us know if **you** would like us to do so at no cost. We will **accept** your Purchase Order 450 in replacement **of** the original purchase order sent in May.

Sincerely,   *(Closing should be at left margin.)*

Nancy Jones

lm   *(Reference initials should be lower case.)*

Transcription Preview: Self-Check 1

1. We understand the strict adherence to the no-smoking policy, and we will advise our staff to follow this policy and the other restrictions that Mr. Andrews gave us regarding use of the building.

2. We look forward to serving Orange City Association's catering needs, and we hope that our quality professional service and outstanding cuisine will result in repeat business.

3. The festival backyard tent, which until this week was only available in blue and white, is now available in a variety of colors.

4. Your office manager, Ms. Martha Anderson, faxed her entry in to our "Delivering the Best" contest last week; and her entry was chosen as one of ten lucky winners.

    1. six menu selections

    2. C

    3. C

    4. C

    5. C

    6. mouth-watering cuisine

    7. C

LESSON 2: THE CAMBERLEY ANDERSON RESORT

Word Usage Review 2

1. air		**12.**	aide, aloud
2. aisle		**13.**	effect
3. aid		**14.**	heir
4. a lot		**15.**	ally
5. affect		**16.**	aloud
6. already		**17.**	a lot
7. allot		**18.**	Isle
8. aide		**19.**	already
9. I'll		**20.**	aid
10. allowed		**21.**	Err
11. all ready		**22.**	almost

Language Review 2

1. Correct as written or a better solution would be to change "black" to African-American and "white" to Caucasian. (GP 10.12)

2. Only 10 percent of the photographs came out. (GP 14.1)

3. The merger took place on Thursday, May 18, 2001. (GP 3.9)

4. Correct as written. (GP 3.3C)

5. Consequently, he was able to apply the profit he made on the sale of the house toward paying his college loan. (GP 3.3C)

6. Of the three new employees, Mary is the best qualified to assume Beth's duties. (GP 3.2A)

7. Because he missed the meeting, it is important that you get the minutes to him. (GP 3.2D)

8. Sally's mother, of course, will be there to see her get the award. (GP 3.3A)

9. According to my records, she was absent **seven** times this month. (GP 12.1, GP 3.3A)

10. It is vital, therefore, that she signs the contract before tomorrow. (GP 3.3C)

11. If you are a college student, you can get a **15** percent discount on the first month's rent. (GP 3.2D, GP 14.1, GP 8.2)

12. Finally, she was able to take her vacation. (GP 3.3C)

13. Striving to become a better transcriptionist, she spent hours reviewing grammar and punctuation rules. (GP 3.2B)

14. The lower sales in our department, in my opinion, were caused by inexperienced staff. (GP 3.3A)

15. Correct as written. (GP 3.2B)

16. Correct as written. (GP 3.8)

17. She is an expert in corporate management, portfolio development, and stock analysis. (GP 3.7)

18. The new president will take office on Monday, May 10. (GP 3.9)

19. She is a very well-known consultant and speaker. (GP 7.1)

20. The quartz clock, which was given to him as a retirement gift, was stolen. (GP 3.4)

Format Review 2

T 1. This is the correct abbreviation for U.S.A. (In an address, it is acceptable not to include periods.)

F 2. **No** space should be after the first period in a.m.

T 3. One space is used after the period in a person's title, such as Mr.

T 4. This is the correct form of the abbreviation post office: PO. According to the United States Postal Service, Postal Addressing Standards, it is acceptable to abbreviate post office like this in addresses.

T 5. If initials are used in a name, one space should be left after the period in the initials.

T 6. Space once after a semicolon.

F 7. **No** spaces should be left after the colon in 6:20 p.m.

F 8. **One** space is now commonly used after a period at the end of a sentence.

F 9. **No** space should be left after an asterisk and the text that follows.

F 10. **No** space should be left before and after a dash.

T 11. There should be no space left before and after a hyphen.

T 12. When parentheses are used, there should be no space left after the first parenthesis and before the last parenthesis.

F 13. Letters are **always** single spaced.

T 14. Double space between the last line of the inside address of a letter and the salutation.

T 15. The complimentary close is typed a double space below the last line of the body of the letter.

F 16. After the writer's typed name in a letter, press return (enter) **twice** and type the reference initials.

T 17. The enclosure notation is typed after the reference initials.

T 18. The enclosure notation is always typed at the left margin.

Proofreading Exercise 2

Current Date   *(Date should be at left margin or closing should be moved to center.)*

Mr. Thomas Henson
598 East Elm Street
Atlanta, GA 85093

Dear Mr. Henson: **("Thomas" should be deleted.)**

This is to confirm your registration for the week of October 24. We have reserved a suite on the fourth floor close to the **aisle** leading to an outdoor balcony**,** which overlooks the Atlanta skyline. We have reserved an **adjoining** suite for your **aide.** According to the schedule we received, your assistant will **already** be in Atlanta prior to your visit**;** so we will be able to handle any last-minute details or changes regarding meeting rooms and accommodations.

We are certain that you will enjoy the warm, friendly atmosphere of the community and the spectacular nightlife and activity Atlanta has to offer. We look forward to your visit.

Sincerely,

(Additional lines between Sincerely and Martha)

Martha Barlow

slm   *(Reference initials should be typed a __double__ space after the writer's typed name.)*

Transcription Preview: Self-Check 2

1. At the request of Mr. Randy Simms**,** we are submitting a bid to host the Regional Association of Information Systems Supervisors**'** 2010 conference.

2. Since we are a five-star resort**,** you can be assured that we pamper our guests and do everything possible to make their stay enjoyable and memorable.

3. First**,** we're offering an incentive travel award that could put you**,** your boss**,** or a superstar attendee on an **eight-day/seven-night** vacation anywhere in the United States.

4. As a result, we are offering your group a $5,000 Bonus Dollars Certificate that may be applied towards your master account for guest and meeting room charges, banquet food, beverage expenses, and audiovisual rentals.

    1. C

    2. Bonus Dollars Certificate

    3. **five-star** resort

    4. C

    5. C

    6. 8,500 **square** foot ballroom

LESSON 3: SWEET HOLLOW LANDSCAPING

Word Usage Review 3

1.	alter	16.	anyway
2.	analyst	17.	alternative
3.	assistance	18.	alternate
4.	apprised	19.	awhile
5.	annual	20.	annual
6.	assistants	21.	annalist
7.	Any one	22.	illusion
8.	alternate	23.	all ready
9.	altogether	24.	always
10.	annul	25.	arrange
11.	a while	26.	attendants
12.	appraised	27.	allusion
13.	altar	28.	already
14.	anyone	29.	attendance
15.	apprise	30.	anti-

Language Review 3

1. We apologize, Mrs. Anderson, for the delay in filling your order. (GP 3.5)

2. She was transferring the information from Brochure No. 576 to the new multimedia format. (GP 10.10)

3. The new supervisor suggested that every employee become familiar with the book *Merriam Webster's Guide to International Business Communications.* (GP 6.3)

4. The problem we found is, many of the new employees don't know the policy. (GP 3.11)

5. She worked in a cold, dreary office. (GP 3.6)

6. To become a good transcriptionist, you should practice listening and using good grammar. (GP 3.2C)

7. We could not locate Purchase Order No. 578. (GP 10.10)

8. The top ranking salesperson is a hardworking, conscientious employee. (GP 3.6)

9. You should be delighted to know, Susan, that you have met your transcription quota. (GP 3.5)

10. Correct as written. (GP 3.2C)

11. Correct as written. (GP 6.3)

12. Correct as written. (GP 10.10)

Format Review 3

T   1. Do not space before or after a dash.

T   2. Space twice after a colon except when it is used in a time context. (Example: 6:30).

F   3. Do **not** space before and after a hyphen.

T   4. In the Simplified letter, all lines begin at the left margin.

F   5. The complimentary closing and the date are typed **not** centered in modified-block style letters. They are typed **beginning** at the center.

T   6. The first and second pages of a letter usually have a 1″ top margin.

F   7. Numbers ten and **below** used as street names are spelled out.

T   8. This is the correct format to use in a street name: 6200-23rd Avenue North.

F   9. This is <u>not</u> correct (Third should be spelled out.) Numbers 1–10 should be spelled out when used in street names. (GR 7)

Proofreading Exercise 3

Ms. Paula Atkinson   Page 2   April 10, 20—
                                                        (Delete comma after April)

We will send **(delete the word out)** your merchandise for Order **No.** 3760 by United Parcel immediately, so it should arrive about the time you receive this letter. We are sorry, Ms. Atkinson, for any inconvenience this delay has caused you.

You are a very loyal, dependable customer; and we strive to make our service as efficient as possible. Once in **a while,** however, we slip up as we did in this case. Please accept our apology, and let us know if we can be of **assistance** in **any way.**

Sincerely,   **(Indented paragraphs and second page heading indicate that this is a modified block letter and closing should begin at center.)**

Peggy Jones

lm

Transcription Preview: Self-Check 3

1. The bedding plants arrived in excellent condition, and we were able to plant them at a client's house within hours of your delivery.

2. These are majestic trees that are hardy to the cold and are able to survive drought, flooding, smoke, and soot.

3. I have chosen **eight** perennials interspersed with annuals to add color to the courtyard and garden area.

4. Since the restaurant business is as competitive as the landscaping business, I know you understand that although there are many competitors, not just **anyone** can provide you with quality.

5. From touring other developments built by your company, I notice that large picture windows, glass walls, glassed-in sun porches, and terraces all combine to make the outdoors part of the house.

6. Beautiful gardens, luxuriant turf, and healthy blossoming trees add as much to the exterior appeal of a home as the wallpaper and other amenities add to the interior appeal.

   1. C
   2. C
   3. C
   4. 1890 Seventh Avenue
   5. first-class eating establishment
   6. 10 percent
   7. 350 acres

LESSON 4: EVERGREEN PRODUCTS, INC.

Word Usage Review 4

1. breaks	14. basis
2. bazaar	15. bear
3. bare	16. bizarre
4. border	17. brakes
5. beside	18. brooch
6. breadth	19. breathe
7. biannual	20. biennial
8. bored	21. bated
9. besides	22. build
10. bread	23. born
11. broach	24. baited
12. beat	25. borne
13. boarder	26. billed

Language Review 4

1. Mr. Smith and his nephew, John Jones Jr., did not attend the conference. (GP 3.10 & GP 3.4)

2. Because there were so many customers interested in the sale, it was extended. (GP 3.2D)

3. The outgoing president will not leave office until May; the incoming president will begin her term then. (GP 4.1)

4. Since she had so much experience, she was promoted to manager; and John became her assistant. (GP 3.2D & GP 4.2)

5. JoAnne took the CPS exam in August, and she passed on her first try. (GP 3.1)

6. If you continue to practice, you will become a good transcriptionist. (GP 3.2D)

7. Sally attended night classes to get her associate degree; as a result, she got a salary increase. (GP 4.1, GP 3.3A)

8. If he doesn't improve his proofreading, he will be fired; and then we will have to do his work. (GP 3.2D, GP 4.2)

9. Correct as written. (GP 3.10)

10. How much money did it cost to operate the booth at the conference? the meeting afterward? the transportation shuttles for board members? (GP 2.1)

11. Unless the product has better sales, we will discontinue manufacturing it; and then some consumers will be angry. (GP 3.2D, GP 4.2)

12. Although it took us nine months to prepare the report, we were able to meet the deadline; but we still were unprepared for some of the questions. (GP 3.2, GP 4.2)

13. We will be going to the office at noon; therefore, we should be finished before dinner. (GP 4.3)

14. In addition to the pay increase, some of the operators received a bonus for exceeding their quota; and this enabled them to have extra money at Christmas. (GP 3.3B, GP 4.2)

15. I don't remember the book's name, but I think it was written by Paul Jones Jr. and sells for $1.98. (GP 3.1, GP 3.10, GP 8.2)

16. She donated $6 to the school fund. (GP 13.1)

17. The deadline for applying was August 10. (GP 12.4)

18. Each employee was asked to bring one of the following items to the party:

    Dessert

    Casserole

    Soft drinks

    Chips

    (No periods in listed items. Review Rule GP 1.2)

Format Review 4

F   1. **Always** spell out the name of the city in the inside address.

F   2. The word "Saint" **should** be abbreviated in American cities.

T   3. Due to space restrictions on an envelope, it is acceptable to abbreviate some items that should not be abbreviated in the inside address.

F 4. **Fort** Lauderdale is the correct style to use in the inside address.

F 5. **Fort** Lauderdale is the correct style to use on the envelope.

T 6. If the individual to whom the letter is addressed is no longer working for a company and an attention line is used, someone in the company may open the letter.

T 7. It is better to address a letter directly to an individual rather than use an attention line.

T 8. An attention line is frequently used when the writer does not know the name of the individual but knows the title of the person such as marketing director.

T 9. The attention line may be typed as the first line of the address.

T 10. Enumerated items are single spaced if they are more than one line.

T 11. One blank line is left before and after each enumerated item.

F 12. Enumerated items usually **are** indented from the left and right margin.

Proofreading Exercise 4

July 10, 20—

Attention: Sales **M**anager
Applehouse Magic
3899 **Tenth** Street
Mount Dora, **FL** 3392   **(Digit missing in ZIP code)**

Gentlemen: **(Sexist salutation. Ladies and Gentlemen should be used.)**

We recently **sent** you a demo copy of **(delete extra our)** our CD-**ROM**, *The Rolling Que*, which provides instructions for making music. To date, we have not heard from you regarding the introductory offer outlined in the brochure that accompanied the demo CD-**ROM.** Because this introductory offer is only for a limited amount of time, we need a response from you within the next few weeks if you would like to purchase the software at the **15** percent discount. If you do not wish to take advantage of quantity discounts for a site license, you may purchase single-user versions of the software; however, this is more costly.

Sincerely,

(There should be three blank lines between "Sincerely" and "George Markham" for the signature)

George Markham, Marketing Manager

lm

(Note: Since Marketing Manager is not a long title, it is correct to place it on the same line as the writer's name. It would also be acceptable to place the job title on the line below the writer's name.)

Transcription Preview: Self-Check 4

1. You have the largest wholesaling operation in the state, and Evergreen appreciates your business.

2. Upon the basis of your payment record, we are increasing your line of credit by $10,000.

3. The newsprint, school and office paper products, and computer printout paper should be at your Matanuska warehouse in five days; but this schedule may be altered if this bizarre weather continues.

4. For instance, each mass-produced T-shirt exacts a toll on the environment either through the pesticides used by farmers to produce the cotton or the chemical bleaching and dyeing of the fabric during manufacturing.

5. Our dilemma, however, is how to take advantage of this interest after the Eco-Expo convention.

6. We know that in addition to your catalog, you also produce the *Enviro Business Letter*; and an article in this newsletter might educate the general consumer about the environmental hazards of standard clothing manufacturing.

7. We would like to advertise our clothing line, Enviro Duds, in your *Green Business* catalog.

8. The carrier, Ptarmigan Fast Freight, called our Anchorage representative, Tom Broers, who contacted three private insurance appraisers to determine the extent of the damage.

9. When Tom called me about this shipment, I immediately made these decisions: (1) to offer the furniture on the next salvage sale, and (2) to send a duplicate shipment by air freight.

10. Bob, we have had a long and cordial business relationship; and I am truly sorry about having to submit this claim.

    1. C
    2. 30 percent
    3. your June 15 order
    4. Pier 14
    5. C
    6. C
    7. three appraisers' fees

LESSON 5: PC ANSWERS/MULTIMEDIA, DESKTOP PUBLISHING, AND PC SUPPORT

Word Usage Review 5

1. senses	6. choose
2. carrots	7. caret
3. can not	8. cannot
4. capitol	9. ceiling
5. canvass	10. cease

11. canvas
12. capital
13. seized
14. serial
15. choose
16. sealing
17. cannot
18. chose
19. canvass, census
20. borough
21. calendar
22. cache
23. colander, a lot
24. cash

Language Review 5

1. The transcription handbook did not include the procedures for reporting absences, making personal telephone calls, or working overtime. (Note no colon is used after procedures.) (GP 5.1 & GP 3.7)

2. All of the department heads failed to request reimbursement for travel, meals, and supplies. (Note no colon is used after *for.*) (GP 3.7, GP 5.1)

3. **You're** the main candidate for the promotion. (GP 8.1)

4. Since we arrived after 1 P.M.; since we had no idea of what our responsibilities were; since we did not know where to display the computer equipment; the conference day was of little value. (GP 4.5)

5. If **it's** approved, we will get a salary increase in June. (GP 3.2D, GP 8.1)

6. The supplies were shipped to Kansas City, Missouri; Orlando, Florida; Maryville, Tennessee; and Dayton, Ohio. (GP 4.4)

7. The new advertising logo stressed one theme: relaxation. (GP 5.1)

8. The name of the CD was Rock Rap' N' Roll. (GP 8.1)

9. Do not tell **your** supervisor that you will be gone that week. (GP 8.1)

10. The members of the quality circle were Agatha Eastrurn, Nancy Evans, and Samantha Robinson. (Note no colon should be after *were.*) (GP 5.1, GP 3.7)

11. Correct. (GP 10.1)

12. When she was offered the opportunity to transfer from the Finance Department to the Personnel Department, Sally decided to stay with our company instead of taking a position with a competing firm. (GP 3.2D, GP 10.2)

13. When Jon transferred to the Becker Corporation**,** he was put in charge of the **f**inance **d**ivision. (GP 3.2D, GP 10.2)

14. Many transcription operators were unprepared when the company went through its "downsizing." (GP 6.2)

15. It was Jon—not Mary, who transcribed the document. (GP 11.2. The word *and* or a semicolon could also have been used.)

Format Review 5

T 1. The memorandum templates found in some word processing software programs do not conform to traditional memorandum format.

F 2. Titles such as Mr., Mrs., or Ms. should **not** be used in the "To" and "From" sections of a memorandum.

T   3. No matter what style is used for a memorandum To, From, Date, and Subject are always included.

F   4. Memorandums are sent to people **inside** the company.

T   5. If a memo is going to more than one person, a distribution list may be used at the bottom of a memo or the names can be listed after the word "To."

F   6. If the memo is confidential, the word *confidential* is typed in **all capitals** in bold.

F   7. The body of a memorandum is **single** spaced.

T   8. Usually memorandums do not include signature lines.

T   9. Reference initials are typed on the memo a double space below the last line of the memo.

T 10. The same second-page heading format used for letters is used for memos.

T 11. Triple or double space after the word *Subject* before typing the body of the memo.

T 12. The heading information (To, From, Date, Subject) is typed in all capitals.

T 13. The body of the memo is typed at the left margin.

F 14. The body of a report is **double** spaced.

F 15. The first page of a report should **not** be numbered.

T 16. The first page of a report should have a 2″ margin.

Proofreading Exercise 5

MEMORANDUM

TO: Mary Thompson *(Dr. should not be included.)*
John Anderson
Aretha Fain

FROM: Alison DeChant

DATE: *(Date was missing from heading.)*

RE: New Procedures for Submitting Payroll **I**nformation

There are new guidelines that will be used beginning on the first of next month for turning in payroll information. These guidelines are explained in the attached documentation.

It's important that **everyone** in your department be familiar with these guidelines and **follow** them. Failure to follow these procedures will result in possible delay in paychecks. If you have questions concerning these procedures, please contact the supervisor in the Accounting **D**epartment, Martha Jeptson, at extension 876.

lm

Attachment   *(Attachment should not be in all capitals.)*

Transcription Preview: Self-Check 5

1. Technology-enabled information exchange is now the lifeblood of an organization. Information and the growing knowledge base of an organization have become increasingly audiovisual in nature.

2. Via voice, data, and video links, users can see and speak with customers and competitors.

3. Interactive brainstorming can be instantly E-mailed, printed, or stored.

4. Electric copyholders with foot-pedal control of copy movement, text-magnifying lens, place-keeping line cursor, and built-in task lighting

5. Adjustable modular desks with shelves, file cabinet, and personal locker

6. Works not owned by anyone through an expired copyright or those that have been identified as such are public domain.

1. PDAs
2. in-depth analysis
3. touch-screen panel
4. C
5. C
6. built-in wrist support
7. full-motion video
8. CD-ROM
9. C
10. Web-streamed content
11. E-mailed (E-mailed and e-mailed are both acceptable formats. In this textbook E-mailed will be used for consistency.)
12. C
13. If the "essence" or "expression" of the work

LESSON 6: ROCKY MOUNTAIN HIGH REALTY

Word Usage Review 6

1. confidant
2. comments
3. chronic
4. sight
5. course
6. site
7. confident
8. cords
9. clothes
10. commence
11. cite
12. cloths
13. chronicle
14. compliment
15. command
16. confidentially

17. close

18. complement

19. confidently

20. coarse

21. comptroller's

22. corpse

23. clique

24. Click

25. collision

26. commended

27. cliché

28. command

29. collusion

30. controller

Language Review 6

1. You are requested to bring the following items with you:

   Minutes of the last meeting

   Comprehensive report

   Schedule of projects (GP 1.2)

2. We couldn't find any of the old, old houses shown in the book. (GP 3.12)

3. Several branch offices will open in:

   Florida.

   Maine.

   California. (GP 1.2)

4. Can you please pass along the information in the memo to Jim. (GP 1.1)

5. The water level in the lake was very, very high due to the heavy rain. (GP 3.12)

Format Review 6

F   1. The subject line always **starts at the left margin.**

T   2. The salutation comes before the subject line.

T   3. The titles "Subject," "In re," "Re," or "Refer to" are used at the beginning of the subject line.

T   4. Double space before and after the subject line.

T   5. In a block-style letter, the subject line begins at the left margin.

T   6. A colon is used after the word *subject* in the subject line.

T   7. The subject line may be typed in initial caps or all caps.

F   8. The second-page heading of a letter should start **1** inch from the top of the page.

F   9. It is **not** acceptable to put the complimentary close and signature line on the second page alone.

T 10. Triple space between the second-page heading and the body of the letter.

F 11. The **name of the person the letter is addressed to** is the first thing to put in the second-page heading.

T 12. There should be at least two lines of a paragraph left at the bottom of the first page and at least two lines carried over to the top of the second page.

F 13. Leave at least **1** inch at the bottom of the first page.

Proofreading Exercise 6

Date

Ms. Mary Hamilton
One Anderson Street
Sharpsburg, GA 3027   *(Digit Missing from ZIP code)*

Dear Mary:

Subject: Performance Evaluation

Tuesday morning at 9:30 a.m. has been set aside for us to go over your yearly performance evaluation. Please bring the following items with you to this meeting:

(Periods not needed in list
list should be indented.)

      Portfolio of work
      Transcription monthly log reports
      Attendance record
      List of questions or concerns

Your immediate supervisor can give you the log and **attendance** reports. You may **choose** to postpone this review if you **cannot** obtain these documents by the deadline, but you **can not** postpone the review for more than three weeks. This is because we are on a very, very tight schedule to discuss **performance** reviews for **150** employees.

Could you please notify your supervisor if a conflict exists with prior commitments that you may have made for next Tuesday that cannot be changed.

Sincerely,

Peggy Jones

lm

Transcription Preview: Self-Check 6

1. Teresa Puglisi, who designed our Web site, is no longer with our firm; she is presently operating her own Internet service in Houston. (A period instead of a semicolon can be used after *firm*. When transcribing the letter, however, use a semicolon.)

2. As marketing manager, I recommend that we become part of Realtor.com, which is the official site of the National Association of Realtors.

3. Hoping to save their homes, several neighbors and your mother hired a lawyer to fight the location of the beltway.

4. Since your mother gave you power of attorney during her illness and named you as executrix of her estate in her will, you should be able to sell her property consisting of the house she lived in and several rental properties if you so choose.

5. At the conclusion of a six-month listing agreement with Monery Real Estate in North Carolina, she chose not to sell the property; and it has not been on the market since.

6. Through legal pressure, this group of citizens was able to obtain a stay on the building of the beltway while alternate routes are reviewed.

7. In view of the owner's arrangements with the current tenants, I cannot believe that the home will be put on the market.

8. This couple, Mr. and Mrs. Edward Elsman, qualified for a loan on the house at a local bank; but the money that they would have to pay in mortgage discount points was high.

9. The state could employ the eminent domain rights at a future time, so it is important that you discuss the status of this real estate problem with your mother's attorney.

10. In order to capitalize on maximizing your capital investment, you can not delay the sale of this real estate.

    1. six-month lease
    2. C
    3. three-bedroom, two-bath home
    4. $575
    5. C

LESSON 7: THE CITY OF GENEVA

Word Usage Review 7

1. detract	13. corps
2. conscious	14. consul
3. correspondents	15. queued
4. councils	16. descent
5. conversation	17. difference
6. cue	18. diary
7. deference	19. dissent
8. dairy	20. counsel
9. correspondence	21. defer
10. conscience	22. differs
11. core	23. deposition
12. conservation	24. disposition

Language Review 7

1. Some of the heavy equipment is going to the **Middle East**. (GP 10.8)

2. Each one of the transcription operators **has** been late. (GP 17.1, GP 17.5A)

3. Either the new department chairman or the old department chairman **has** the book. (GP 17.2)

4. Neither Molly nor her replacement **knows** where to get their checks signed. (GP 17.2)

5. One of his many duties **is** to train the supervisors. (GP 17.3)

6. The East Coast is beautiful, but it can be dangerous during hurricane season. (GP 10.8, GP 3.1)

7. Only one of the boxes **is** small enough to store the files. (GP 17.3)

8. Correct. (GP 7.2)

9. She lived in **West** Texas for a short time before she moved to the Midwest. (GP 10.8)

10. Correct. (GP 10.3)

11. Correct. (GP 10.3)

12. When the companies merged, the **p**resident from our company became **p**resident of the new firm. (GP 10.3, GP 3.2D)

13. Either our Engineering Division will sponsor the event or the Advertising Department will. (GP 17.2, GP 10.2)

14. Ginger did not know Council **R**epresentative Juan Perez's extension. (GP 10.3)

Format Review 7

F 1. In the simplified letter style, the date **is** included in the letter.

F 2. In the simplified letter style, the writer's name is typed at the end of the letter in **all** capitals. It is becoming acceptable, however, to use initial capitals.

T 3. There is no salutation included in the simplified letter style.

T 4. There is no complimentary close in the simplified letter style.

T 5. Only open punctuation is used in the simplified letter style.

T 6. All lines in a simplified letter are typed at the left margin.

F 7. The word *confidential* is typed after **the date** in a letter that is confidential.

F 8. The word *confidential* is typed at the left margin **in all capitals with bold print** to show that only the person to whom the letter is addressed should read the letter.

F 9. The word *subject* is **not** included before the subject in a simplified letter.

T 10. The main headings in an itinerary are dates.

T 11. A two-column format is usually used in an itinerary.

F 12. The information in the body of an itinerary is **single** spaced.

Proofreading Exercise 7

Current Date

CONFIDENTIAL
Ms. Terry Carter
278 **Fifth** Ave. SW
Decatur, **GA** 37891

COUNCIL ADVISORY BOARD

This is to notify you, **confidentially,** that you have been selected to serve on the Council Advisory Board. Since the announcement will not **be** made until next week, we are asking that you not share this news until the public announcement is made.

It is an honor to be selected to serve on this board, and I can assure you that you will find serving on the board to be a very rewarding experience. We are hoping that this letter will give you enough advance notice to schedule time to fly to Southern California for the installation ceremony next month. I will send you **correspondence** with more details regarding the installation ceremony next week.

The members of our Council **A**dvisory **B**oard have a diverse **breadth** of knowledge and experience, which **aids** us in deciding company policy. We **cannot** thank our board members enough for sharing their expertise.

JANE MCALPINE   (Writer's name should be at left in all capitals although initial caps are becoming more common)

lm

Transcription Preview: Self-Check 7

1. Every one of the candidates possesses the qualities needed; however, three candidates stood out.
2. Operators on the 7 **a.m.** to 3 **p.m.** shift have requested a meeting.
3. Correct
4. We believe this expense is justified because the City would benefit by an improvement in the quality of communications; labor, material, and overhead costs would decrease; and the morale of dictators and transcription operators would improve.
5. Scheduling conflicts exist because of the limited number of computers, the workflow requirement, and the need to retain the 3 **p.m.** to 5 **p.m.** part-time people on those hours for which they were hired.
6. (1) we already have qualified individuals on our staff, (2) payment of moving and transfer costs is expensive, and (3) promoting from within promotes good morale.

7. Tangible savings would accrue in the categories of labor, material, and overhead; and intangible benefits in the area of personnel satisfaction should also bring about savings necessitated by hiring employees to replace those who quit due to stress from conflicts arising between supervisors and transcription operators.

    1. **80** percent of the employees

    2. Could you please verify the attached information and comment on her performance in these areas.

    3. **N**orth **C**entral area

    4. **24-**hour schedule

    5. C

    6. select the **p**urchasing **m**anager

LESSON 8: TRL TESTING & RESEARCH

Word Usage Review 8

1. elicit, illicit
2. envelope
3. fair
4. every one, every day
5. insured
6. envelop
7. imminent, devise, fair
8. farther
9. emerge
10. fare
11. diary, illegible
12. immerge
13. Illicit, everyday, do, assure
14. device
15. eminent, further, everyday

16. do, dues
17. every day, ensure, eligible
18. discreet, everyone
19. disperse, already
20. dual, allowed
21. elusive
22. duel
23. discrete
24. disburse, done
25. illusive, a lot
26. dun
27. expend, expand
28. Every one
29. immigrate
30. due, due

Language Review 8

1. When discussing the new contract, he commented, "The 4 **percent** pay increase is not acceptable." (GP 3.2D, GP 6.5, GP 14.1)

2. "I will attend the training session on Monday night," reported Martha, "but Alice will go on Tuesday after work." (GP 6.5)

3. Anyone can attend the classes if **he or she** signs up in advance. (GP 17.5)

4. C (17.6)

5. Either the instructor or his assistant **has** been given the test forms. (GP 17.2)

6. You **are** not going to graduate if you don't get better grades. (GP 17.6)

7. The vice president reported that he had many chances to be promoted; but, in his words, didn't take them because, "I didn't want to transfer, change positions, or work longer hours for little extra pay." (GP 3.3A, GP 10.3, GP 3.7, GP 6.1, GP 6.5)

8. "Something has to be done, and done soon, about the network problems," complained the transcription operator. (GP 3.3A, GP 6.5)

9. No one on the committee **was** informed about the meeting. (GP 17.5)

10. "Did you go to the orientation?" asked Mary. (GP 6.6)

11. Mr. Harper reported that the merger is imminent. (GP 6.1)

12. Every employee should bring **his or her** report. (GP 17.1)

13. "Your main responsibility," the supervisor instructed the new employee, "is to answer the phone." (GP 6.5)

14. We did not get the information in time to make the deadline; consequently, we did not submit the grant. (GP 4.3)

Format Review 8

T **1.** The copy notation is typed underneath the enclosure notation or reference initials.

F **2.** The notation **"bc"** is used when the writer does not want the addressee to know that someone else will also receive a copy of the letter.

F **3.** A colon **may or may not be** used after the copy notation.

T **4.** Either one or two *c's* may be used in the copy notation. The preferred style, however, is a single *c*.

T **5.** If there is room, the copy notation is typed a double space below the enclosure notation or reference initials.

F **6.** Words should be divided according to **syllabication based upon pronunciation** instead of roots and derivations.

T **7.** Dates may be divided between the day and year.

T **8.** It is correct to divide this word as shown: *estima-tion*.

F **9.** It is **not** correct to divide this word as shown: *em-pty*. (Empty shouldn't be divided because only two letters would be carried.)

F **10.** It is **not** acceptable to divide the last word on a page.

F **11.** Names may be divided **after** the first name and the middle initial.

T **12.** If you do not know the sex of the person to whom you are writing, it is acceptable not to use Ms. or Mr. in the inside address.

T **13.** If you know the addressee is a woman but do not know if she is married, use Ms. as a title.

T **14.** Use figures instead of spelling out words for building and house numbers in the address unless the number is 1.

F **15.** This is **not** the correct form to use in an address: Ms. Paula Anderson, M.D. (Use either the title Ms. or M.D.)

T **16.** If you were addressing a letter to an organization with both male and female members, the salutation would be "Ladies and Gentlemen."

F **17.** This is the correct form to use in addressing a letter to a husband and wife: Mr. **and** Mrs. Tom Royal. (Always spell out "and.")

T **18.** The newer trend in addressing a letter to a husband and wife is to not use titles such as Mr. and Mrs. and to only use the husband's and wife's first and last names.

Proofreading Exercise 8

Current Date

Mr. **and** Mrs. Jon Andersen
4 Glendale Blvd.
Sarasota, FL 37871

Dear Mr. **and** Mrs. Anderson**:**

Some of the information on the form you completed regarding your availability to volunteer to register voters at the mall was **illegible** due to water stains from rainy weather. We need to **ensure** that the information we have deciphered is correct. Please review the enclosed card to see if the information is correct so that we may process your application correctly.

(Paragraph below should not be indented.)
According to policy guidelines, everyone who is eligible to work will receive information about the proper procedures to follow and **further** information will be sent closer to the actual volunteer day. We try to be **fair** in our assignments and try to assign you to a mall close to your house. Our supervisor has asked us to inform you that volunteers will be treated to an appreciation dinner in June**.** *(No quotation marks needed.)*

Sincerely,

Jane McAlpine

Ref. Initials

Enclosure

cc Mr. Tony Peterson   *(one c without a colon would also be correct.)*

Note: If space were a factor, reference initials, enclosure notation, and copy notation could be single spaced.

Transcription Preview: Self-Check 8

1. So far this therapy of using coral and cloned proteins to rebuild crushed**,** brittle**,** and broken bones appears to be positive in **100** percent of the cases we have been monitoring for five years.

2. In his presentation three years ago, the **eminent** orthopedic trauma surgeon, Dr. Cole Ricks predicted, "By using coral, orthopedic trauma surgeons nationwide will create walking miracles among people injured in sports and near-death accidents."

3. The new bone melded with the implant, and a limb-lengthening device stretched the limb to match the length of her other leg.

4. The **everyday** contact with latex products, ranging from disposable diapers to buttons on calculators and TV remotes, is making the problem of latex allergies very widespread.

5. We have had success with a topical cream that treats the rash, but the only relief we have found so far for severe sensitivity is a self-injected dose of epinephrine.

6. With regard to the No Sugar Added product, I can inform you that, in fact, to our surprise it has reacted differently to market storage conditions than our prereleased studies indicated; and we are already taking steps to remedy the situation.

    1. for five years
    2. Foxley's No Sugar Added Ice Cream
    3. prereleased studies
    4. deep-sea coral implant
    5. career-ending ailment

LESSON 9: ECHO FAMILY INSURANCE

Word Usage Review 9

1. later
2. incidents, indicted
3. libel
4. It's, formally, hiring
5. legislator, liable, instances
6. latter, implied
7. formerly
8. implied
9. formally, legislator, legislature
10. higher
11. instants, later
12. inditing
13. incidence
14. It's, its
15. inferred, indicted, libel, formerly
16. flair
17. forgo
18. hear, lead, leased
19. here, hoard, hall
20. herd
21. holy
22. least, haul, wholly
23. human
24. flare
25. horde
26. insinuate, correspondence
27. forward, lesson
28. lay
29. allowed, holey
30. foreword, humane
31. incinerate, everyone

Langauge Review 9

1. The auditors' findings showed that the accounting procedures were being followed. (GP 8.3)

2. The new employees started on the first of the month, rather than beginning work in the middle of a pay period. (GP 3.3B)

3. We will not be able to have the meetings in Conference Rooms 301–308 because they don't have teleconferencing capabilities. (GP 7.4)

4. The supervisor changed the arrangement of the reception area, not the work area, in order to make it more convenient for individuals to pick up completed work. (GP 3.3A)

5. He was asked to **reevaluate** his position on refusing to accept payroll turned in late from self-employed contractors. (GP 7.2)

6. Mary's typing was so good, it earned her a promotion. (GP 8.2, GP 3.11)

7. Please return the forms in the self-addressed envelope. (GP 7.2)

8. Correct. (GP 7.4)

9. Rather than transfer to our company, she stayed in the **f**inance **d**epartment at her company where her job was secure. (GP 3.3B, GP 10.2)

10. Correct. (GP 10.3)

11. **His** understanding of the project enabled them to complete the job on time. (GP 8.4)

12. Mr. Williams was willing to transfer to another state, but only if the company would pay moving costs. (GP 3.3B)

13. Two years' experience is required before employees can be considered for a promotion. (GP 8.3)

14. She was given a salary increase, but only after she questioned her evaluation. (GP 3.3B)

15. Before employees can be considered for a promotion, they must work for the company for two years. (GP 3.2A)

16. All of the department managers' salaries were increased. (GP 8.3)

Format Review 9

T 1. The U.S. Post Office prefers that two spaces be left between the two-letter state abbreviation and ZIP code.

F 2. This is the correct format:

Ms. Nancy Abteron
Research and Development Manager
Regional Sales
376 South Avenue
Salem, NC 78432

T 3. This inside address is correctly formatted:

Ms. Janie Thompson, Coordinator
Medical International Laboratories
6 Park Lane
St. Petersburg, FL 33710

F 4. Postscript notations are used to add information that was thought of after the letter was composed.

F 5. The information below is correctly formatted:

PS: We have the items needed for your next shipment. Please call our Order Department immediately to have the order shipped.

T 6. If the letter is block style, the postscript is not indented.

T 7. If the letter style uses indented paragraphs, the postscript should be indented.

F 8. If the writer wants the receiver of the letter to know that it is his or her personal views reflected in the letter, he or she would **not** use the company name in the letter's closing.

F 9. If a modified block-style letter is used and the company name is requested to be included in the closing, it is typed **starting at the center point.**

F 10. The company name is typed in **all** capitals on the second line below the closing.

F 11. If an apartment building or number is used in the address and is put on a separate line, it should be typed on the line **before** the street address.

T 12. This address is formatted correctly:

Dr. Paul Smith
765 East Street, Apt. 87E
Cleveland, OH 86409

F 13. This address is formatted correctly:

Peter and Elaine Smith
Apartment 86B
301 West Amelia Street
Orlando, FL 32801

Proofreading Exercise 9

Current Date

Ms. Mary Halloran   (**Delete comma and put job title on next line**)
Southeastern District Conference Coordinator
MS Office Products
Building 83B
878 23rd Avenue North
Decatur, GA 50812

Dear **Ms.** Halloran:

Putting on a conference can be a major headache as well as **a** major accomplishment. A subscription to our magazine **Conferences & Conventions** can help you take some of the "headache" out of the sometimes overwhelming planning involved in setting up a conference.

Rather than spending hours trying to pull together all the elements of putting on a good conference, let *Conferences & Conventions* do all the networking and information gathering for you. This versatile monthly magazine covers everything **from** destination guides, free information, **planning** portfolios, hot ideas, and important news to convention managers and planners. Not only are issues such as **cancellation** clauses and political concerns associated with conference planning covered, but also topics such as international updates are covered.

We are sending you a complimentary issue of *Conferences & Conventions.* Return the enclosed subscription form to commence having a monthly issue delivered to your doorstep. We are certain that you will see the tremendous value from this complimentary issue.

Sincerely,

CONFERENCES & CONVENTIONS   **(Company name goes before the writer's name.)**

Ted Liberman

lm

PS: If you return the enclosed subscription form between **May 10** and **May 20,** you will have the option of accessing *Conferences & Conventions* online.

Enclosure notation missing

Transcription Preview: Self-Check 9

1. To provide prompt payment of your claim, please submit the following information as soon as possible.
2. We cannot process this claim, however, without your assistance.
3. Therefore, the damage to the paint or waterproofing material applied to the exterior of your residence is not covered.
4. Although there is a short grace period, I suggest that we meet prior to this renewal deadline to help you select the option most appropriate to cover your commercial needs.
5. Each question must be answered; and the affidavit must be signed, witnessed, and notarized.
6. Since you have changed the conditions under which the policy was originally issued, I believe that you should consider updating the coverage under this policy.

    1. June 5 through June 10
    2. C
    3. $1 million
    4. renewability
    5. self-addressed

LESSON 10: POTOMAC NATIONAL BANK

Word Usage Review 10

1. patients, personal, everyday
2. past, passed
3. perspective, may be, quite, confident, assistance
4. loss, annual, every day
5. principal, prospective, personnel
6. quiet, presence
7. peruse
8. a lot, personal, bazaar, presents, patients
9. proceed, everyone, quiet
10. prosecute, quite
11. pursue, lose
12. past, loose, personnel
13. principles, complimenting
14. precede
15. loose, may be, personnel, peruse
16. lose
17. moral, peace
18. morning
19. piece, plane, peak, piqued, annalist
20. morale, due, mourning, physical
21. precedence
22. prophesy
23. plain
24. perfect, prefect
25. fiscal
26. pier
27. peer, piece
28. precedent, lead
29. prophecy
30. plain, plane
31. plain, planes

Language Review 10

1. The **S's** did not print on the hard copy although they showed on the screen. (GP 8.8)
2. The question the new employees wanted answered was, "When will we be eligible for a raise?" (GP 3.13, GP 6.5, GP 6.6)
3. Hilary Thompson**'s** salary was $8.50 an hour—or was it $9.50 an hour**?** (GP 8.2)
4. During the last committee meeting, he was asked to bring the **auditor's** final report in which the question, "Did any employees violate accounting procedural rules?" was answered. (GP 3.2D, GP 8.2, GP 6.6)
5. Sally shrieked with delight when told that she had won the contest and shouted, "I can't believe I won!" (GP 6.5, GP 6.6)
6. We attended Vernita **Hotlz's** engagement party; and the host of the party predicted, "Vernita you will have a long and happy marriage." (GP 8.5, GP 4.2, GP 6.5, GP 6.6)
7. The department manager asked the vice president the following question: "If we went on a flextime schedule, would all departments have the option of choosing their schedules?" (GP 6.7, GP3.2A, GP 6.6, GP 10.3)
8. At the orientation did the vice president say, "All new employees are eligible immediately for health care benefits"? (GP 3.13, GP 6.6)
9. We will see if Tom can watch the **Prez's** dog when they are vacationing. (GP 8.5)
10. All the students attending school in the '**90s** took part in technical-preparation training. (GP 8.2)

11. The new ice cream, **Minneapolis Delight,** will be available in June. (GP 10.5, GP 3.4)

12. We won't know if many people will take advantage of the **Circle of Friends** long-distance telephone service. (GP 7.1, GP 10.5)

13. When you select our fixed rate option, you can finance up to **95%** loan-to-value on owner-occupied purchases at a **9%** interest rate. (GP 3.2D, GP 14.1, GP 7.1)

Format Review 10

F 1. If the word *Southeast* is used *before* the street name in the address, it should **not** be abbreviated.

F 2. The name of the department should be put on the line **before** the company's name.

F 3. If the word *Northwest* is used in the street address and appears *after* the street name, it **should be** abbreviated.

F 4. If the word *West* is used after the street name, a comma should **not** be placed before it. Do not use a comma after the street name with North, South, East, and West.

T 5. Compound directions (Northeast, Northwest, Southeast, and Southwest) should be abbreviated when they appear after a street name.

T 6. If a compound direction is used in the street address after the street name, a comma is placed before the compound direction.

F 7. The correct abbreviation for Southwest is **SW.** Do not use periods in the compound direction abbreviations.

F 8. The individual's job title should be placed on the line **below** his or her name.

Mr. Paul Anderson
Research Director
Research and Development Department
769 East Rochester Drive
Warren, MI 39812

F 9. A comma should be inserted after the street name and South should be spelled out.

Mr. Paul Anderson
Vice President Production
Research and Production Division
8700 30th Street, **South**
Warren, MI 39812

F 10. Southwest should not be abbreviated because compass points coming before the street name should be spelled out.

Mr. Paul Anderson
Vice President Production
Emerging Technologies Department
6200 **Southwest** Oakridge Road
Warren, MI 39812

Proofreading Exercise 10

June **30,** 20— *(**June does not have 31 days**)*

Mr. Robert L. Morrison, Manager
Purchasing Department
Capital Manufacturing Company
2199 Essex Knoll Drive
Stone Harbor, NJ 03247

Dear Mr. Morrison:

Many firms spend thousands of dollars annually to purchase fin**e** letterhead**,** which will carry the **(delete the)** image of **their** company to **their** readers. Many companies insist on expensive paper and print that is **legible** and **up to date.** Some require a letterhead **in two** colors of a highly artistic nature. This touch of individuality, they feel, will create a lasting impression on their customers and leave **a** feeling of confidence about **their** firm. We understand this need to set yourself apart in order to establish a strong client base. For this reason**,** we offer our customers that individualized touch.

Our company just moved **into** a **new** building adjacent to the Winterside Mall. This new location allowed us to **expand** our inventory, and we now have a complete line of office **supplies.** Because **past** experience has shown us that many customers need to shop after they have finished working, we are open from 9 a.m. (**delete** *in the morning*) until 9 p.m. *(**delete** in the evening.)*

We invite you to take advantage of our expert, courteous staff, and quality merchandise. The enclosed coupon will give you a **10** percent discount on your first purchase.

Very **truly** yours,

Don Patterson   **(Delete Mr.)**

lm

Enclosure notation missing

Transcription Preview: Self-Check 10

1. As a valued Potomac Bank customer**,** you've earned special recognition**;** and we're saying "Thank You" by offering you a **preapproved** Potomac Gold MasterCard with no annual fee**,** a low**,** fixed 7.9% APR, and a credit limit of $8,000.

2. For instance**,** All-In-One customers can write any number of checks without a service charge**;** and the interest on MasterCard balances is 13%, which is lower than competitive cards with 15% to 20% interest rates.

3. You may, however, pay the $5,000 at any time before the due date and reduce the amount of interest proportionately.

4. You will receive a statement prior to that date, which will show the term, maturity date, current balance, interest rate, and earned interest on this certificate.

5. For current rate information, please call our 24-hour rate line (919-468-7889) on the day your certificate matures.

6. Many banks offer online computer banking services; but our service allows you to choose how you access your accounts, such as from America Online, Microsoft Money, Quicken, or from Potomac National Bank's Cyberbanking.

1. C

2. Acceptance Certificate

3. $5 service charge

4. C

5. postcard

6. C

7. C

LESSON 11: AUNT DEE'S KIDS KAMPUS

Word Usage Review 11

1. respectfully
2. role
3. soar
4. rights
5. Someday,everyone, respectfully
6. sore
7. write, scene
8. roll
9. stationery, than
10. respectably
11. some day
12. rites
13. seen, their
14. lose, stationary
15. Sometimes
16. there, pursued
17. stationery, they're
18. route
19. statute, too
20. two, statue
21. sweets, root
22. stature, root, to
23. suite, two

Language Review 11

1. The Purchasing Department's, Personnel Department's, and Production Department's reports were all turned in on time. (GP 8.2)

2. The new form was changed to include categories for high-, medium-, and low-priority ratings. (GP 7.3)

3. The new assistant only met Mary when they both attended the reception for his son-in-law's graduation. (GP 8.6)

4. Anderson, Smith, and Johnson's report on the new surgery procedure was printed in the latest journal. (GP 8.7)

5. Hotels in the AAA book receive a one-, two-, three-, four-, or five-diamond rating. (GP 7.3)

6. Mary's, Susan's, and Tim's typing speeds were all more than 55 wpm. (GP 8.2)

7. The six word processing operators' and four transcriptionists' productivity logs showed that the majority of the work processed was for the Accounting Department. (GP 8.3)

8. The notary public's seal was missing from her desk. (GP 8.2)

9. The "do-it-yourself" book's format made it easy to follow. (GP 6.2, GP 7.1, GP 8.2)

10. Over 50 people attended the parents' and teachers' reception at the beginning of the school year. (GP 8.3)

11. The team's red, white, and blue banner could be seen from a distance. (GP 3.6, GP 8.2)

Format Review 11

F 1. A press release is **not** lengthy and usually is sent **before** the time of the event.

F 2. The body of a press release is usually **double** spaced.

F 3. A press release should have a **1-inch** top margin.

T 4. Either "End" or "###" is typed a double space after the message to signify the end of the press release.

T 5. The 1-inch default side-and-bottom margins are used for a press release.

F 6. The heading lines of a press release are **single** spaced.

T 7. A triple space should be used after the heading in a press release.

Proofreading Exercise 11

Current Date

Paul and Teresa Roderberg
East **Third** Street
Bangor, ME 86329

Dear Paul and **Teresa:**   (**There should be consistency in spelling Teresa.**)

It has been **some time** since we met to discuss **your** financial planning. I am not sure if I should **proceed** with the changes we agreed upon. Please let me know your wishes on this matter as soon as possible**,** so I can determine what the current APR is in order to quote you new rates.

I look **forward** to hearing from you.

Respectfully,

(*Another line should be added between Respectfully and Laura.*)

Laura Ashley

(**Reference initials are missing.**)

Transcription Preview: Self-Check 11

1. Please contact me or my office assistant, Karen Smith, to arrange a time when we can meet.

2. If a cake in this design is too complicated, perhaps cupcakes with wrappers that have teddy bear stickers could be used.

3. Some students, although they have excelled in different child development courses, have difficulty applying what they have learned in regard to teaching and nurturing young children in a formal setting.

4. The date you noted in your letter, October 25, does not present a conflict with my schedule.

5. Aunt Dee's offers a secure, loving environment where children develop socially, emotionally, physically, and intellectually.

6. Refreshments will be served, and information about our age-appropriate learning activities will be available.

7. I would like to design a coupon with our "teddy bear" logo and motto: "Where Creativity and Children Flourish."

    1. C

    2. one and seven

    3. ZIP codes

    4. C

    5. C

    6. C

    7. sign-up roll

    8. C

LESSON 12: SNAPSHOTS, INC.

Word Usage Review 12

1. threw		11. thorough
2. whose		12. vise
3. whether		13. you're
4. vice		14. undo
5. where, were		15. waver
6. weather		16. Whether, vain, undue
7. Who's		17. week, weather
8. there		18. waiver
9. through, threw		19. vein
10. trail		20. weather, vane, weak, vain

Language Review 12

1. Here is the perfect solution—how could we have missed it for so long.(GP 11.2)

2. He waited for his turn to interview—nervous, apprehensive, and well pre-pared—ready to sell himself as the best candidate for the job. (GP 11.1)

3. The United Way Drive was successful because all the employees—support staff, supervisors, and divisional representatives—contributed. (GP 11.1, GP 3.7)

4. Strong grammar, typing, punctuation, and word processing skills—all of these are essential for success as a transcriptionist. (GP 11.1, GP 3.7)

5. The manager's old office—the tiny room in the back of the building—has been turned into a storage area. (GP 8.2, GP 11.1)

6. The company offers several services—consulting, purchasing, typing, and re-modeling. (GP 11.1, GP 3.7)

7. Do the newly employed transcription operators have strong communication skills—listening, speaking, and writing? (GP 11.1, GP 3.7)

8. The new **All-In-One** Account only costs **$25** more a month. (GP 10.5, GP 13.1)

9. The new medicine—Proctramle—will go on sale next week. (GP 11.2)

10. We went fishing last week at **E**agle **R**un and caught **five** fish. (GP 10.4, GP 12.1)

Format Review 12

F   **1.** **Either** the post box number or the street address should be used—not both.

T   **2.** The United States Post Office prefers the all-capital abbreviation PO BOX to be used on the envelope.

F   **3.** The abbreviation for mail stop code used in the envelope address is **MSC.**

F   **4.** The **street address** should be used for Express Mail.

T   **5.** The mail stop code goes on the first line of the address.

F   **6.** Mail Stop Code should be **abbreviated** MSC.

T   **7.** It is correct to include both the mail stop code and street address in the address.

Proofreading Exercise 12

Ms. Luz Castiblanco   Page 2   April 22, 20—

(Order of Date and Page Number should be reversed.)

conference schedule will be to our advantage.   *Carry over at least two lines to the next page.)*

The flight leaves at 6 **a.m.,** so we will have to pick up **Dr.** Thomas before **5** a.m. in order to get to the airport in time. This airline does not use tickets, and seats are assigned on a **first-come-first-served** basis.

If we get **there** early enough, we may be able to get an **aisle** seat. I have **already** encouraged Dr. Thomas to **take only carry-on** luggage, so we can save **a lot** of time by not checking baggage. If for some reason our luggage gets lost, Nancy should be notified at the following address:

MSC 543
Ms. Nancy Drew   *(Placement of MSC and Post Office Box should be reversed.)*
Post Box 95
Orlando, FL 32891

Sincerely,

Gene Atkinson

lm

Transcription Preview: Self-Check 12

1. Please let me know if you have any questions regarding the photos, payment policy, or if you would like to have the photos of the building.

2. Many of the slide show programs have TWAIN support, so you can import images directly from the scanner without switching to another imaging program.

3. Photo processing software, such as Corel's Photo-Paint Digital Camera Edition, includes a slide show utility that allows the creation of basic slide shows.

4. Another option, if video-editing software is used, is to output the project to VHS or DVD for playback on television.

5. In addition to the photo contest, award-winning photos by local professional photographers will be on exhibit; and a workshop on digital cameras and digital photography will be offered at no cost between 10 a.m. and noon.

6. If you are able to position yourself ahead of time, the action will come to you, rather than you having to run around trying to follow it.

7. I don't know what model point-and-shoot camera you own, but many have an action feature that selects a fast shutter speed.

   1. C
   2. award-winning photos
   3. 5 percent
   4. C
   5. C
   6. Recordable CDs (GP 8.8)

LESSON 13: NOVA TRAVEL

Word Usage Review 13

1. bring, take
2. defer
3. may
4. take
5. between
6. differ
7. can, may
8. intrastate
9. badly
10. desert
11. export
12. well, lie
13. import
14. among
15. bring, dessert
16. good
17. well
18. badly
19. bad, well
20. among
21. anxious
22. trial, mad
23. eager, angry

Language Review 13

1. The proposed contract contained the following: (1) one more paid vacation day, (2) a 5 percent pay increase, and (3) a 45-minute lunch. (GP 9.1)

2. Sometimes in legal documents monetary amounts are written in words and then in figures enclosed with parentheses, such as one hundred dollars ($100). (GP 3.3A, GP 9.2)

3. Between the two companies, one thousand dollars ($1,000) was raised for the United Way. (GP 9.2)

4. She had no indication that she was to be transferred. (Neither did any of us for that matter.) (GP 9.3)

5. Did Edward Allen receive a pay increase? (If so, this should cause a demand for a pay increase from every employee in his department.) (GP 9.3)

6. The managers of the Legal Department, Finance Department, and Personnel Department stayed within their budgets. (The Production Department failed to do so.) (GP 9.3)

7. The tour includes: (1) one week of sightseeing, (2) air transportation, and (3) five dinners, three lunches, and six breakfasts. (GP 9.1)

8. The supervisor said she was busy. (How busy could she really have been, though, if she read a novel for an hour?) (GP 3.3C, GP 9.3) An exclamation point could also be used instead of a question mark after *hour*.

9. Who should conduct the orientation for the new employees? (Should it be the new manager or the previous manager who already is familiar with the organization?) (GP 9.3)

10. She gave the message to Larry (or was it Sally?). (GP 9.3)

11. There **are** a number of students who qualified for the new grant. (GP 17.13)

12. The number of students passing their board tests **is** increasing. (GP 17.13)

Format Review 13

T   **1.** An itinerary is a schedule of activities used by individuals when traveling.

F   **2.** Usually an itinerary is typed in **two** columns: **date and time,** activity or event.

F   **3.** Itineraries are typed **single** spaced.

T   **4.** An itinerary usually includes travel directions.

T   **5.** An easy way to format an itinerary is to use columns or tables without lines.

T   **6.** Except on the first page of an itinerary there should be a heading that includes the name of the person the itinerary is for, page number, and date.

Proofreading Exercise 13

MEMORANDUM

TO: Art Dallas

FROM: Dorothy Lynch

DATE: **Current date should be part of the heading and not at top of memo.**

SUBJECT: Required Training for **N**ew **E**mployees

(Paragraphs should not be indented.)

You are required to attend an orientation session next Monday, August 10, at **10** a.m. in **R**oom 7B on the second floor of the Professional Development Center. The meeting should last **three hours.** Please take the following to the meeting: (1) social security card, (2) insurance card, and (3) fingerprint clearance.

Prior to the meeting, you should view the **video** at your worksite concerning company benefits. You **may** check the video out, but be sure to return it to your supervisor within a **one-day** period since there **are** a limited number of copies to share **among** several departments.

Transcription Preview: Self-Check 13

1. Do you think it would be possible to put together a full-scale expedition along the trail from Dyea, Alaska, to Bennett, British Columbia?

2. Since most of the major tributaries on the Yukon have roadside access, trips can vary depending on which roadside access points are used.

3. Since you work with our clients most directly, you know their needs; and I value your evaluation of the courses and their content.

4. For instance, Don, if you design a wilderness hiking tour, we could offer a course on survival tactics, such as how to endure unpredictable weather conditions (such as snow, sleet, fog, and thunderstorms) and what emergency rations should be packed.

5. It is also important that a traveler who has diabetes or a physical condition, which might require emergency care, wear a medical card, tag, or bracelet.

6. Take shuttle transportation to Marriot International Hotel, International Drive, Orlando, Florida. Phone (407) 354-2778.

7. Nova tour escorts in Europe will assist you in exchanging United States money into foreign currency during your European visit, but it is a good idea for you to obtain European currency before leaving the United States.

8. Unless travelers are aware of these restrictions, they may unknowingly violate laws, such as taking unauthorized pictures and items as souvenirs.

1. C
2. prepackaged
3. C
4. company's headquarters' staff
5. C
6. traveler's checks

LESSON 14: AMERCIAN PUBLISHING CO.

Word Usage Review 14

1. morning, rising, leave	13. Who, bring
2. peace, between	14. Who's
3. least	15. least, let
4. sit	16. in-depth
5. morning, which, mourning	17. learn
6. leased, well, which	18. in spite of
7. set, lease	19. teach
8. leave	20. in spite of, in spite
9. rise, leave	21. an, interstate
10. shall, let, set	22. intrastate
11. whose	23. Fewer
12. piece, which, will	24. Less

Language Review 14

1. **Number** 653 was the first number to be called. (GP 12.3)

2. The advertising campaign was going into its **fifth** season. (GP 12.5)

3. The supply order showed that the **five 20**-pound trays were ordered. (GP 12.7, GP 7.1)

4. Correct. (GP 10.11)

5. Correct. (GP 10.11)

6. **Three hundred fifty** people attended the conference. (GP 12.3)

7. The report was dated May **5,** but he received it on May **10.** (GP 12.4, GP 3.1)

8. The new employees had to take a course called **C**ustomer **R**elations in the **W**orkplace. (GP 10.11)

9. The purchase order showed that **six 5-**ounce tubes of ointment were ordered. (GP 12.7, GP 7.1)

10. Did Mae say she wanted **four 15-pound** hams for the Thanksgiving party, or did she say she wanted ten 15-pound turkeys? (GP 12.7, GP 7.1, GP 3.1)

11. The author of the article, Rose Episton, RN, was not able to be the keynote speaker. (GP 10.11)

12. Correct. (GP 12.5, GP 7.1, GP 12.1)

13. Her parents celebrated their **fiftieth** wedding anniversary with a party attended by **150** guests. (GP 12.5, GP 12.1)

14. Correct. (GP 12.5)

15. Correct. (GP 10.11, GP 12.5)

Format Review 14

1. C
2. Incorrect (STA)
3. C
4. Incorrect (ANX)
5. Correct
6. Incorrect (TER)
7. Incorrect (JCT)
8. C
9. C
10. C

Proofreading Exercise 14

Current Date

MSC 769 *(Mail Stop Code goes on first line.)*
Ms. Alice Jones
Anderson University
PO Box 87 *(Should only use street address or PO Box.)*
23 East Bayshore St.
Dayton, OH 67307

Dear Ms. Jones:

I feel **bad** that I haven't written sooner. This is a very busy time of year for **our** company, so it has been very difficult for me to respond to your request to serve on your School Advisory Board. I will be honored to serve in this capacity for a second term; however, I will not be able to participate until the **first** of the year when things have calmed down.

I have had an opportunity to **peruse** the comprehensive, indexed catalog and am impressed with the variety of programs offered at the university. I am glad to see that **H**umanities 509 was added as we recommended last year.

In **regard** to your request to be a guest speaker for the graduating business students in the *Bachelor of Science Environmental Engineering program, I will have to decline **due** to a conflict with a previous engagement; however, I will be able to attend the university's **fiftieth** anniversary celebration on August **10.** Please give my administrative assistant, Doug Peterson, the details on this event so that I can plan accordingly.

Sincerely,

(Should be 4 returns after Sincerely)

Ronda Perez, **Ph.D.**
(A blank line should be between the reference initials and the writer's name.)
lm

Bachelor of Science is capitalized in this instance because it is part of the name of a specific program.

Transcription Preview: Self-Check 14

1. They will be wrapped for long-term storage, and I ask only that you keep them in a warm, dry place.
2. A fax machine is also available; and I leave the fax and answering machine on at all times, so please feel free to leave a message or send a fax 24 hours a day.
3. Depending on manufacturing costs, it will cost between **$2** and **$5** more to purchase the student CD with the simulation.
4. If the contract looks all right to you, please sign and initial all copies and return them directly to Charlotte at our home office in Hammond, Louisiana.
5. If this is not possible, please send the original camera copy page along with the marked copy; and we will try to match the corrections to the original typeface.
6. The target audience for this magazine is self-employed individuals, entrepreneurs, and freelance employees who are hired on an outsourcing or consulting basis.
7. The project has many innovative features and sales "handles" and will be a lot of fun to sell.

    1. C
    2. **100** sheets

3. our **p**roduction supervisor, Cheryl Jimenez,

4. C

5. **fax** machine (Sometimes *fax* is used in all capitals when referring to the document itself, but the common trend is to use lowercase letters when referring to both the process and document.)

6. **M**odel 15 **C**amera **C**opy paper (name of a specific type of paper)

7. form entitled "What to Submit and How"

LESSON 15: METROPOLITAN COUNTY PUBLIC SCHOOLS

Word Usage Review 15

1. facade

2. a la mode

3. encore

4. connoisseur, hors d'oeuvres, circa

5. coup d'état

6. faux pas, finesse, aplomb

7. ad hoc

8. facade

9. debut

10. ex post facto

11. carte blanche, esprit de corps

12. a la carte, au jus, intoto

13. ad valorem, avant-garde

Language Review 15

1. Because she was such a good employee, she was given a $50 a month raise; but he only received a **$.25** an hour raise. (GP 3.2D, GP 13.2)

2. Correct. (GP 14.2)

3. Only **three-fourths** of the employees voted to change their hours. (GP 14.3)

4. **Colonel** Anderson won a medal for his bravery. (GP 16.1)

5. Mary contributed $5; Suzie, **$.50;** and Joan, $8.50. (GP 13.1, GP 13.2)

6. In order to change the bylaws, a **two-thirds** membership majority had to be present. (GP 3.2D, GP 14.3)

7. We couldn't remember if Mrs. Thompson paid her **50 cent** donation. (GP 13.2)

8. The assistant dean asked his colleagues to support **Professor** Roder's research. (GP 8.3, GP 16.1)

9. The average age of the students attending the community college was **thirty.** (GP 12.8)

10. The 15-pound laptop cost $944.50, but the battery cost **$15.** (GP 3.1, GP 7.1, GP 13.1)

11. There are eight months and **five** days before the holidays. (GP 15.2)

12. The bookstore had to start charging **60 cents** for bookmarks. (GP 13.2)

13. Martha couldn't wait until she turned **twenty-one.** (GP 12.8)

14. The book was given to Doctor Johnson to review. (This is technically correct, although the common abbreviation *Dr.* is usually used—GP 16.2.)

15. She did not have the **35 cents** needed for the toll, so she took the long way home. (GP 13.2, GP 3.1)

Format Review 15

F   **1.** If correspondence originating in the United States is being sent to China, this is the correct address format: (Country should be in **all capitals.**)
Dr. Paulette Parkway
870 East Robinson
Taipei, Taiwan
REPUBLIC OF CHINA

F   **2.** If someone in Tallahassee, Florida, sent a letter to someone in Buffalo, New York, the words, "United States of America" should **not** be typed in all capitals on the last line of the address.

F   **3.** There are **ten** provinces in Canada.

F   **4.** The abbreviation **YT** in Canadian mail stands for Yukon Territory.

T   **5.** New Brunswick is a city in the United States and a province in Canada.

T   **6.** The country's name should be typed in all capitals as the last line of an address for correspondence from the United States to another country.

Proofreading Exercise 15

Date should start at center to match closing position or closing should start at left margin.

Paul Anderson, **M.D.**   *(Both Dr. and MD should not be used.)*
Tri-County Medical
2867 Eastwood Dr.
Fort Lauderdale, FL 32851

Dear **Dr.** Anderson:

Ms. Dorothy DeChant has applied for a position at our medical lab. Her application shows that you were her last employer, and we would like to have **your** input in regards to the following:

1. Ms. DeChant's attendance
2. Work performance
3. Job Responsibilities
4. Initiative

We understand the legal issues in giving us this information and **assure** you that your response will be strictly confidential. You may wish not to comment on the above requests. If so, please just drop us a note to this **effect. Ms.** DeChant's application shows that she has the skills we are looking for, but we must check her credentials to make sure that she is a bona **fide** physician's assistant and that all her references are accurate. Being in the medical profession, I am sure you can understand our need to screen employees.

Please respond as soon as possible as we have a deadline **for** filling this position. Because our practice is growing and we take care of such a diverse group of individuals, we need individuals who are team oriented. Please comment on Ms. Dechant's attitude in these areas.

Sincerely,

Charlotte Morgan, M.D.

xx
(Enclosure notation should be deleted.)

Transcription Preview: Self-Check 15

1. We further realize that inconveniences are created for many as a result of the court order, and we regret our inability to assist you at this time.
2. Correct. (Note that commas should be inserted around Amanda Andrews if she is an only child. If her parents have more than one child; however, Susan Jones is essential to the sentence's meaning in order to know what child is being tested if there were more than one child in the family. Since the circumstances are not known, don't use commas.)
3. Correct. (In this instance, Initial FTE is referring to the name of a report and not the *first* FTE report.)
4. Since the Intermediate FTE report will be finalized the evening of February 8, all corrections and additions should be entered by that afternoon.

    1. reapply
    2. online system
    3. Payroll Department
    4. C
    5. Ext. 2856 (The word *extension* is generally not spelled out when a telephone number is given.)

LESSON 16: BED AND BREAKFAST AROUND THE WORLD

Word Usage Review 16

1. status quo
2. passé
3. per se
4. vis-à-vis
5. verbatim
6. pro tempore
7. per capita
8. vice versa
9. per diem
10. R.S.V.P.
11. laissez faire
12. rendezvous, tete-a-tete
13. motif
14. sans
15. non sequitur

Language Review 16

1. The bylaws had to be changed because they were not in keeping with the Articles of **I**ncorporation. (GP 10.6)

2. The **S**chool **A**dvisory **C**ouncil is responsible for the school improvement plan**;** therefore**,** the members take their duties seriously. (GP 4.3, GP 10.2)

3. The new employee received a **VIP** welcome. (GP 16.6)

4. The box was shipped **UPS,** but the letter was mailed **F**ederal **E**xpress. (GP 16.6, GP 10.1)

5. The merchandise was shipped **c.o.d.,** but he didn't have money to pay the bill when it arrived. (GP 3.1, GP 16.6)

6. Half of the employees **have** passed their examination for certification. (GP 17.12)

7. **Has** the instructor's information been given to the students? (GP 17.4)

8. Most of the employees **have** attended the required workshop. (GP 17.5C)

9. The **C**urriculum **R**eview **C**ommittee**,** which was composed of members from **30** states**,** are independently evaluating **16** courses. (GP 12.1, GP 10.2, GP 17.7)

10. In addition to the new medical coverage **are** new insurance plans that include new benefits for all employees. (GP 17.4)

Format Review 16

T   **1.** Most reports include a table of contents and title page.

T   **2.** Many word processing software programs include report templates.

F   **3.** If side headings are used in a *traditional* report style, a **triple** space is placed before and a **double space** is used after the side heading.

F   **4.** **The first** page in a report should **not** have a page number on it.

T   **5.** The body of the report should be double spaced.

F   **6.** The first page of the report should have a **2**-inch top margin.

T   **7.** Usually the default margins are used for typing a report.

F   **8.** Enumerated items are single spaced **and** indented.

T   **9.** The title of the report may be used as a header on all pages.

F   **10.** If the title is used as a header, it should be typed in **initial capitals.**

T   **11.** Footnotes or endnotes are used to show referenced text in the report.

F   **12.** Long quotations are **single** spaced and indented.

T   **13.** The title should be centered in all capital letters on the first page of the report.

F   **14.** The top margin on the second page of the report is **1** inch.

Proofreading Exercise 16: Subject/Verb Agreement

(1)   _C_   The computer <u>components</u> <u>are</u> in the storage room.

(2)   _I_   <u>You</u>, as well as Andy, **have been** chosen to serve on the Advisory Council.

(3) _C_ <u>Somebody</u> on one of the swim teams <u>is</u> going to give him a ride home.

(4) _I_ Neither the band <u>director</u> nor his <u>students</u> **are** responsible for the missing money.

(5) _I_ <u>One</u> of the students **receives** a monthly check to cover school expenses.

(6) _C_ The band <u>members</u> <u>are</u> in disagreement over who should be their captain.

(7) _I_ <u>Everything</u> stored using computers **is** easy to retrieve.

(8) _C_ The <u>report</u> about the word processing operators <u>was</u> sent to the supervisor for review.

(9) _I_ The <u>number</u> of transcription operators working in medical records **determines** the speed of document turn around.

(10) _C_ The <u>band</u> <u>plans</u> to rehearse for the concert.

(11) _I_ <u>Each</u> of the new jobs **pays** a higher salary.

(12) _I_ The <u>number</u> of software spreadsheet programs **has** increased.

(13) _I_ Either the <u>judge</u> or his staff <u>members</u> **were** responsible for the break down in communication.

(14) _C_ <u>Was</u> the facsimile <u>machine</u> with <u>the</u> computers that were stolen?

(15) _I_ <u>One</u> of the fields **was** deleted when Jon entered the data.

(16) _I_ <u>Answers</u> to the student survey **show** that many students leave home by the time they are 18.

(17) _C_ Where <u>is</u> the <u>secretary</u> for the two men?

(18) _I_ **Do** <u>Mary</u> and <u>Jane</u> **like** their class?

(19) _I_ <u>Each</u> department branch and home office division **was** audited for compliance with software copyright laws.

(20) _I_ Neither a reporting delay nor several power <u>failures</u> **are** reason for the manuscript not being completed on time.

(21) _I_ <u>Either</u> of those dresses **is** appropriate.

(22) _C_ <u>Most</u> of the report <u>contains</u> information we already know.

(23) _I_ **There are** several <u>types</u> of word processing software available.

(24) _C_ <u>Many</u> of the company's 500 employees <u>are</u> at a sales conference.

(25) _I_ <u>Mathematics</u> **is** not her favorite subject.

Proofreading Exercise 16: Pronoun/Antecedent Agreement

(1) _I_ The collaborative consultation process requires training on both the speech and consumer education teacher**s'** parts.

(2) _I_ "The key determinant of the quality of an early childhood program", she further states, "**is** trained staff who have knowledge and ability to implement developmentally appropriate curriculum."

(3) _C_ It was his hat.

(4) _I_ As principal, he or she must choose the kind of leader **he/she** wants to be—no one else can make the choice.

(5) _I_ The child is an individual, and we need to help **him/her** to be successful.

(6) _C_ Many students didn't bring their books.

(7) _C_ The style of leadership chosen by a principal will have a great influence on the kind of person he or she will become.

(8) _I_ Teachers must design their programs so that each child can gain confidence in **his/her** own ability.

Proofreading Exercise 16: Verb/Tense Answers

1. associated
2. repeated
3. eliminated
4. committed

5. determined
6. eliminated
7. required
8. mastered

Proofreading Exercise 16: Final Agreement Self-Check

1. There are many advantages offered by Telex. The messages usually get immediate **attention** and response. They can be cleared for security through sender and receiver codes. Detailed monthly billing as well as multiple polling is also offered by Telex. Another feature being **offered** is a 57-page memory for sequential broadcasting.

   Some of the benefits are the ability to leave a message without conversing with the recipient, transmitting messages to one or more recipients, and adding comments to messages. These benefits **integrate** with a wide range of E-mail services.

2. Computer-based messaging systems and services (CBMS) **provide** the base for E-mail. During recent years, E-mail has **proven** a cost-effective way of communicating. It is used by all **types** of organizations and millions of consumers who have PCs.

3. It will be beneficial for you to review the mortgage insurance on your home. You told me that you have not **changed** the beneficiary on the policy since your divorce.

4. Susan Jones will retire after working with our firm for 40 years. She started as a part-time clerk when she was a college student. She **has** always been a person who is loyal and hard working.

5. The **enclosed** report, as well as the appropriate tables, may give you a simply written bit of information that you could use with the students in your next presentation.

6. Insurance companies **classify** the value of an automobile through a process whereby a symbol is assigned to the various makes and models of cars. The enclosed chart **provides** a clear picture of how value and age of automobile are figured.

7. Both of these women will be rechecked in six months. Further violations will mean the end of their coverage. We are willing to reinsure, but only on our terms. Coverage for these drivers **is** high **priced;** and only they, not you, can act to lower the cost. Only the absence of hazards **incurred** in their driving will warrant a reduction in premiums.

Transcription Preview: Self-Check 16

1. We have connoisseurs, individuals who have experience in evaluating inns and hotels, visiting several bed and breakfasts that have been nominated for selection as one of our best 150.

2. She was impressed with Kathy, the gregarious hostess. She reported that each of the four guest rooms is decorated with colorful motifs that have transformed the rooms into portraits of Victoriana.

3. During this same time period, 55 clients did not renew their contracts.

4. We have retained all our reservation specialists and have hired only one new staff member, Marie Fierro, from California.

5. As part of your contract obligations, we would like you to develop a B & B bonus package for the 150 B & Bs selected.

1. C
2. best 150 B & Bs (GP 8.8 abbreviations)
3. one-minute video
4. Greek **R**evival home
5. our "family" of **b**ed and **b**reakfast sites

INDEX